FREEDOM OF ARTISTIC EXPRESSION

This book presents a unique and comprehensive examination of the human and moral rights of artists. In what is arguably the first exhaustive book-length account of artists' rights, Paul Kearns explores the problems associated with censorship, both from philosophical and legal perspectives, and focuses on the various ways in which the morality of art is legally regulated in different jurisdictions. In relation to human rights, English, French and American law, the law of the European Convention on Human Rights, European Union law and public international law are all closely scrutinised to discover the extent to which they offer protection for artistic freedom. The author also examines domestic and international law in respect of artists' moral rights, the law of copyright and related laws. In short, the book provides an original, and sometimes controversial, analysis of persistent concerns regarding the legal regulation of the arts universally, doctrinally and theoretically, and seeks to offer an holistic treatment which will appeal to art lawyers, artists and those interested in the future of the arts.

Freedom of Artistic Expression

Essays on Culture and Legal Censure

Paul Kearns

•HART•
PUBLISHING
OXFORD AND PORTLAND, OREGON
2013

Published in the United Kingdom by Hart Publishing Ltd
16C Worcester Place, Oxford, OX1 2JW
Telephone: +44 (0)1865 517530
Fax: +44 (0)1865 510710
E-mail: mail@hartpub.co.uk
Website: http://www.hartpub.co.uk

Published in North America (US and Canada) by
Hart Publishing
c/o International Specialized Book Services
920 NE 58th Avenue, Suite 300
Portland, OR 97213-3786
USA
Tel: +1 503 287 3093 or toll-free: (1) 800 944 6190
Fax: +1 503 280 8832
E-mail: orders@isbs.com
Website: http://www.isbs.com

British Library Cataloguing in Publication Data
Data Available

ISBN: 978-1-84113-080-4

Typeset by Hope Services, Abingdon
Printed and bound in Great Britain by
Lightning Source UK Ltd

Preface

I came to the School of Law, University of Manchester, in 2000, as its City Solicitors' Trust Lecturer in Human Rights Law. Since 2003, I have also been teaching my niche interest as a course there called *Law, Literature and Art,* which supplements my interests in Freedom of Expression, Public International Law, and Legal Theory. My student numbers are relatively high for such a specialism, and the course is built around my monograph *The Legal Concept of Art* (Oxford, Hart Publishing, 1998). The instant book, *Freedom of Artistic Expression*, concerns new ground: the human and other rights of artists, with specific reference to the legal censorship of art. My interest in Art Law emanates from my PhD at the European University Institute, Florence, Italy, and was, prior to that, ignited during my Oxbridge degrees, notably my Cambridge LLM in Public International Law and Legal Theory, that was founded on my Oxford BA degree in Jurisprudence.

Thanks are due to many concerning this book of essays on artists' freedoms and their legal control. Apart from my immediate family in Denbigh, north Wales, who have dutifully and lovingly supported me at an emotional level, I wish to thank Jackie Boardman, Julia Bradshaw and Myra Knutton for their timely practical typing skills (connected with this particular enterprise), which occasionally supplemented my own. My publisher, Richard Hart, has always been extremely pragmatic and kind during the course of this enterprise, and, indeed, long before that. Professor Norman Palmer and Ruth Redmond-Cooper have open-heartedly provided me with many welcome opportunities in the Art Law field, particularly in connection with their thriving Institute of Art and Law; and my two main supervisory influences, at the seminal stages of Art Law studies, Professors Bruno de Witte and Gunther Teubner, have always generously inspired, and continue to inspire, my Art Law initiatives.

Friends and colleagues in the law and culture area, notably Professors Reza Banakar, Costas Douzinas, Peter Goodrich and Dora Kostakopoulou, have always been encouraging and supportive; and I also wish to thank Sir Christopher Greenwood, Professor Tony Bradney, Professor Fiona Cownie, and Professor David Milman for, at different professional junctures, mentoring me, and nurturing my juridical enthusiasms during my initial legal studies, and thereafter. Finally, many thanks are also owed, collectively, to the various personnel involved in legal journals and reviews who, over 20 years, have seen fit to publish my legal-academic work.

This book is dedicated to my beautiful cat, Jude (1993–2010), still alive in our hearts and beyond, who, as his name might suggest, was of obscure origin. My father and I keenly look forward to being reunited with him (less remotely) in the fullness of time.

Dr Paul Kearns, Easter 2013.

Contents

Introduction

THIS BOOK OF essays comprises a history of artistic freedom of expression, drawing on the author's specialised legal scholarship from just before 2000 to the present day, hence why some of the individual papers are specifically dated. An essay can be defined as 'a piece of writing which reveals an author's personal point of view', and this is largely the impressionistic definition adopted here. As well as being legal-analytical, the essays presented in this volume are also literary, and it is hoped that they will appeal to intellectuals as well as artists, the art-interested, human rights lawyers, and lawyers and legal academics in general. As essays, they are relatively lightly footnoted, where footnotes are necessary, and some of the articles are necessarily longer than others, as dictated by the precise nature of the subject-matter. The table of contents itemises the specific legal dimensions examined in each essay.

The notion of 'art' in these collected articles is construed broadly, to include, inter alia, visual art, creative writing, and film. Some of the essays were first published as pieces in peer-reviewed law journals, and, within them, the words 'article' and 'paper' are used interchangeably with the word 'essay'. It is the dictionary that informs us that the meanings of these terms can overlap.

Some of the essays traverse socio-legal, jurisprudential, and inter-disciplinary ground, and cover, quite exhaustively, the interaction of public-moral laws and art, in various jurisdictions, according to each essay's overriding argument. Others emphasise other connected cultural concerns. In some instances, English, French and US laws are analysed, together with pertinent aspects of EU law, European Convention on Human Rights law, and other international human rights law. The individual articles present different perspectives on sometimes similar legislation and case law, but the central theme of each is unique.

Regarding this, it is important to understand the text's distinctive methodology. Some of the later essays clearly build on the earlier ones. In this and other ways, the essays may not function exactly like chapters in the average legal monograph, especially where legal recurrence tends to be avoided. However, in the law relating to specifically artistic freedom, there is a very small amount of directly pertinent case law, for example, yet several relevant autonomous essays here testify to a broader picture of how, sometimes, essentially similar or complementary law can generate different legal and cultural insights within separate original themes. By using an epistemologically cumulative method, inter alia, a gradual pedagogical as well as holistic effect naturally accrues, and is ultimately systematised. This may be particularly useful for newcomers to this particularly challenging branch of art law.

One objective of the essays is to seriously question the need for legal-moral constraints on artistic freedom, especially at a time when that freedom can be rarely constrained in practice, because of, in particular, the ubiquity of the Internet, and the difficulties involved in successfully monitoring that phenomenon's moral and legal parameters. The need for any such legal paternalism regarding art law subjects is itself also contested, mainly on philosophical grounds. However, the need to protect children from exposure to morally heinous artistic, and allegedly pornographic, imagery, is strongly affirmed in these essays, as is the general need for the legal proscription of conspicuously 'extreme' pornography, that may prompt, and promote, serious sexual offences, notably in relation to victims who are women. The essays, as a thematically integrated group, aim to show support for the liberty of the arts, and the co-extensive desirability of an art-informed art audience. The latter suggests a development which might obviate, at least in theory, the possibility of inappropriate, and unreflective, responses to controversial artworks that, allegedly, have important and pressing immoral implications.

It is intended, additionally, that the more general essays on culture, artists' rights, and free speech, will set in relief the information derived from the more specialised area of the legal-moral control of art. What is also not neglected here is the recognition of ways in which the law actually embraces, and fosters, the arts, even in the course of the regulation of their freedom. This is perhaps most overtly apparent in the area of intellectual property rights.

Finally, the essays in this monograph are arranged thematically, rather than strictly chronologically. Critically, though, they reveal the key developments in the relevant art law sphere over time. More precisely, as mentioned above, the individual articles almost exclusively draw on the author's legal scholarship from just before, and then into, the new millennium, which is an era of rapid legal-moral change. This, consequently, affords the collected critiques a very concentrated historical profile, that invites much detailed commentary. This, in addition, is not least because the years from the fin-de-siecle into a brand new millennium are commonly a period of much importance in art history, constituting an époque that witnesses the eradication of traditional positions, and the imposition of new cultural strategies, artistically, politically and legally. At the beginning of the twenty-first century, the interface between art, morality, sociology, politics and law has never been as significantly protean; and it is because this era is such a catalyst for change that art is now as volatile as it is. Accordingly, the details of art law and censorship become not just interesting, but trans-culturally pivotal. It is also, quite logically, but equally, quite inappropriately, why the law might sense that it has a particularly urgent obligation to circumscribe contemporary art's seemingly audacious transgressions. In attempting to control something as uncertain as art, and to create a precarious balance between conservative and liberal forces, the law is not assisted by Thomas Mann's warning that 'poets are prone to excess', or, indeed, by Ralph Waldo Emerson's telling aphorism that 'a genius knows nothing of consistency'.

Dr Paul Kearns, The School of Law, University of Manchester, England.
Easter Sunday, 2013.

Part I

A Contemporary Overview

1

*A Critical and Historical Study of English Legal Restraints on Artistic Liberty**

I INTRODUCTION

THIS ESSAY EXPLORES, historically and holistically, the neglected, ramified and problematic theme of freedom of artistic expression in England. It begins by examining, as a backcloth, the complex underlying issues affecting the legally-relevant inter-relationship of censorship, pornography and art; then it presents a history of the evolution of English legal regulations that impinge on the liberty of artists. Amongst the public-moral crimes of relevance, now or in the recent past, in potentially and actually curbing artistic freedom in various instances, are obscenity law, the former law of blasphemy that still resonates in trials involving cognate offences, the common law offence of outraging public decency, the Indecent Displays (Control) Act 1981, and the very recently enacted legislative provisions on 'extreme' pornography. These measures are counterpoised by the Human Rights Act 1998 (hereinafter sometimes referred to as the 1998 Act). A prominent middle section of the essay comprises a very close critique of the four most important cases[1] involving the balancing of artistic freedom against the constitutional need for the enforcement of morality in England. This particular aspect of the essay explores judicial approaches to the legal censorship of art to illustrate the general and specific problems that face the judiciary in applying public-moral legal measures to art, given the lack of a conclusive definition of it,[2] which threatens

* This essay was written in 2013. A shorter precursor of this essay, on a narrower theme, appeared in print as 'Controversial Art and the Criminal Law' (2003) 8 *Art, Antiquity and Law* 1, 27–56. The style of the article is socio-legal, inter-disciplinary and jurisprudential, including some close literary analysis of legal judgments containing mainly the author's own original ideas. The term 'English law' is replaced by the term 'UK law' when that is more accurate, especially in relation to the Human Rights Act 1998, which is a piece of UK, not solely English, legislation.

[1] For a close critique of the judicial approach to artistic appreciation in art law cases in England, France and the USA, see P Kearns, *The Legal Concept of Art* (Oxford, Hart Publishing, 1998) ch 2, 40–60.

[2] The difficulty of defining art is not a task confined to legal personnel. The problem of art's definition has never, of course, been completely resolved by philosophers, even those whose specialism is aesthetics.

to cause legal uncertainty and inconsistency. Another related concern the author raises here is whether judges are equipped with sufficient intellectual expertise in the area of art law to render justice for art when it is confronted with antipathetic legal-moral controls. The next part of the essay adumbrates European law's relevance to our theme,[3] and concludes by evaluating the efficacy and justice of English laws protecting public morality when art is alleged to contravene them.

In England, the laws compromising artistic freedom in favour of protecting public morality are wide-ranging in terms of both content and age, and are now set, at least prima facie, in opposition to the Human Rights Act 1998. This Act guarantees freedom of expression as a positive right, and consequently implicitly protects, under that generic freedom, freedom of specifically *artistic* expression as an important dimension of free speech law. However, we will discover that the legal position is far from that simplistic in practice, since under Article 10[4] of the European Convention on Human Rights (hereinafter sometimes referred to as the Convention), Contracting States of the Convention are able to place legitimate restrictions on freedom of expression to protect morality, and this includes local[5] as well as national morality within the state. The Human Rights Act, which incorporates the Convention into the domestic law of the United Kingdom, ensures that such restrictions, as well as artistic liberty as a right, are observed when our domestic courts take into account[6] the Strasbourg jurisprudence under Article 10.[7] In relevant cases, this duty is a judicial obligation even though such case law is not binding. Because the Strasbourg Court is generally unsympathetic to protecting artistic freedom over moral concerns,[8] our national judges are more or less obliged to follow suit under the Human Rights Act, so artistic liberty is in practice co-extensively limited here. This makes artists frustrated since their positive freedom is in fact undermined under

[3] The objective of this essay is to state the law that prevails in England (or the UK) alone. European law, especially that relating to the European Convention on Human Rights, has art law dimensions, but is not the chosen focus of extensive scholarly analysis here.

[4] For the rubric of Art 10, see n 27.

[5] The protection of provincial, in addition to urban, morality is significant, not least because moral evolution in a rural or parochial place does not develop as quickly as in a metropolitan or cosmopolitan locality. It is a truism that avant-garde, postmodern art, with its sometimes morally provocative aspects, is less favourably appreciated outside cities. It is particularly important, therefore, that the European Court of Human Rights thoroughly reviews any legal constraints on art that operate in a relatively quiet and conservative environment, that may be more antipathetic to morally challenging art than a vibrant liberal one. As apparent from the main text, below, the margin of appreciation doctrine does not currently accommodate the operation of such a distinction by the Court.

[6] Under s 2 of the Human Rights Act 1998, UK judges are obliged to take into account, inter alia, Strasbourg jurisprudence. It is important to note, however, that they are not bound by such case law. They merely have to take it into account when relevant to the court proceedings.

[7] For more information on Art 10, see n 27.

[8] In all the cases dealt with by the Court where artistic freedom has been pitched against the morality laws of the relevant Contracting State to the Convention, artistic freedom has lost. This is remarkable, not least because the very raison d'etre of the Strasbourg system is to endeavour to uphold such freedoms.

the Act, via the Convention, when, fundamentally, the opposite should be occurring. However, the relatively tender age of the 1998 Act, and the lack of relevant case law relating specifically to *artistic* freedom under it, means that this conundrum has, as yet, only had a slight formative influence on artistic freedom in the UK's legal practice.

II CENSORSHIP, PORNOGRAPHY AND ART

Philosophers of art have, for a long time, distinguished pornography from non-pornographic (if erotic) art. The typical arguments have been constructed in different ways. Firstly, pornography can be considered inherently bad (because, for example, it involves shameful exploitation and denigration of those who participate in it). Secondly, pornography can be considered to be instrumentally bad (because, for example, it supports offensive assumptions about women's inferiority to men, or promotes violence against women). Unsurprisingly, counter-arguments have been constructed that not all pornography involves inherent or consequential harm, however unpopular such arguments are with certain feminist writers and conservative moralists.[9] If a work seems solely designed to arouse a sexual response, with its content and related effects subordinate to that aim, it is often considered that the work is not in the category of art but, rather, straightforwardly pornographic; and pornography has always presented a special problem in the distinguishing of art from reality because its effects do not engage the meditative interest associated with high art, but instead instil an actual physiological response.

Entangled with the issue of pornography's alleged ill effects, and legal and other legitimacy, is the obvious concern for what is right and good. The right to free speech does not usually specifically prescribe that any given speech must achieve morally palatable ends. More commonly, it is advocated by free-speech proponents that the necessity of freedom is one principal reason not to prevent the making and dissemination of certain pornographic entities. However, this liberty presumption is unavoidably open to exceptions and so any such presumption can be rebutted in certain instances.[10] Emphasising the intrinsic evil in pornography is the approach behind most censoring legal mechanisms, and this is accentuated by the habitual use of some law as a paternalistic defender of the best moral values in order to set an example for the pursuit of decent moral behaviour by citizens in society. More subtle arguments follow from this position. Bernard Williams,[11] for example, has argued that if art is censored on

[9] It is not the purpose of this essay to expound the details of such positions, not least for practical reasons of available time and space.

[10] Certain 'extreme' pornography may precipitate sexual violence, especially towards women and children. The mere possibility of this suggests that that pornography should not be available, least of all on the easily accessible Internet.

[11] B Williams, 'Censorship' in DE Cooper (ed), *Companion to Aesthetics* (Oxford, Blackwell, 1992) 68.

moral grounds, it is senseless to make an exception when the work has significant aesthetic merit. Its merit, he has opined, may make it even more dangerous.[12] Nevertheless, the approach taken in English obscenity law is that art that is held to be legally obscene may be subsequently vindicated by the successful use of a specific defence that the art, despite being deemed obscene, is for the public good. In this way, the obscenity is in effect negated by its sufficient artistic merit. This balancing of factors is undertaken by the jury, and is not an easy exercise for them. The appreciation of this difficulty means that expert witnesses may be called upon to assist the jury in their task. So, *pace* Bernard Williams, a relatively commonsensical position is reached for practical purposes by the appreciation of a meritorious dimension in some art that is prima facie obscene.

Artists and those interested in art, however, may not be satisfied with the legal position in English obscenity law. They point to art's inherent value despite whether it is meritorious or not. Amongst the considerations here is the fact that morally controversial art plays a crucial role in challenging the moral status quo that often then opens a pathway to a new moral order in society. It is often overlooked that contentious art played a central role in promoting the case against slavery in England, for example, and that 'art therapy' is an established form of psychological assistance, whether the art used or produced is morally challenging or not. Art is therefore not as 'useless' as writers such as Oscar Wilde have claimed.[13] It is just that art's usefulness is complicated and refined, rather than simple and banal. Other virtues of art will be explored in due course but it is important to understand, even at this early juncture, that (moral) virtue and (artistic) virtuosity share a common semantic root. Moreover, morally (and legally) transgressive art can be furnished with defences based on its own ontology. It is arguable, for example, that when art is shocking, that is for a sound reason. Through the shock, we begin to understand some truth about our world, including about art and ourselves. We are thus temporarily alienated from the safety of our common preoccupations and embark instead on questioning what has been previously accepted. This prevents society's mores from being unprogressively static. Moreover, the art experience also has to be put in its own context. Art that is controversial is part of an orthodox pattern of general artistic development. Such art, to be appreciated properly, must be seen as part of artistic tradition: morally challenging art must be considered within art's unique historical process, where it co-exists with other disturbing works, together with less provocative peers. Related also to art as a distinct mechanism

[12] Williams seems to miss the point regarding the aesthetic merit component in the argument. Artistic merit (for the public good) in English law, for example, is what can redeem obscene material once it has been found to be obscene; it is not part of that legal balance, established under s 4 of the Obscene Publications Act 1959, for the jury to weigh up whether the artistic appeal of the publication somehow actually palliates the material's obscene content.

[13] Wilde was prone to such generalisations, which were rarely wholly accurate. See, eg, in the preface to Wilde's *The Picture of Dorian Gray* (London, Penguin Classics, 2003).

is its singular mode of formal existence: art's form marks it apart from other cultural phenomena, and that in itself should ensure a certain autonomy; but that form sometimes goes unrecognised outside art's own internal field of reference. If it is art's form that crucially best defines it, constant legal anxiety about its sometimes morally revolutionary content is not just misplaced, it is also harmful to art's cultural legitimacy as a prominent societal feature, resting alongside others such as politics and religion. In order to function freely, each social sector needs its independence and respect for its own immanent rules. This is particularly the case in egalitarian postmodernism,[14] where sub-sets of society ideally co-reside equally justifiably.

Less apparently routine arguments can be used to support the pornographic in relation to art. From an artistic perspective, rather than invading art's canon, pornography adds to the range of art's contents. Pornography can be used to invigorate more conventional art, or to question that art's accepted worth, or to suggest transgression when art lies too safely within its own existing parameters. Moreover, the erotic dimensions of an artwork increase the ambit of art's aesthetic effects such as its sensuous appeal.[15] The addition of pornography to artistic formulae of being augments the engagement of the viewer; and pornography can be an antidote to the pretensions of established art, which is sometimes complacently within the confines of a pre-determined, hierarchical, recalcitrant academy.[16] Significantly, pornography can be iconoclastic and break rules, and it is arguable that the best new art, of necessity, also infringes rules. However, pornography's 'sedition' in the artistic realm can be overstated. It may test certain conventions, but the sexuality it tends to favour, not least in terms of quantity, is classical heterosexuality. However, in the interior world of art's mechanism, pornography can crush elevation and genre (as part of art's aesthetics). It can in this respect be equated with assault, but only as a crime in an artistic sense and context, not in the wider, literal landscape. Nevertheless, even there, to allow the oxymoron of 'obscene art'[17] to be made possible is not necessarily to condone it. The literal world habitually makes concessions to art since art evokes reality by being like it but not identical to it; and a similar thing could be said of pornography. It is also arguable that visual pornography is not involved in a one-way, real-life impacting of power on the innocent; it is, rather, simply one aspect of role play, and, as such, a particular type of artistic enactment. When Robert Mapplethorpe,

[14] See further, D Harvey, *The Condition of Postmodernity: An Enquiry into the Origins of Cultural Change* (Oxford, Blackwell, 1990).

[15] That appeal is most successfully encapsulated in the German term *Sinnlichkeit*.

[16] The French art establishment famously dismissed the artistic worth of Impressionism when its exponents wished to exhibit their new style. Their paintings, now revered, could then only be formally viewed in a salon for rejected works.

[17] Being obscene can only be a property of a work viewed out of context. Art cannot be obscene when viewed in its proper aesthetic context. The correct aesthetic psychic approach to the work excludes the possibility of it having a depraving or corrupting effect because an appropriate meditative attitude to the work creates a reflective distance from it (that puts into perspective any immediate, more visceral response to it). See further, 'The Legal Concept of Art' n 1, 193.

for example, photographed the apparent degradation of gay sadomasochism,[18] it could be contended that he was showing the difference between real fetishism and art, even though his art was using fetishism as its subject. In other words, it could be proffered that he was consciously illustrating, albeit indirectly and subtly, art's (only) oblique relationship with the real world, and simultaneously emphasising very heavily the difference between them by the particularly provocative theme he chose.[19] Some liberals defend pornography, even if they might personally loathe it, in order to protect equality in processes through which the moral environment is formed. Every curtailment of speech, even the abhorrent, they suggest, carries the risk that democracy and individual freedom in self-expression[20] may be both subsequently jeopardised. In the case of morally controversial art, in particular, a disadvantage censorship brings is that it is not visionary: allegedly obscene artworks that the present era is indifferent about may be destroyed even though in the future they could have been considered very important, intrinsically or historically. Moreover, it is arguable that the finished artwork represents a creative result that is implicitly positive, and that the triumph of creativity overwhelms any potentially offensive dimension of the work, which is minor in comparison. Although with pornographic depictions it is sometimes argued that a line has to be drawn somewhere, putting limits on freedom of expression is, for many, simply counter-intuitive. A further consideration, however, is that although the mere fact that a work is deemed to be of the artistic order may, for some, actually neutralise concerns about its content, while, for others, in favour of censorship, the assertion that something is art may be questioned, together, perhaps, with a denial that it has been created by a bona fide artist.[21] The pro-censorship lobby, whether comprising legal moralists or concerned feminists, may object to apparent pornography not just because of its possible (or proven) harms but because, firstly, unlike art, it is not a serious, cognitive attempt to cast light on the human condition, and because, secondly, it does not present the same opportunities for the intellectual or sensory complexity arising from the contemplation of art.

Arguably, the most difficult area to penetrate in the freedom of artistic expression field is the degree to which (art-related) pornography can be actually harmful. Can art of a sexually-arousing type cause paedophilic fantasies leading to the harm of children? Anti-'child pornography' laws would seem to suggest so;

[18] For example, in his exhibition 'The Perfect Moment' which caused controversy across the world. In the USA, in 1990, an exhibition of 175 of Mapplethorpe's photographs took place at the Contemporary Art Centre in Cincinnati. Some of the photographs were alleged to be obscene because five detailed homosexual acts and two showed children with their genitals uncovered. Obscenity proceedings followed but, largely because expert witnesses testified that the photographs were works of artistic merit, the defendants (among them Dennis Barrie, the Centre's Director, and the Centre itself) were acquitted.

[19] Mapplethorpe initially became famous as a result of exhibiting his exquisite collection of photographs of flowers (a more innocuous subject).

[20] Censorship can lead to auto-censorship, and have a chilling effect on the creative ideas and scope of others.

[21] In postmodernism, a prevailing philosophy is self-legitimacy. If one labels oneself an artist, for example, one is *ipso facto* an artist, irrespective of the judgement of others.

and in England it is highly unusual to advocate that children should not be protected from those in consumption of child-related venal art. It is also certain, for the vast majority, that children should be protected from exposure to pornography.[22] But what if certain pornography features only adults, and is consumed only by adults? Here, feminist philosophers have elaborated fierce attacks on the pornographic, some even considering that pornographic concerns are not even a free speech issue. A principle of freedom of speech surely cannot be used to defend actual harm or coercion, but is it accurate to state that pornography actually inspires such evils as rape? It appears so according to some commentators; and it seems indisputable that 'extreme' pornography is definitely linked to violent or other aberrant sexual activity, hence, for example, recent legislation against its possession in England. Such pornography is proscribed here largely because sexual violence against women was explicitly emphasised by the Government as a significant factor behind its proposals to outlaw it. It is still unclear whether art of an associated extreme type comes within the ambit of the offence in theory, or for practical purposes, since the legislation is very young. But it is difficult to imagine a work of art as sharing the same characteristics as extreme pornography, linked as the latter is to such objectively despicable imagery that latently appears to legitimate the activities it is based on between real people in ordinary society. With respect to this, it is easy to see how Andrea Dworkin came to the conclusion that the sex act is inherently an act of occupation and colonisation by a hostile force, a stance embracing even symbolic aggression as a type of sadism.[23]

Finally, there tends to be an assumption, notably in democratic societies such as England's, that freedom of artistic expression is a good thing. However, this view is challenged by those worried about what they regard as the imposition of Western values on non-Western cultures. They submit, for example, that other values, such as self-determination, equality, and freedom from racial and religious hatred[24] and prejudice, should render all types of freedom of expression as matters of much less urgency and importance. Artistic expression became part of this debate following the publication of Salman Rushdie's allegedly blasphemous novel, *The Satanic Verses*.[25] The details of this debacle are given later in the essay. For present purposes, it is sufficient to note that at the centre of the anti-Rushdie position is that it is morally unacceptable to cause offence to other

[22] For the 'Sensation' exhibition at the English Royal Academy in September 1997, the Academy took the unprecedented step of making one of its galleries an 'adults only' space. Exhibited there, inter alia, was a work by Jake and Dinos Chapman called *Zygotic Acceleration*, which comprised models of androgynous children with aroused genitalia instead of faces. Those under the age of 18 were not admitted.

[23] Together with Catherine McKinnon, Dworkin drafted a civil rights ordinance that employed the concept of 'pornography' as a basis for legal control, and which was passed by the Indianapolis City Council. Later, the ordinance was struck down by the Supreme Court. See *American Booksellers v Hudnut* 475 US 1001 [1986].

[24] In England, the Racial and Religious Hatred Act 2006 provides protection against such unjustifiable enmity.

[25] S Rushdie, *The Satanic Verses* (London, Viking Press, 1988)

cultures even through art: a view now widely accepted, especially in our Muslim community. However, others in England warn that, after the Rushdie controversy, the spirit of the fatwa (amounting to a death sentence) issued in Iran against the novelist for, inter alia, defaming Mohammed, has been dangerously internalised in England to the extent that free speech, a fundamental tenet of our unwritten constitution, has been clearly undermined in favour of meticulously attempting to promote all aspects of racial and religious harmony in our now pluralist society. This casts a relatively new perspective on freedom of artistic expression in England, precise attention to which will be paid later in this essay.

III THE EVOLUTION OF FREEDOM OF ARTISTIC EXPRESSION IN ENGLAND

Freedom of expression in the United Kingdom is in a transitional phase, courtesy of the coming into force on 2 October 2000 of the Human Rights Act 1998.[26] As stated earlier, UK courts now take into account European human rights law that has accrued under the European Convention on Human Rights, notably Strasbourg jurisprudence. Specifically, freedom of artistic expression has a comparatively short case law content under the Convention,[27] but it is not the objective of this essay to examine that in detail. But as a preliminary point, it can be said with some certainty that there are few grounds for considering that art as expression is well protected under that international instrument.[28] The resultant effect in the UK, under the Human Rights Act 1998, is therefore not dissimilar to the situation in the UK prior to the Act, because under the Act

[26] Section 12 expressly covers freedom of expression issues, including a provision that particular regard must be paid to freedom of expression in a case where it conflicts with another interest (especially, in practice, privacy). The phrase 'particular regard' has, somewhat strangely, not been judicially interpreted to mean that any balancing of such interests is tipped in favour of freedom of expression. See further, s 12(4) of the Act. The rubric of s 12 is set out in n 112.

[27] Artistic expression is not explicitly mentioned in the rubric of the freedom of expression provision, which comprises Art 10. This Article reads as follows: '1. Everyone has the right to freedom of expression. This right shall include freedom to hold opinions and to receive and impart information and ideas without interference by public authority and regardless of frontiers. This Article shall not prevent States from requiring the licensing of broadcasting, television or cinema enterprises. 2. The exercise of these freedoms, since it carries with it duties and responsibilities, may be subject to such formalities, conditions, restrictions or penalties as are prescribed by law and are necessary in a democratic society, in the interests of national security, territorial integrity, or public safety, for the prevention of disorder or crime, for the protection of health or morals, for the protection of the reputation or rights of others, for preventing the disclosure of information received in confidence, or for maintaining the authority and impartiality of the judiciary.'

[28] Art is usually given low priority in Strasbourg jurisprudence when it allegedly contravenes other social interests, especially the protection of morals. In practice, contrary to what some commentators believe, artistic freedom is even less well protected under the Convention system than commercial speech. It is not within the ambit of this essay on domestic law to examine in detail the Convention case law giving rise to this conclusion; but to prove its verity, see further, P Kearns, 'Art's Demise in the European Court of Human Rights' (2007) 12 *Art, Antiquity and Law* 2, 137–69.

the equally art-indifferent human rights law of the Convention is applied, which is rather dismaying for those interested in art. The disadvantaged status of artistic expression under the Convention emanates largely from the European Court of Human Rights being too generous in endowing Contracting States with a virtually unreviewed discretion or 'wide margin of appreciation'[29] regarding the establishment of public morality laws, enabling them to be priorities that in practice prevail over freedom of artistic expression as a more weakly supported conflicting interest. From a national perspective, it is well worth examining the comparable position of artistic expression in UK law prior to the 1998 Human Rights Act, to determine for the first time as a matter of legal history English law's real commitment to it as a civil liberty. For these purposes, the sixteenth century is an apt starting point. By a Star Chamber decree of 1538, English printers were prevented from publishing without first acquiring a licence,[30] because Tudor monarchs wished to prevent the circulation of heretical or seditious literature that might cause constitutional instability. Consequently, draconian penalties were in force for breaching the licensing rules. At the beginning of the Civil War, this licensing system waned but a decree was issued in 1643 to reinvigorate and galvanise it.[31] The system then proved unworkable, and was abolished in 1695. Criticism of government was then regulated *after* publication using the legal mechanism of seditious libel,[32] and, at the beginning of the eighteenth century, two relatively minor unreported cases tested the efficacy of its cognate offence, obscene libel. James Read's *The Fifteen Plagues of Maidenhead* was prosecuted in 1708, but the work did not focus specifically on any person or persons so Read was exonerated.[33] In 1727, Edmund Curll was similarly prosecuted, this time successfully, for the publication of *Venus in a Cloyster*, which was deemed obscene for tending to corrupt its readers and disturbing the peace.[34] As the century progressed, common law principles of this type grew increasingly at odds with public opinion, but the ancient crimes of outraging public decency and corrupting public morals were not used against artistic works, more by chance than design, because their most common variants took

[29] The margin of appreciation doctrine has been developed by the European Court of Human Rights since 1976. The idea behind it is that where sensitive subjects, such as morality, are in issue, the Court will operate a type of subsidiarity, whereby a discretion is afforded to a Contracting State to the Convention to decide a matter for itself without a full review of that decision by the Strasbourg Court. The margin of appreciation in the area of morality is wide but, particularly where there is a consensus amongst the Contracting States on an issue, a narrow margin may operate, such as in the area of sexual orientation, which is a crucial aspect of private life that must be firmly safeguarded. As stated in n 27, it is not within the remit of this essay, largely because of the pressure of available space, to examine Strasbourg jurisprudence in detail on this or other matters.

[30] See further, D Thomas, *A Long Time Burning – The History of Literary Censorship in England* (London, Routledge and Kegan Paul, 1969).

[31] F Schauer, *Free Speech: A Philosophical Enquiry* (Cambridge, Cambridge University Press, 1982) 15.

[32] See, eg, *R v Tutchkin* (1904) 14 ST 1095.

[33] B Williams, *Report of the Committee on Obscenity and Film Censorship* (Cmnd 7772, 1979) Appendix 1, para 2 (The Williams Committee).

[34] ibid para 3.

the form of little-prosecuted conspiracy offences.[35] The public exhibition of obscene prints was made a summary offence under the Vagrancy Act of 1824, and the Metropolitan Police Act of 1839 and the Town Police Clauses Act of 1847 reinforced the general censoring emphasis on indecent public displays and the sale of obscene material. By 1851, the law of blasphemous libel had become virulently unpopular, especially when the Government was instructed that the celebrated John Stuart Mill could realistically be prosecuted for delivering a lecture that was purportedly agnostic.[36] Nowhere in the common law at this time could we find notions of free speech or liberty of the press and, in 1857, Lord Campbell's Obscene Publications Act was passed, which, though aimed at offensive products of teeming mass culture rather than serious artworks, had unfortunate effects for art.[37] It was not Lord Campbell's intention for the Act to apply to high culture[38] or art's private enjoyment, but no safeguard appeared in the bill to protect the supposedly legitimate cultural digestion of erotic art imagery, and once again a very real fear of the enforcement of cultural philistinism arose. The latter part of the nineteenth century fell under this generally repressive cloud, and artistic freedom was jeopardised by the notions of corruption and indecency despite Lord Campbell's initial vociferous assurance that the private possession and assimilation of explicit books, and items of visual cultural value, were protected as matters of taste, and not subject, therefore, to the threat of legal interference.

The twentieth century was the first era in which commentators categorically acknowledged the countervailing notion of human rights protection of freedom of expression as a matter of legal regulation, notably in the international sphere. Nevertheless, even as late as 1958, before the advent of the Obscene Publications Act 1959, individuals' expressive freedoms in England were characterised merely as residual civil liberties, framed in the negative way that citizens in England were free to do all, and only, that which was not legally prohibited. It is arguable that this position persisted (despite the liberalising provisions of the Obscene Publications Act 1959) until the Human Rights Act 1998 came into force on 2 October 2000, investing UK citizens and residents for the first time with distinct, constitutionally-enshrined rights that they could only now legally activate as a basis for defending and reinforcing their freedoms effectively. But, even as late as May 1999,[39] Lord Steyn referred to freedom of expression as a right that must yield to other cogent social interests whilst simultaneously venturing the rather contradictory, optimistic view that there is no difference in principle

[35] These offences achieved renewed vigour in their conspiracy and non-conspiracy forms from the 1970s onwards.

[36] See, more generally, G Robertson, *Freedom, the Individual and the Law* (Penguin, 1993).

[37] See further, L Nead, 'Bodies of Judgment: Art, Obscenity and the Connoisseur' in C Douzinas and L Nead (eds), *Law and the Image: The Authority of Art and the Aesthetics of Law* (The University of Chicago Press, 1999).

[38] It is arguable that there is no longer a meaningful distinction between 'high' and other culture; such is the equalising tendency of postmodernism.

[39] *R v Secretary of State for the Home Department, ex p Simms* [1999] 3 WLR 328.

between the UK law on free expression and the protection of it under Article 10 of the European Convention on Human Rights. Valid reservations about the true efficacy of that Convention law in preserving free artistic expression make the tenor of such statements particularly disappointing for the art community. Nevertheless, in *Broadmoor Hospital Authority v R*,[40] the only domestic legal case in this era specifically centred on art and freedom of expression, free artistic expression was successfully upheld in the UK even prior to the application of the Human Rights Act. This is promising for artists and is a precedent that should be followed in spite of the current intolerant spirit of Strasbourg case law. In the *Broadmoor* case, the Health Authority applied for an injunction to restrain the publication of a literary work, *Armageddon Ahoy*, written by R, a Broadmoor patient, who was suffering from paranoid schizophrenia and who had been convicted of manslaughter. The book referred to fellow patients and detailed the patient's motives for killing his victim. In refusing to grant an injunction, the Court of Appeal noted that free artistic expression was an important consideration but, like Lord Steyn, it equated the UK stance on free speech with that of the Strasbourg institutions, prompting again the question of whether the parallel is truly accurate and valuable in terms of ensuring the protection of artists' rights of free expression, especially given the European human rights law case of *Wingrove v United Kingdom*,[41] which is explored in depth later in the essay, where the European Court of Human Rights deprioritises artistic freedom (previously endorsed by the European Commission of Human Rights) in favour of the enforcement of local-national public morality.

Before exhaustively analysing contemporary crimes that affect controversial art specifically in England, it is finally also necessary to put those, and the relevant case law, in brief current sociological perspective. All the pertinent crimes and case law examined here come within a period known in social philosophy as postmodernism,[42] which is an era that began in the 1940s as a reaction to modernism. Sociologically, it is arguable that the inter-relationship of art and legal morality should not involve conflict if the theory of postmodernism works in tandem with practice under it. In postmodernism, there is deemed to be a dynamic equilibrium of different identities, all co-existing in a homogeneous state of respect for difference. Under this scheme, art should be equivalent to law in terms of importance because, in postmodernism, there is a compelling claim to equal significance on the parts of all societal players. Within the legal construction, art should enjoy equal compositional value with other regulated factors. The non-recognition by law of the distinctive ontology of art threatens this ethos because art cannot then be differentiated from other facts as an entity of special cultural value distinct from other social phenomena. If the social reality of postmodernism is the respectful treatment of the 'unlike' only cosmetically

[40] *Broadmoor Hospital Authority v R* [2000] 2 All ER 727.
[41] *Wingrove v United Kingdom* [1997] 24 EHRR 1.
[42] See 'Postmodernism: A Critical Guide' (n 1) 185.

rather than actually, the law is even further obligated to ensure that there is no practical legal indifference to art by recognising art as a specific, substantive legal category, and, in so doing, compensating for the lack of depth to postmodernism's evolved praxis in effectuating merely surface ideals. Law's success in such a role can be pertinently evaluated here in the course of analysing the legal treatment of art in what artists regard as the most acutely contentious legal area, namely the enforcement of public morality.

IV CONTEMPORARY CRIMES AND CASE LAW

The area of law that most prominently restricts, or attempts to restrict, controversial art is public morality law, which, in English law, comes in many guises. Obscenity laws and other related public morality provisions regulate activities and facts that contravene certain legally-determined essential moral values. They embody state paternalism to keep public moral standards intact. They are not usually specialised monitors of morality in art but art is frequently caught by such laws, which do not generally accept, or even consider, the cultural distinctiveness of art as a factor in the assessment of legal-moral constraints. There are several art-relevant offences that therefore require analysis, excluding race relation offences and seditious libel, which have a less central relation to art issues. Of the principal relevant offences, the key one is obscenity legislation in the form of the Obscene Publications Act 1959. Its section 1 proscribes publications that have a tendency to deprave and corrupt. Initially, obscenity was an ecclesiastical offence, like blasphemy, and the current law retains atavistically in its basic *modus operandi* a conspicuously Christian hypostasis. Under the 1959 Act, whether an item is obscene or not is a question for the jury, and expert evidence is not admissible on that matter. The jury must decide if the publication has or does not have a tendency to deprave and corrupt. The legislative formula of 'deprave and corrupt' connotes, albeit imprecisely, a *serious* illegal tendency, and the common law has in its development deemed that to 'deprave and corrupt' (a phrase that is legally used disjunctively, and that is considered to convey something deeply immoral) is not equivalent to merely to shock and disgust (a phrase that is in practice used conjunctively, and that is considered to convey something less grave). Also, if an item is adjudged to have a tendency to deprave and corrupt a significant proportion of its audience, the actual intention of its author is legally irrelevant. Nevertheless, section 4 of the Act does provide a defence of 'public good':

> (1) Subject to subsection 1(A) of this section a person shall not be convicted of an offence against section 2 of this Act if it is proved that publication of the article in question is justified in being for the public good on the ground that it is in the interests of science, literature, art and learning, or of objects of general concern.

As provided in section 4(2), this ground can be established or abrogated by the opinion of experts as to the entity's artistic or other merits. The evolved process is therefore that the jury is directed to first consider whether an item is obscene within section 1 and, if it is not satisfied of that beyond reasonable doubt, it must acquit. However, if, on the contrary, the jury is so satisfied, it should proceed to consider whether, on a balance of probabilities, the publication of the item, though obscene, is nevertheless for the public good. The onus of establishing the defence in section 4 is on the accused.

Due to limited space, one can only summarise here certain factual contexts where action under the Obscene Publications Act 1959 has been taken or contemplated in relation to art, including creative writing. The English publication of Vladimir Nabakov's classic *Lolita*[43] in 1959, for example, potentially attracted legal censure based on its treatment of under-age sex but went unprosecuted; and other obscenity cases have included the famous *Lady Chatterley's Lover*[44] and *Oz* trials. The *Chatterley* trial, that first tested the 1959 legislation in a significant way, is examined in detail later in this essay; in the *Oz* trial, the magazine of that name was the object of a prosecution in England in 1971. *Oz* advocated sex and drugs as liberating forces, and detailed homosexual, lesbian and sadistic activities. Its publishers were found guilty under the 1959 Act. In 1976, the *Inside Linda Lovelace*[45] obscenity trial took place because that book contained steamy descriptions of orgies, but its publishers were acquitted because the jury found that the work would not 'deprave and corrupt' the type of person likely to buy it. The touring exhibition of Robert Mapplethorpe's sadomasochistic photographs caused controversy, notably in the USA in 1989, whilst in England in 1997–98 a book in the library of the University of West England of explicitly sexual Mapplethorpe photographs nearly led to the Vice-Chancellor of that University being charged under the 1959 Act. In 1989, the last novel to be banned under that legislation was *Lord Horror* by David Britton, and it can be inferred from the lack of more recent prosecutions that novels are now outside the remit of police interest.[46] Photographs of Brooke Shields as a naked child have also caused moral controversy, and police consideration of an obscenity prosecution in England in late 2009. This had resonances of art-photographer Tierney Gearon's potential prosecution under the 1959 Act in the 1990s for taking photographs of her own children naked, and the difficulties Marcus Harvey encountered with the potential censorship of his artwork *Myra*, in the 1997 'Sensation' exhibition in the Royal Academy in London, because of the alleged glorification of the child murderer Myra Hindley in a work made from a child's handprints. The taboo subject of child sexuality has been the theme of a very recent controversial Von Trier film called *Nymphomanic*, but, as yet, no

[43] V Nabakov *Lolita* (London, Penguin Group, 2006)

[44] DH Lawrence *Lady Chatterley's Lover* (London, Penguin Group, 2011)

[45] L Lovelace *Inside Linda Lovelace*, 1st edn (New York, Oceana Press, 1973)

[46] The last cases when French law applied obscenity legislation (*outrage aux bonnes moeurs*) to serious literature concerned Flaubert's *Madame Bovary* and Baudelaire's *Les Fleurs du Mal*. This was in the middle of the nineteenth century. Now, the objectives of French law in this area are to protect children and to proscribe undue violence in films. Sexual representations for adults' consumption are currently very rarely prosecuted.

prosecution relating to it has been instigated. The topic of gay pornography's legitimacy in relation to the Obscene Publications Act 1959 has also been closely monitored in England in recent years, not least because differences in principle appear to be necessary when gay pornography is contrasted with its heterosexual counterpart, which is more traditionally the subject of censure, including on feminist grounds – arguments which arguably have less relevance when men not women are the subject of the medium.[47] Equally controversial has been the content of the recent film *Shame*, which some feminists consider attempts to palliate pornography by relating it to the depiction of illness, notably 'sex addiction'. The 'Body Worlds' exhibitions of Gunther von Hagens that apply the scientific technique of plastination to human and animal corpses to reveal the bodies' workings have so far avoided prosecution under English obscenity law even though some find the exhibits distasteful or disgusting. Under the Obscene Publications Act 1959, the test of depraving or corrupting, rather than shocking and disturbing, is the legal barometer used. The latter-mentioned, lower standard is reserved for the analogous ancient and recently resurrected crime of outraging public decency. Because of the advent of the Internet, certain very contemporary jurisdictional problems have arisen, but it is now settled law that if a website is hosted abroad, and sufficiently offensive material is downloaded from it in England, the publication of such electronic data (such as relevant artistic matter that comes under our obscenity legislation) is deemed to take place when such images are both loaded *and* downloaded.

Blasphemous libel was a sister offence to obscene libel but it was not in its most recent form enshrined in legislation. It has now been repealed, and therefore removed from our common law, but it still resonates through public-moral English law due to it being a cognate offence to obscenity: cases connected with blasphemy are still routinely referred to in other public morality cases and contexts. Blasphemy was an oppressive common law offence forbidding the vilification of Christ and the fundamental tenets of Christianity. If the jury decided that the putative libel published was blasphemous, the intention of the publisher merely to publish was sufficient for a conviction. The publisher did not need to even think, let alone intend, that the material was blasphemous. In addition, unlike under the obscenity legislation, no defence of artistic or other merit was available to the accused. In England, various publications attracted the actual or possible application of the old blasphemy law, which is no longer extant. For example, the editor of the magazine *Gay News* was successfully prosecuted for blasphemy when a poem by James Kirkup, and an accompanying illustration, in one particular issue, had as their theme the sexual interference

[47] This is a very sensitive area. It appears from most sociological studies and media coverage that men are much less likely to be concerned about the sexual exploitation of other men in pornography than women are about other women in comparable circumstances. In 1989, the New Zealand Committee of Inquiry into Pornography observed: '[t]he term "pornography" in its now common and useful meaning, derived from feminist writings . . . refers . . . to sexually explicit material which is demeaning or degrading to women (and sometimes to children or men). See further, *New Zealand: Report of the Ministerial Inquiry into Pornography* (1989) 27.

with the body of Christ by a centurion at the foot of the Cross. This was the case of *R v Lemon, R v Gay News Ltd.*[48] This was a rare case because blasphemy law had not been applied for decades. The crime was later resurrected when a Mr Choudhury applied for a summons against Salman Rushdie for alleged blasphemy in his novel *The Satanic Verses*. This case, detailed later in this essay, involved alleged blasphemy against the tenets of Islam, and that theme was later of relevance in Denmark when cartoons that caricatured Mohammed, allegedly offensively, were the subject of a blasphemy complaint. In England, the author Philip Pullman escaped prosecution in England for blasphemy when it was still an existing crime here, despite the blatantly anti-Christian content of some of his books. In a similar vein, in 1997, Jeremy Springer came under attack for alleged blasphemy in his sexually outrageous production *Jeremy Springer: the Opera*, but its attempted private prosecution failed in an action brought under section 2(4)(a) of the Theatres Act 1968.[49] In a more legally famous case, elaborated upon later, Nigel Wingrove, a British film-maker, had a licence refused for the distribution, and concomitant showing, of his video film *Visions of Ecstasy*, because it was thought that it could infringe English blasphemy law. It depicted Saint Teresa of Avila engaging in erotic activity with Christ during her famous ecstatic religious experiences. In 1997, the European Court of Human Rights upheld the decision of the English Video Appeals Panel to enjoy its right to in effect censor the film as an aspect of the margin of appreciation doctrine. However, when blasphemy law in England was abolished, Wingrove was invited in early 2012 to re-submit his film to the British Board of Film Classification (hereinafter sometimes referred to as the BBFC). In the USA, in 1989–90, the artist Andres Serrano caused religious controversy when he exhibited his artwork *Piss Christ*, a photograph of the crucifixion immersed in a tank of what was taken to be urine. Charges in relation to this work against the Cincinnati Contemporary Arts Centre's Director, Dennis Barrie, in 1990, were only dropped because the exhibition was terminated. In 2011, in Avignon, France, the same artwork was physically attacked because certain Christians considered it blasphemous.

In recent years, an equally draconian common law offence relating to public morality has suspiciously reappeared. This is the ancient offence of outraging public decency (as alluded to earlier). The jury simply ponders whether the relevant entity outrages public decency and, if it so decides, there is a conviction. As

[48] *R v Lemon, R v Gay News Ltd* [1979] 2 WLR 281.

[49] As judicially interpreted, this provision dictated that the ancient offence of blasphemous libel was to be distinguished from criminal defamatory libel, which was the offence specifically preserved by the Theatres Act. The aim of criminal defamation had to be a living person, it was held, and Christ could not be regarded as a living human being for these purposes. This approach raises interesting theological questions. Are we to conclude, following the Court's reasoning, that Christians do not worship a living God? Why was it only the prerogative of blasphemy law to preserve a living God's reputation? Defamation of a living God was at the root of blasphemy law in England, and one of the key tenets of Christianity is the resurrection, by which the eternal living status of Christ is assured. See further, R *Green, v The City of Westminster Magistrates' Court* [2007] Divisional Court, [2007] EWHC 2785 (Admin).

was the case in blasphemy law, the *mens rea* of this crime is tantamount to strict liability, with no provision or possibility of an artistic merit defence. The notable case is that relating to the 'foetus earrings' (which is later considered in some detail). An action using the offence of outraging public decency was also contemplated, in 2009–10, by a group of Christians following the exhibition of an artwork by Terence Koh in Gateshead art gallery. The work depicted Christ with an erection, and its allegedly negative impact occurred after the repeal of English blasphemy law. It is interesting to note that, if the action had gone ahead, the group would have used outraging public decency as an alternative to the more appropriate, but by then defunct, law of blasphemy. This highlights the possible overlapping nature of public-moral offences, a situation that does not lead to legal consistency or certainty. Moreover, such overlapping is considered not just antinomic or undesirable but illicit by the English judiciary. Outraging public decency's revival from being a dormant, archaic offence has been accompanied by that of the equally ancient common law offence of corrupting public morals.[50] This strict liability crime has not featured in any case involving art but, if it were to do so, it is highly likely that art would again be denied a suitable defence based on any inherent merit, which is the established position in relation to its sister offence, which seeks to prevent public outrage.

The next offence adumbrated here as most relevant to art concerns is the Indecent Displays (Control) Act 1981. Its section 1(1) prescribes that if any indecent matter is displayed in public, the person making the display, and any person causing or permitting the display to be made, shall be guilty of an offence. However, significantly, the Act does not apply in relation to any matter included in a display of an art gallery or museum and visible only from within the gallery or museum. Art is consequently somewhat idiosyncratically exempted from prosecution here, based exclusively on its physical context rather than on its intrinsic qualities, although it is true that underlying such a provision a favourable value judgment about art has evidently been made by the legislators.

Visual artworks can be affected by other, more miscellaneous areas of law that in a direct way relate to immorality. One such example is section 42 of the Customs Consolidation Act 1876, as amended, which makes it a criminal offence to import into the United Kingdom indecent or obscene prints, paintings, photographs, books, cards, lithographs or other engravings, or any other indecent or obscene articles. Another example is section 54(10) of the Metropolitan Police Act 1839, which prescribes that every person who sells or distributes or offers for sale or distribution, or exhibits to public view, any profane book, paper, print, drawing, painting or representation, in any London

[50] The crime of corrupting public morals clearly overlaps in content with the statutory obscenity test formula that proscribes, in a given publication, a tendency to deprave and corrupt. This is antinomic. Both offences aim to prevent the same (legally unspecified) deleterious effect on an individual arising from alleged 'corruption'. See further, C Manchester, 'Obscenity, Pornography and Art' (1999) *Media and Arts Law Review* 70.

thoroughfare or public place, shall be guilty of an offence. A provision with broadly comparable objectives is section 28 of the Town Police Clauses Act 1847. All of the above-mentioned, seemingly archaic crimes are still extant, and artwork in a public place could also, in theory at least, be caught by the 1986 Public Order Act (which reinforces the 1936 Public Order Act, hence its chronological position here) in certain, admittedly practically unlikely, circumstances. In addition, section 11 of the Post Office Act 1953, as amended, provides that it is an offence for a postal packet to be sent through the mail which encloses any indecent or obscene print, painting, photograph, lithograph, engraving, cinematograph film, book, card or written communication, or any indecent or obscene article; or for a postal packet to have on it outside grossly offensive, indecent, or obscene matter. Section 2 of the Theatres Act 1968 provides that a performance of a play shall be deemed to be obscene if its effect is such as to tend to deprave and corrupt persons likely to attend it. This broadly deliberately parallels the Obscene Publications Act 1959, as does section 3 of the 1968 Act, which provides the defence of 'public good' if the performance in question is in the interests of drama, opera, ballet or any other art, or of literature or learning.

Much more recently, section 63 of the Criminal Justice and Immigration Act 2008 criminalised possession of what it refers to as 'extreme pornographic images'. The law came into force on 26 January 2009, and is not retrospective. It applies to pornographic images of such a nature that they must reasonably be assumed to have been produced solely or principally for the purpose of sexual arousal, which are grossly offensive, disgusting or otherwise of an obscene character, and which portray in an explicit and realistic way any of the following: an act which threatens a person's life; an act which results, or is likely to result, in serious injury to a person's anus, breasts or genitals; an act which involves or appears to involve sexual interference with a human corpse; and, finally, a person performing or appearing to perform an act of intercourse or oral sex with an animal (whether alive or dead), such that a reasonable person looking at one of the above-mentioned images would think that any such person or animal was real. Although it is difficult to imagine much artwork[51] to include the type of material that this legislation proscribes, the 'extreme' pornography provisions do render art of an extreme nature vulnerable to equation with morally reprehensible, more literal representations of genuinely heinous activities. The extension of the public good defence in section 4 of the Obscene Publications Act 1959 to this legislation would potentially guard against the conviction of artists for 'extreme' art (presumably containing sufficiently severe pornographic imagery to cross the 'extreme' pornography legislation's immorality threshold). Admittedly, it would take a particularly esoteric artistic mind-set to fulfil an artistic project of such pornographic extremity and to still expect to receive a

[51] It is suggested by some that the only art-related media that would in practice be adversely affected by the 'extreme pornography' legislation would be 'art films'.

substantial audience. Nevertheless, the possibility exists, not least because the general public tends to be intrigued by such controversial material. Moreover, in the era of postmodernism, self-legitimation is of key importance, so that a pornographer can characterise himself or herself as an artist without having to receive objective confirmation of that title or label. Since the 'extreme' pornography legislation is so young, it is as yet difficult to predict how art will be accommodated as a probable exception to its general measures of prohibition, but other legislation clearly supports the tenor of this legal censorship. The Coroners and Justice Act 2009, for example, makes it illegal to own any picture depicting under-18s participating in sexual activity in the presence of someone under 18; and another, older, offence that can relate to artistic images regarding minors is section 1(1)(d) of the Protection of Children Act 1978, which rightly penalises the making, distribution, showing and advertising of indecent photographs of children.

V FOUR MAJOR CASE PARADIGMS: THE JUDICIALISATION OF ART IN ENGLISH PUBLIC-MORAL LAW

A Obscenity Case Paradigm

The first major case that was brought under the Obscene Publications Act 1959 was the prosecution of Penguin Books Ltd[52] for the publication of DH Lawrence's novel *Lady Chatterley's Lover*.[53] The case presents the prototype judicial approach to an artwork that is the subject matter of an obscenity charge under the Obscene Publications Act 1959, and the judgment, being seminal, and not atypical, requires detailed examination. The legal relevance of such analysis is to reveal by example potential difficulties judges may have with respect to the efficient working of the obscenity legislation and to expose as somewhat justified the scepticism some artists have about judicial antagonism to the artistic medium, resulting from ignorance of the imaginative dimensions to the artistic process. The instant case demonstrates that legal literalism is inappropriate when a judge tackles difficult and specialised moral and artistic issues with insufficient expertise. *Lady Chatterley's Lover* was the subject of obscenity proceedings in England, America, Canada, India and Japan. In England, the novel met with Justice Byrne,[54] who, from the start, was obviously very hostile towards it. He was squarely against the jury founding its views on those of experts called under section 4 of the Act to defend it, an attitude which conspicuously undermined the whole rationale supporting the newly-established statutory right to

[52] See further, CH Rolph, *The Trial of Lady Chatterley's Lover* (Penguin Books, 1961).

[53] See further, P Kearns, 'Obscenity Law and the Creative Writer: The Case of D.H. Lawrence' (1998) 22 *Columbia-VLA Journal of Law and the Arts* 4, 525.

[54] It is unknown as to why Justice Byrne personally felt so strongly about the necessary censorship of the novel in question.

call them. The judge's stance towards the novel was that of a proud non-specialist, and he exhorted the jury to approach the book with similar mind-sets, unenlightened about what he considered to be only narrowly academically appreciable elements of the creative writing process, such as the writer's purpose. He wanted the jury to react as their 'normal' selves (assumed by him to be art-ignorant). He told them to separate the work from its apposite artistic context and to deflect rather than digest the learned appraisals of experts allied to what he perceived to be Lawrence's ignoble endeavour. From a hermeneutical standpoint, this stance could be justified on the grounds that, though antipathetic to art, it embraced the common position of the man-in-the-street who would not have expert appraisals at hand to better inform him about the novel. Nevertheless, the approach Justice Byrne adopted was antithetical to the intentions behind the obscenity statute, which expressly demanded an artistic appraisal from the jury to satisfy the exigencies of section 4[55] of the Act. The judge's adverse treatment of the issue of literary merit also cast doubt that justice was actually being seen to be done in terms of proper interpretation and the sound use of the obscenity statute's unique new mechanisms for art protection.

The first day of Justice Byrne's summing up in the trial of *Lady Chatterley's Lover* was on 1 November 1960, and was very censorious.[56] The judge instructed the members of the jury that they were exercising their minds not about questions of taste but about moral standards: the question, he asserted, was whether the novel was immoral, not whether it was likeable. He also warned the jury that the wisdom that morality should be fundamental to the wellbeing of a community must conquer the desire for apparently wayward self-expression. However, one might argue that, since morality defies definition except relatively, that might beg the question as to how one can ever know in advance what is likely to jeopardise it. But Justice Byrne was hardened against such abstract thinking. He instructed the jury to read the novel 'dispassionately', even though the very systemic existence of art requires an emotional, as well as purely cerebral reaction to it. He was inappropriately condescending towards the expert witnesses in favour of the book, uttering the dismissive statement that 'nobody, of course, for one moment questions the honesty of their opinions'. His clear implication was that candour was their only virtue. The judge also displayed no real interest in the novel's details saying, for example, that the heroine was 'living with her husband in the dreary place of Wragby, I think it was called'. He had a better memory for the details of the descriptions of sexual intercourse, which could be explained sympathetically by the fact that the focus of the trial was the question of obscenity. Less conscientiously, Justice Byrne failed to accurately explain to the jury the 'public good' defence: he said that if the jury was satisfied that it was an obscene book, it had then to go on to consider the further question: 'Have the defendants established the probability that the

[55] The rubric of s 4 was set out earlier in the essay.

[56] My analysis here follows the content of the judgment sequentially, from point to point.

merits of the book as a novel are so high that they outbalance the obscenity, so that its publication is for the public good?' In law, the defendants only had to establish that on the balance of probabilities their case was the stronger one. The judicial use of the phrase 'so high' is inept because it suggests merit has to significantly outweigh obscenity, whereas it only has to outweigh it slightly. In addition, although Justice Byrne acknowledged that all the witnesses subscribed to the fact that *Lady Chatterley's Lover* was a book of literary merit and that Lawrence was one of the greatest authors of the twentieth century, he asserted that the jury was to appraise the book only by itself rather than in comparative relation to other books. However, one might submit that in the course of the necessary ascertainment of an obscene tendency, it would seem particularly profitable to compare the text in issue with other books of a similar genre so as to better decide the threshold of condemnation.

The second day of Justice Byrne's summing up in the trial was on 2 November 1960. On this occasion, the judge again exhibited inadequate comprehension of artistic processes. For example, he chose to adopt a strictly legal idea of marriage and its associated Christian duties, which differs from the concept of marriage often found in creative literature, which tends to be less rigid. One creative illustration occurs in Virgil's *The Aeneid*, Book four, for example, when the 'marriage' of Dido and Aeneas occurs spontaneously when they are hunting in the mountains. Justice Byrne went on to condemn promiscuity and adultery as the central evils for legal purposes, whereas the specialised legal concept of obscenity per se, and any countervailing redemptive merit, should have been emphasised as the jury's prime focus. Additionally, the judge was clearly against artistic realism: he was disapproving of Lawrence's use of words as a gamekeeper might use them; he also said, incorrectly, that the 'dirty' language could only be redeemed if its purpose was scientific rather than artistic. There was no basis in law for such an assertion. In response to Dame Rebecca West's testimony for the defence, Justice Byrne intoned disrespectfully: 'That was her view, for what that is worth.' He circumvented any notion that sex could be exciting rather than simply congenial and procreatively necessary. He also doubted whether the sexual passages in the book were founded on a 'holy' basis, and whether a couple's union in a non-legal sense could ever have 'sacred' importance. One might have been forgiven for thinking it was a blasphemy trial in part, so inappropriate were these obiter dicta.

Ultimately, despite Justice Byrne's strenuous efforts, the verdict the jury delivered was an emphatic not guilty, which was a triumph not just for literary art but for art in general. It was a conspicuous defeat for legal literalism. The jury had appreciated *Lady Chatterley's Lover* was of the artistic order and upheld that canon. It dismissed the judge's literal attitude of taking the allegedly offending passages out of their appropriate artistic context. For the lawyer who specialises in obscenity law, or who is interested in the field of law and literature, it is regrettable that we will never know more precise details of this notable verdict: it was never recorded whether the jury found that the novel was simply not obscene or obscene but justified under section 4[57] of the Act. This reporting oversight does not of course detract in any way from the novel's unqualified legal victory.

B Blasphemy Case Paradigms

i The Rushdie Debacle and Contingent Considerations

There is an arguably erroneous belief that art can be blasphemous and appropriately detailed attention to the nature and operation of art in the blasphemy context is rarely given in legal proceedings, even when it is imperative in order to respect art's distinct and unique ontology. The importance of the art issue in English blasphemy law arose in the wake of the controversy stirred by the publication of Salman Rushdie's novel *The Satanic Verses*, which was alleged by some, especially Muslims, to be blasphemous.[58] On 13 March 1989, the Chief Metropolitan Magistrate, sitting at Bow Street Magistrates' Court, refused to grant the applicant, Abdul Hussain Choudhury, summonses he had applied for against Salman Rushdie, the author, and Viking Penguin Publishing Co Ltd, the publishers, alleging the commission of the offences of blasphemous libel and seditious libel at common law. The said novel won the Whitbread Prize for literature in 1988 and has been translated into at least 15 languages. It has been banned in all Muslim countries, China, India and South Africa.

The applicant sought summonses alleging that the author and publishers had published or caused to be published 'a blasphemous libel concerning Almighty God (Allah), the Supreme Deity common to all major religions of the world . . . and the religion of Islam and Christianity' and a seditious libel in that it raised widespread discontent and disaffection among Her Majesty The Queen's subjects. The relief the applicant sought was an order of *certiorari* to quash the decision of the magistrate and an order of *mandamus* directing him to issue the summonses as applied for. The magistrate had refused to issue the summonses on the grounds that the common law offence of blasphemy was restricted to the Christian religion and the applicant had failed to show that the alleged seditious libel was an attack on Her Majesty the Queen or the State. The magistrate made no finding as to whether in fact the book was blasphemous of the Islamic religion; he found as a fact that its allegedly blasphemous passages did not amount to a scurrilous attack on Christianity.

On application for judicial review of the magistrate's decision, the Divisional Court dismissed the application.[59] It held that although it was empowered to grant judicial review of the magistrate's decision to refuse to issue the summonses on the recognised principles that the magistrate had misdirected himself in law or

[57] The rubric of s 4 is set out earlier in the essay.

[58] See further, P Kearns, 'Art, Freedom and the Christian Law of England' (1994) 1 *Maastricht Journal of European and Comparative Law* 3, 307.

[59] *R v Chief Metropolitan Stipendiary Magistrate, ex p Choudhury* [1990] 3 WLR 986.

that his findings were perverse or unsupported by any evidence, the legal history of the English common law offence of blasphemy clearly indicated that the offence is restricted to a scurrilous vilification of the Christian religion only. It also held that where the law is clear, it is not the function of the court to extend it, particularly in criminal law where offences cannot be created retrospectively. It was, moreover, a question solely for Parliament whether the law of blasphemy was to be altered. The right to freedom of religion, as protected by the European Convention on Human Rights, did not require the law of blasphemy to be extended to other religions. The United Kingdom was consequently not in breach of the Convention but, rather, at liberty to legislate on the matter as it itself saw fit. The Divisional Court also held that there had been no seditious libel as there had been no incitement to violent attack on constituted authority. Before analysing the specific art issues involved in this case, two preliminary general observations must be made about the offence of blasphemy in English law. First, although the law of blasphemy was in theory designed to protect the reputation of God from defamation ('vilification'), the justifications for its existence became highly secularised. For example, it was sometimes said to safeguard 'the internal tranquility of the kingdom',[60] to protect 'the civil obligations whereby society is bound together'[61] or minors from 'wrong influences'.[62] The importance of God Himself became in practice subsidiary within blasphemy law in an age where religious matters tend to be treated more hermeneutically and agnostically in the 'Christian' West, rather than with serious passionate belief. Secondly, the case under examination raised the question whether a conscientiously plural society could justify maintaining a blasphemy law providing such selective protection. As it stood, the law indicated the inchoate nature of constitutional protection for minorities in a structure that remained basically 'traditional' in its workings.

In this case, the Divisional Court established that the law of blasphemy was clear in its exclusive protection of Christianity.[63] It was less definitive about its operation on art. However, it did disclose the contentious view that an attitude expressed in the medium of art was not necessarily prevented from being a blasphemous libel simply because of its artistic context: 'simply because the statement is put into the mouth of a character, even a disreputable character, in a novel'.[64] This approach has serious negative implications for art and artists because it ignores not only the autonomy of voices in art but the autonomy of art as a cultural category, and the (only) oblique relation of art to life. All art is essentially ambiguous in the sense that the interpretation it invites includes an imaginative aspect. Art cannot occur without there being room in an object's reading or viewing for our own creative activity, making us its internal co-creators. Any offence for which art is the alleged stimulus is the result of an

[60] *Lemon* (n 48) 658.
[61] *Rex v Williams* (1797) 26 St Tr N S 654, 714.
[62] *Regina v Hetherington* (1840) 4 St Tr N S 563, 590–91.
[63] The branch of the Christian religion protected is Anglicanism rather than Catholicism.
[64] *ex p Choudhury* (n 59) 990.

incorrect psychic approach on the part of the reader or viewer (a regrettable situation adequate art education would preclude). In addition, as an acknowledged higher medium of human achievement, at least in modernist and much pre-modern thought, art, especially, should not be condemned for inappropriate relations and responses to it. In the case of *Lemon*,[65] a poem for a gay or bisexual readership about homosexual acts with the body of Christ was successfully prosecuted for blasphemy at the instigation of the late Mary Whitehouse. No judicial attention was paid to the poem as art rather than literal factual statement. In addition, an argument can be put forward that in a society comprising people of diverse sexual orientation, it is unfair for the law to impose religious standards allied to heterosexual mores on art for the particular enjoyment of gay and bisexual people. It would appear that English blasphemy law not only permitted the silencing of art in favour of enforcing a religious belief, but disfavoured art (which is more universally participated in) in favour of what was in practice a small censoring lobby (which happened to be religious in its justification). Moreover, England is a democracy not a hagiocracy. Freedom of expression is as intrinsic to democracy as freedom of religion, and art, treated as art, in no way rules against the latter, and does not purport to. Art, not necessarily even cognitive, simply offers itself and invites the appropriate meditative (aesthetic) attitude. It is thus generous not constricting, and it is not the exertion of a will that its contemplation results in real-life disaccord. Art is an option for its reader or viewer, not an imposition.

When couched in decent and temperate language, a publication could not constitute blasphemous libel according to English law. The publication of opinions hostile to the Christian religion was insufficient for the offence; the test to be applied was as to 'the manner in which the doctrines are advocated and not as to the substance of the doctrines themselves'.[66] There seems no good reason why the manner should not have covered the (artistic) medium. If coarse and scurrilous attitudes are expressed in the medium of art, can it be realistically and reasonably said that the art (or its maker) is scurrilous, indecent or intemperate? Chaucer, for example, presumably did not portray either the views or tones of his characters as either his own, or as correct: rather, they were conceived within his exceptional artistic frame of thinking that produced each of them as authentic for the purposes of art. Moreover, voices from the artist are

[65] *Lemon* (n 48).

[66] JF Stephen and LF Sturge, *Stephen's Digest of the Criminal Law*, 9th edn (London, Sweet & Maxwell, 1950) 163. In the original 1877 edition of the *Digest*, at 105, Stephen stated: 'A person is justified in exhibiting disgusting objects . . . if their publication is for the public good, as being necessary in the pursuit of . . . art . . .'. In contemporary Western Australia, a standing advisory committee assists the police in their assessment of art. No appropriate committee performs a comparable role in England, France or the USA, for example, which is disappointing for the causes of artists, and those interested in art, in these states. In no state do art-law tribunals exist, that could expertly examine art-law cases, in keeping with the specialised legal attention art requires. Such attention is especially needed in the criminal law environment, where art is particularly vulnerable, even to the point (in English law, for example) of its destruction (following a relevant conviction, such as in an obscenity case).

from him but not necessarily of him. Even in non-fiction in the first person, the 'I' of the author is (only) the 'paper-I'. A fortiori, to speak of art 'attacking' something 'coarsely or scurrilously' is to be oblivious to the highly specialised artistic *modus operandi*, which is more congenially and metaphorically gestural and pacific at its real-life inception. Art may, of course, reflect the artist's own views, but enquiry into the precise form and extent of this reflection (if it exists at all) is a complex enquiry even for an expert biographer or literary psychologist. The strict liability of English blasphemy law put the artist and his publisher in a position whereby the very nature of the cultural exercise they were fostering precluded just process – the law ignored *artistic* intent, not just depriving art of a fair hearing but invalidating as immaterial art's distinct ontology, including a specialised cultural purpose and concomitant mental impetus.

The creative writer's intent is to create a work of art. This is not malice. Moreover, any allegedly subversive sub-intent is subsumed under the artistic intent, the final artistic product being the embodiment of innocuous and creditable creativity. Rather than being viewed as flatly blasphemous by any deity, a demonstrably creative God would surely *favour* man's creativity. Regrettably, God's interest in art is little-researched in the Christian and Islamic traditions. What is certain, though, is that it is not just in the ontogeny and product of creative genius that we sometimes witness what looks from a human perspective to be religiously iconoclastic tendencies. Many now established religions, including Christianity and Islam, are based on the teachings of prophets who radically altered existing religious practice following inspiration subsequently accepted as of God's volition. In the specific context of the Rushdie scenario, the ignoring of subtle intellectual approaches to religion and art in courts of law precluded the desired reconciliation of what were legally caricatured as necessarily competing claims. A very salient observation in the context of the Rushdie affair is that Islam is a younger religion than Christianity and it acknowledges Christ in its hierology, the Koran equitably voicing the contribution of Christ as well as Mohammed to God's truth. This equity did not find reflection in the exclusively Christian English law of blasphemy. Neither was there equity, if political sense, in what, during the height of the Rushdie crisis, was seen by some as the selective non-prosecution of certain members of society for incitement or conspiracy to murder a novelist. Such sad circumstances deeply threatened the rule of law and illustrated the highly inconsistent enforcement of 'Christian' principles within the English legal system. Within that system, during the Rushdie debacle, neither Mohammed nor art nor the individual human life was held sacred; and it is arguable that they all should have been, by using a more cerebral juridical approach to matters of acute cultural importance.

ii Visions of Ecstasy by Nigel Wingrove

Before the appearance of Salman Rushdie's *The Satanic Verses*, blasphemy was considered something of a dead letter in England. Prosecutions for blasphemy had been extremely exiguous for over 100 years, yet several attempts at its abolition had failed. Nevertheless, in 1996 a controversial video film by Nigel Wingrove gave added momentum to the blasphemy revival[67] inaugurated by *The Satanic Verses*. The facts are straightforward. Nigel Wingrove produced an 18-minute video film exploring the experiences of St Teresa of Avila, a sixteenth-century Carmelite nun who experienced ecstatic visions of Jesus Christ.[68] The film was objected to by the British Board of Film Classification (hereinafter sometimes referred to as the BBFC) on the grounds that the treatment of an ersatz St Teresa's erotic encounters with a presented Christ figure comprised an unacceptable interpretation of a sacred subject, and would constitute an infringement of the criminal law of blasphemy if deliberated upon by a properly directed, reasonable jury. Accordingly, the BBFC refused to grant a certificate permitting the sale, hire or supply to the public of the said film, *Visions of Ecstasy*. On appeal to the Video Appeals Committee, the panel upheld the BBFC's decision by three votes to two. Consequently, Nigel Wingrove made an application to the European Commission of Human Rights claiming a violation of the right of freedom of expression contrary to Article 10[69] of the European Convention on Human Rights. Article 10(1) sets out the fundamental right to freedom of expression, and Article 10(2) indicates permitted state derogations from it in certain fixed circumstances, including in the interests of the protection of morals and the rights of others. The Commission concluded by 14 votes to two that there had been a violation of Article 10.[70] It reported that Wingrove's film was a video not a feature film and of unusually short length, and that its blasphemous parts were 'fleeting'. It added that it was unlikely that members of the public would unintentionally find themselves viewing the video in the same way that they might walk into an art gallery or cinema, or browse through magazines. A person would have to make a conscious decision to view the applicant's video and it was unlikely that it would have been seen by anyone who was unaware of the film's probable subject matter. The fact that certain Christians might be outraged by it did not, in the Commission's opinion, amount to a sufficiently compelling reason to prohibit its lawful supply. Moreover, the BBFC could have given the film an '18' certificate, thus limiting its viewing to people over that age. The Commission added that the refusal of the classification certificate for the film did not correspond to a pressing social need, and considered that the interference with the applicant's freedom of expression was disproportionate to the aim pursued, and could not be deemed necessary in

[67] See further, P Kearns, 'The Uncultured God: Blasphemy Law's Reprieve and the Art Matrix' (2000) *European Human Rights Law Review* 5, 512.

[68] A sculpture by Bernini, 'Saint Teresa in Ecstasy', was first displayed in public in 1651, provoking the comment in a contemporary pamphlet that a pure virgin had been prostituted. Modern scholarship has since proclaimed the sculpture as amongst the most important creations of its period.

[69] See further (n 27).

[70] *Wingrove v United Kingdom*, Report of the European Commission of Human Rights adopted on 10 January 1995.

a democratic society within the meaning of Article 10(2).[71] The case was then referred to the European Court of Human Rights for its judgment.

In the Strasbourg Court's judgment,[72] it was pronounced that the applicant's freedom of expression was clearly violated, and this was not disputed. The pertinent remaining question for the Court was whether such a violation was justified under Article 10(2)[73] or was, instead, an unwarranted violation of Article 10.[74] The Court first had to decide if the interference with Nigel Wingrove's exercise of freedom of expression was 'prescribed by law'. It pronounced that English blasphemy law could not be said to deny adequate protection against arbitrary interference, so was therefore prescribed by law: there was no general uncertainty or disagreement as to the definition of what constituted blasphemy, and the Court added that, with appropriate legal advice, the applicant could have reasonably foreseen that certain scenes in the film could fall within the scope of the English blasphemy offence. The Court then affirmed the 'legitimacy of the aim' pursued by the censors: the fact that blasphemy law operating in England only protected the Christian faith, and did not treat all religions on an equal footing, did not detract from that legitimacy. Moreover, the aim of the interference, the Court pronounced, was fully consonant with the aims of Article 9[75] of the Convention protecting religious freedom. The Court then considered whether the precise censoring interference was 'necessary'. It noted that blasphemy laws were still in force in various European countries, and though rarely applied, could not be adjudged to be unnecessary in a democratic society. In addition, whereas there was little room for restriction of political speech and questions of public interest, a wider 'margin of appreciation' was generally available to states in relation to matters liable to offend intimate personal convictions in the sphere of religion or morals. The Court further held that national authorities were in a better position to define these requirements, and rule on the necessity of a restriction, than an international judiciary. Its conclusion was that the national authorities' margin of appreciation had not been overstepped and there had accordingly been no violation of Article 10[76]: the reasons given to justify the interference could not be said to be arbitrary or excessive.

Wingrove v United Kingdom[77] is an important case for several reasons. First, it confirms that operating a blasphemy law is a legally valid choice for any state under the Court's jurisdiction. The Court disclaimed its entitlement to 'Europeanise' the notion of blasphemy, leaving the concept and its practical ambit to be interpreted at a local level. This was arguably a dereliction of duty because one principal role of the Court is to provide a useful supra-national

[71] See further (n 27).
[72] *Wingrove v United Kingdom* [1997] 24 EHRR 1.
[73] See further (n 27).
[74] ibid.
[75] For more information on Art 9, see n 80.
[76] See n 27.
[77] *Wingrove* (n 72).

solution for Contracting States' observance whenever appropriate. It is particularly important in the case of a legally ambiguous term like blasphemy to determine its precise import. Although in *Wingrove*[78] the Court admitted that the definition of blasphemy was elusive, it nevertheless said, somewhat disingenuously, that there was no disagreement over its definition. But it is difficult to agree or disagree about the definition of a concept that goes so unclarified at both national and international levels. Secondly, *Wingrove*[79] is important because it implicitly upholds freedom of religion over freedom of expression, even though the freedom of religion encapsulated in Article 9 of the Convention does not extend to protection from challenge to religious stereotypes because in such a challenge there is no detraction from freedom of religious practice.[80] Censorship, though, *ipso facto* curtails freedom of expression. Thirdly, it is clear that the Court found the art aspect of the case unimportant even though blasphemy law had only ever been designed to remedy more literal alleged harms. The symbolic, imaginative, metaphorical and sometimes mimetic dimensions of an artwork's only oblique relation to 'real life' was ignored by the Court, despite the existence of a highly relevant, distinct doctrinal theme in Strasbourg (both in the Commission and the Court) recognising the protection of *artistic* expression specifically.

C Outraging Public Decency Case Paradigm

In the notorious 'foetus earrings' case,[81] Richard Norman Gibson, an artist, and Peter Sylveire, an art gallery curator, pleaded not guilty to charges of outraging public decency and public nuisance. They were convicted on the first count and acquitted on the second. The facts are straightforward. In his art gallery, known as the Young Unknowns Gallery, Sylveire selected for display at an exhibition there in 1988 a work created by Gibson entitled 'Human Earrings'. It comprised a model's head, to each ear of which was attached an earring; each of the two earrings was constructed out of a freeze-dried human foetus of three or four months gestation.[82] The public was invited to the exhibition free of charge, and both press and police were in attendance shortly after the exhibition had opened. Sylveire admitted to police that he did not find 'Human Earrings' very

[78] ibid.

[79] ibid.

[80] Article 9, the freedom of religion provision, does not immunise religious belief from criticism; it merely safeguards religious practice. The Article reads: '1. Everyone has the right to freedom of thought, conscience and religion; this right includes freedom to change his religion and belief, and freedom, either alone or in community with others in public and private, to manifest his religion or belief, in worship, teaching, practice and observance. 2. Freedom to manifest one's religion or beliefs shall be subject only to such limitations as are prescribed by law and are necessary in a democratic society in the interests of public safety, for the protection of public order, health or morals, or for the protection of the rights and freedoms of others.'

[81] *R v Gibson, R v Sylveire* [1990] 2 QB 619, [1990] 3 WLR 595 and Kearns (n 1) 29.

[82] It is a mystery as to where Gibson acquired the foetuses.

attractive, and that he knew the earrings were in fact real human foetuses. He then made a seemingly ingenuous response to the police about his choice of subject matter and its alleged illegitimacy, saying: 'Why, is that wrong?'

When the case reached the appellate level, the Court of Appeal chose not to designate Gibson an artist or his work art in the language of its judgment.[83] This is important because it reveals that the offending enterprise was not characterised as purporting to be of particular cultural value and significance.[84] If a prosecution is brought under the Obscene Publications Act 1959, the legislative provision of the defence of public good on the grounds of artistic merit ensures that the particular cultural status of the defendant(s), and of the offending item, is recognised. The prosecution of the defendants in this case on the common law charge of outraging public decency, where no such legislative provision obtains, made it possible to minimise the significance of the art issue. The Court of Appeal consciously opted for this route, and it could, and arguably should, have chosen otherwise. Regarding precedents, it is also not made clear in the Court's judgment that the leading authority on the crime of outraging public decency is *Knuller (Publishing, Printing and Promotions) Ltd v Director of Public Prosecutions.*[85] The case the Court followed instead was *Lemon.*[86] This was an error since *Lemon*[87] is a less persuasive authority because it is based on the cognate crime of blasphemy only.

In *Knuller,*[88] the appellants published a magazine, *The International Times*, which contained columns of advertisements headed 'Males' on its inner pages. Most of the advertisements were inserted by homosexuals for the purpose of attracting persons who would indulge in homosexual practices. The appellants were charged on two counts. The first count alleged a conspiracy to corrupt public morals. The second alleged a conspiracy to outrage public decency by the publication of the 'lewd, disgusting and offensive' advertisements. No argument for the applicability of the public good defence on either count was submitted and yet the appeal on the second count was allowed. It is antinomic that in subsequent proceedings involving a conspicuous art element, where a defence of public good on the grounds of artistic merit is more obviously relevant, appeals against conviction for outraging public decency should be dismissed. The Court of Appeal in *R v Gibson, R v Sylveire*[89] chose not only to dismiss the appeals but to consider, obiter, that the availability of the defence was 'unlikely', without citing any authority to support that opinion.

[83] *Gibson and Sylveire* (n 81).

[84] See further, P Kearns, 'Not a Question of Art' (1992) 1 *International Journal of Cultural Property* 2, 383.

[85] *Knuller (Publishing, Printing and Promotions) Ltd v Director of Public Prosecutions* [1972] 2 All E R 898 .

[86] *Lemon* (n 48).

[87] ibid.

[88] *Knuller* (n 85).

[89] *Gibson and Sylveire* (n 81).

In *Knuller*,[90] Lord Simon of Glaisdale made it clear that outraging public decency goes *considerably* beyond offending the susceptibilities of, or even shocking, reasonable people. He affirmed that 'public' was to be used in a locative sense, and was of the opinion that the jury should be invited, where appropriate, to remember that they live in a plural society, with a tradition of tolerance towards minorities, and that this atmosphere of toleration is itself part of public decency. Lord Kilbrandon expressly agreed with Lord Simon. Lord Diplock stressed that the courts should be the vigilant guardians of the liberty of the citizen, and Lord Reid held the view that the offence of outraging public decency was 'new' and should not be recognised. Only Lord Morris of Borth-Y-Gest would have entirely dismissed the appeal. However, in *Gibson and Sylveire*,[91] the Court of Appeal in effect affirmed the less liberal, draconian approach of Lord Morris, which their other Lordships flatly contradicted in their majority decision. The Court of Appeal in *Gibson and Sylveire*[92] was obligated to follow, but did not follow, the majority of their Lordships in *Knuller*[93] so as to allow the appeals. It would have been more prudent to distinguish a case specifically involving art in accordance with the liberal reasoning and policy clearly established by the majority of their Lordships in that leading case, mindful of the artistic merit defence prescribed by the Obscene Publications Act 1959 in a closely analogous context.

In short, there is little likelihood of a fair defence for an artist and art gallery curator on a charge of outraging public decency if no provision is made for the consideration of the distinctive ontology of art.[94] If the *mens rea* requirement is as narrow as decided in *Gibson and Sylveire*[95] (cognate with that for the offence of obscenity, and amounting to strict liability), the availability of a defence accommodating the specialised nature of artistic intent is essential. If the Court of Appeal had framed its judgment mindful of this, the long-considered importance of art as a cultural phenomenon, and the concomitant importance of artistic freedom, it could have distinguished art's position from that of other facts. To that end, factors that are highly relevant for that purpose in the instant case include the following observations: that artistic intent is not usually considered base but, rather, noble, and is hardly a committed heterodox attitude but one common to artists in general, and approved of habitually by the art-appreciating general public; that reasonable members of the public would know to approach an artwork thoughtfully, and would respond to it suitably contemplatively; that an inept or inappropriate response to his or her artwork is not something an artist should reasonably have to be made to consider; that reasonable people know that art can, or even must, shock, and that an art gallery is a

[90] *Knuller* (n 85).

[91] *Gibson and Sylveire* (n 81).

[92] ibid.

[93] *Knuller* (n 85).

[94] See further, P Kearns, 'Obscene and Blasphemous Libel: Misunderstanding Art' (2000) *Criminal Law Review* 652.

[95] *Gibson and Sylveire* (n 81).

self-evidently likely place to discover and view art; that it is impossible for outrage to be an effect of art, except if the viewer receives it inappropriately, ie without the necessary psychic distance involved in an aesthetic attitude; that since the publicity requirement in the offence of outraging public decency is locative, the fact that the object is art and appropriately displayed in an art gallery is particularly relevant. Moreover, on 3 June 1964, the Solicitor-General gave an assurance,[96] repeating an earlier assurance, that a conspiracy to corrupt public morals would not be charged so as to circumvent the statutory defence in section 4[97] of the Obscene Publications Act 1959. This implicitly also applied to the crime of conspiracy to outrage public decency, its sister offence. It is lamentable, and arguably a dereliction of duty, that heed was not paid to such a formal declaration in *Gibson and Sylveire*.[98]

VI EUROPEAN LEGAL INFLUENCES: A BRIEF SUMMARY

The details of the effect of domestic public morality laws in the United Kingdom on art are set beneath the umbrella of European initiatives of arguably higher significance. However, they need only a brief examination here, because they have had as yet only a relatively indirect practical impact on specifically *artistic* freedom[99] in the UK, and moreover the focus of this essay is centred on domestic law. In short, there are at least two significant European influences on freedom of artistic expression in the UK, one of which is more important than the other. First, we must put in its European context the Human Rights Act 1998, which came into force on 2 October 2000. To recap, it is a domestic piece of enabling legislation which incorporates the European Convention on Human Rights into UK law. Part of this development, as mentioned previously, is that, under section 2 of that Act, UK courts have to take into account the European Convention law when adjudicating domestic cases that have relevance for human rights. This in practice imports a considerable quantity of Convention law into UK law but it must be remembered that that European law is not binding. The imperative obligation for our national judges is to *take into account* that law only. Nevertheless, that has a radical effect on our constitutional law. Secondly, the law of the European Union (hereinafter sometimes referred to as the EU) also has an influence, albeit more minor, on freedom of artistic expression at a domestic level because the UK is a Member State of that Union, as well as being a Contracting State of the European Convention (which embodies a completely different legal system from that of the EU, that is peculiar to human rights law,

[96] *Hansard*, HC Deb 1964, vol 695, col 1212.
[97] Section 4 is referred to earlier in the essay.
[98] *Gibson and Sylveire* (n 81).
[99] The artistic freedom doctrine of the European Court of Human Rights has had a negligible effect so far under the Human Rights Act 1998 because of the paucity of art-related cases that have come before UK courts post 2 October 2000, when the Act came into force.

and which operates under the aegis of the Council of Europe and its institutions in Strasbourg).

Under the 1998 Act, artists are able to rely directly on Article 10[100] of the Convention, on freedom of expression, when bringing a claim that a domestic public authority has violated that right. This means that all the relevant Strasbourg jurisprudence generated by the European Court of Human Rights under the Convention's Article 10[101] is in principle applicable to all such national cases involving artistic freedom. Moreover, section 12(4)[102] of the 1998 Act in effect prescribes that when a domestic court is considering granting any relief which could specifically affect freedom of expression, that court must have particular regard to the importance of Article 10.[103] The Strasbourg case law involving freedom of expression is well-developed, and matters relating to artistic freedom, though not specifically mentioned in the rubric of Article 10,[104] are in theory protected under it. In practice, this is not the case, because in a range of cases under Article 10,[105] the Strasbourg Court has consistently refused to protect artistic freedom when that is counter-balanced by concerns relating to the protection of morality, including in relation to public morality laws that are extant in the United Kingdom. In the area of morality, it has already been observed that the Strasbourg Court affords domestic authorities a wide 'margin of appreciation', which in practice means a broad discretion to resolve moral issues as they see fit, including by the application of public morality laws that it views as legitimately restricting freedom of artistic expression. This system of operating is arguably a dereliction of duty on the part of the Strasbourg Court, involving as it does the side-stepping of a duty to appraise the relevant domestic law for itself in accordance with the expected role and ethics of its supervisory jurisdiction. The repercussions for artists are severe as the effect is to reinforce the censoring of their morally controversial art in the Contracting State without supra-national revision of that position. This precludes artists from exercising a critical moral role of art, which is to question accepted moral standards as established by the state. This is potentially, and actually, very damaging to artistic freedom, which should be vigilantly protected as an important right under the foundational precepts of the Strasbourg Convention, the observance of which the Strasbourg Court should not be negligent.

Although it is beyond the ambit of this essay to survey the case law of the European Court of Human Rights under Article 10[106] at great length, since the focus of this essay is mainly English domestic law, it is perhaps instructive to reiterate the fact that a legal doctrine on freedom of *artistic* expression specifically, which has become apparent in the Strasbourg case law, is consistently negative

[100] See n 27.
[101] ibid.
[102] For more information, see n 112.
[103] See n 27.
[104] ibid.
[105] ibid.
[106] ibid.

regarding artistic liberty. The Strasbourg Court is surprisingly keen to uphold morality (in the Contracting States) over artistic interests (when art appears to be morally aberrant by those states' standards). The utter subjectivity of what is, and what is not, 'moral' threatens to defeat any attempt to *appraise* opposing value judgements in this art law area empirically and convincingly, let alone to objectively *resolve* the relevant arguments. The fact that the Strasbourg Court fails to try to create and impose an international moral standard in this complicated scenario frustrates the necessary legal endeavour to attain a European moral consensus on artistic freedom. Such unification of legal cultural attitudes in the Contracting States of the Convention is desirable in terms of obtaining justice for artists. This priority cannot be undermined ethically by an insufficiently reflective, and arguably specious, argument that such legal standardisation ignores or reduces cultural variety in Europe.

The way in which, in contrast, European Union law affects the subject of artistic freedom, relates to the importation and subsequent distribution of publications of alleged obscene and indecent content. The relevant topic is the abolition of measures 'having equivalent effect to quantitative restrictions', which is crucial to achieve the single European market. In the EU, provision is made, as a general principle, for the free movement of goods. There can be a derogation from this guarantee,[107] which prescribes, inter alia, that a Member State, such as the United Kingdom, may impose restrictions or prohibitions on imports and exports for the protection of public morality. The now accepted legal position is that a prohibition on imports cannot be justified under EU law on the ground of public morality unless a broadly comparable standard for imports and domestic products is accepted. Consequently, a Member State must show that any national measure really does have the effect of protecting public morality. This is necessary to preclude arbitrary discrimination against foreign products. The practical result is that no Member State can rely on public morality grounds in order to prohibit the importation of certain goods when its national legislation contains no equivalent prohibition on the making and marketing of similar goods on its own territory.

VII CONCLUSIONS AND REFORM

The juridification of art in English public morality law reveals a lacuna in judicial knowledge. When adjudging issues involving art, it is preferable that judges have some awareness of art's cultural ontology. The lack of this results in judgments such as that of Justice Byrne in the obscenity law case of Penguin Books,[108] regarding *Lady Chatterley's Lover*, where indifference to art's unique systemic

[107] Article 30 (ex 36) EC. See further, U Smartt, *Media and Entertainment Law* (London and New York, Routledge, 2011) 281.

[108] Rolph (n 52).

operation leads to unfairness of judicial treatment of it. In this case,[109] this culminated in the jury implicitly having to correct the directions of the judge in an undesirably autodidactic way. To fulfil its role adequately on art-related questions, the judiciary should be required to have sufficient art awareness to instruct the jury from a basis of at least rudimentary knowledge. Under the Obscene Publications Act 1959, the defence of public good on the grounds of artistic merit is established to rectify any dismissive judicial attitude to art as simply an ordinary obscene phenomenon worthy of curt condemnation. The case of Penguin Books[110] illustrates how that mechanism can be abused by an inappropriate judicial appreciation of it. By analogy with the deference frequently shown to medical experts in medical law cases, for example, due respect for the opinions of art experts should be accorded in cases involving art under the Obscene Publications Act 1959. The purpose of calling experts is to illuminate problematic questions for the court, and there should be concomitant positive judicial appreciation of such views. In former English blasphemy law, no defence of artistic merit was ever provided for. This, combined with the strict liability of the offence, not only denuded art of any putative privileged status based on its acknowledged cultural and social standing, but made its inherent symbolic character redundant, and its implicit critical-moral function an inadvertent catalyst for its prosecution. Under the Human Rights Act 1998, freedom of expression is formally protected, and so is freedom of religion; no provision is made in the Act for *artistic* expression specifically, but Strasbourg jurisprudence clearly indicates that this is protectable under the generic head freedom of expression under Article 10[111] of the Convention. It would be interesting to see how freedom of expression (under section 12[112] of the Act) and freedom of religion (under section 13[113]) would interact in a relevant case in the twenty-first century, should such a

[109] ibid.

[110] ibid.

[111] See n 26.

[112] Section 12 reads: '(1) This section applies if a court is considering whether to grant any relief which, if granted, might affect the exercise of the Convention right to freedom of expression. (2) If the person against whom the application for relief is made ("the respondent") is neither present nor represented, no such relief is to be granted unless the court is satisfied – (a) that the applicant has taken all practicable steps to notify the respondent; or (b) that there are compelling reasons why the respondent should not be notified. (3) No such relief is to be granted so as to restrain publication before trial unless the court is satisfied that the applicant is likely to establish that publication should not be allowed. (4) The court must have particular regard to the importance of the Convention right to freedom of expression and, where the proceedings relate to material which the respondent claims, or which appears to the court, to be journalistic, literary or artistic material (or to conduct connected with such material), to – (a) the extent to which – (i) the material has, or is about to, become available to the public; or (ii) it is, or would be, in the public interest for the material to be published; (b) any relevant privacy code. (5) In this section – "court" includes a tribunal; and "relief" includes any remedy or order (other than in criminal proceedings).'

[113] Section 13 reads: '(1) If a court's determination of any question arising under this Act might affect the exercise by a religious organisation (itself or its members collectively) of the Convention right to freedom of thought, conscience and religion, it must have particular regard to the importance of that right. (2) In this section "court" includes a tribunal.'

case arise. The Strasbourg institutions favour religion over expression in most instances where exercise of them as freedoms conflict, which is somewhat surprising given the near-universal acknowledgment that free speech is the pre-eminent fundamental right in democracies. Moreover, as previously stressed, the Strasbourg Court allocates a wide 'margin of appreciation' to Contracting States in matters of morality, a subsidiarity initiative recognising the dubious proposition that states are in a better position than the Court to decide issues of local morality. It is arguable that a supra-national notion of morality from the Court would be preferable to pandering to more parochial moral insight on the part of national authorities, which is usually the very subject of an applicant's complaint. Restricting blasphemy law to the sole protection of Christianity in England has been condoned explicitly by the Strasbourg Court, a stance which was arguably unfair even at that time given the religiously plural nature of English society, and, indeed, that of most contemporary states party to the Convention. The Court's approach in this context is defensible, however, if one uses the argument that blasphemy law is not strictly incompatible with the exercise of freedom of religion per se under Article 9[114] of the Convention. But it is worth reiterating that the Court's persistent adjudication that English blasphemy law prevailed over freedom of artistic expression involved sacrificing art in order to satisfy what was in practice a very small censoring contingent. A fortiori, it represented the silencing of art as a genus in favour of reinforcing only one particular species of religion. The domestic Racial and Religious Hatred Act 2006 now ensures that the sentiments of members of all religions within the United Kingdom are respected rather than overlooked, in recognition, arguably somewhat belatedly, of the religious plurality of our society. In contemporary English law, resurrecting the ancient common law crimes of outraging public decency and corrupting public morals potentially widely retards the artistic liberation from public-moral censure promoted by the Obscene Publications Act 1959, and actually does so in the joined cases of *Gibson and Sylveire*[115] in relation to the former crime, which is a dangerous precedent. That particular case in effect legitimises circumvention of the 1959 Act in blatant disregard of the Solicitor General's clear formal assurances that such a manoeuvre is reprehensible. The problem is compounded by the fact that statutory obscenity and common law's anachronistic offence of outraging public decency essentially duplicate the same prohibition, which is itself inconsistent. Moreover, the Indecent Displays (Control) Act 1981 seeks to strike a fair balance between freedom of expression and public protection by totally exempting displays in an art gallery or museum visible only from within from the ambit of its proscription, and yet in practice, antinomically, art prosecutions persist under the obscenity statute or the aforementioned ancient common law crime. All these factors reveal that policy in this area is lamentably inchoate and incoherent.

[114] See n 80.
[115] *Gibson and Sylveire* (n 81).

The situation is, of course, exacerbated by a lack of tangible human rights for artists. Since the arrival of the Human Rights Act 1998, a reasonable assumption would be that freedom of artistic expression in the United Kingdom is substantively and formally guaranteed. The lack of protection for the arts in the Strasbourg Court's *actual practice* under Article 10[116] is a circumstance that virtually dictates that, under the 1998 Act, which incorporates the Convention, artistic freedom has, at best, a very insecure basis in our domestic law. This state of affairs is further exaggerated by the fact that the Human Rights Act 1998 is only a quasi-constitutional document, rather than fully constitutional, notably because it is unentrenched. This means that, at least in theory, the Act could be repealed at any time, simply by the enactment of appropriate subsequent legislation.

In terms of domestic public-moral laws, the Obscene Publications Act 1959 is rapidly being overtaken in practical importance by the recently established 'extreme' pornography legislation and, with both these statutory regimes running alongside one another, one must question the underlying policy of separate publication and possession offences that regulate differing degrees of immorality. The 1959 Act proscribes publications that have a tendency to deprave and corrupt, whereas the 'extreme' pornography legislation targets much more serious immoral representations, usually of explicitly taboo sexual practices of a clearly damaging as well as unpopular nature. The 1959 Act has been used to try to condemn novels, whereas the 'extreme' pornography legislation targets such vile things as films explicitly portraying bestiality and necrophilia. Times have indisputably changed and our national moral conscience is surely no longer focused on condemning relatively innocent creative writing.[117] The Internet has drawn us closer to much more visceral and offensive imagery of its own, including that relating to heinous 'child pornography'. So the bar for censorship has been significantly raised above the relatively innocuous moral concerns of 1959.

It is also arguable that the 'extreme' pornography legislation is a more fitting measure than the 1959 Act to deal with the highly contemporary pornographic phenomena that the general public finds almost unanimously abhorrent, whether as a matter of publication or possession; and, in practice, the 1959 Act is very seldom used, not least because of the anachronism of what it is aims to proscribe (in inappropriate archaic language). In addition to the common law crimes of outraging public decency and corrupting public morals, a range of miscellaneous, more trivial offences, adumbrated earlier in this essay, simply replicate legal-moral prohibitions found under the ambit of more major crimes. These laws are not even collectively streamlined to achieve their best effect.

In conclusion, the general deficiencies of the protection of artistic freedom are epitomised by its poor protection under the European Convention on Human

[116] See n 27.

[117] In 1979, the Williams Committee recommended that there should be no further prosecutions of creative writing for obscenity in England but this much considered, serious directive was not acted upon by the Conservative Government of the day. See further, The Williams Committee (n 33) 1079.

Rights, an inadequacy that is projected, in turn, under the UK's Human Rights Act 1998, despite the fact that Convention law is not binding on our national judges. Their obligation only to *take into account* Strasbourg jurisprudence under the Act is deceptive, though, because in practice this exercise of judicial duty is observed habitually and uniformly to forcibly ensure the Convention's impact. The consequent gradual effect on art is detrimental, because, following Strasbourg's perpetual dismissive treatment of artistic freedom, our repressive obscenity and related laws become further galvanised, without being really tested in the delicate and controversial area of their (doubtful) moral justification in censoring art. Artists are therefore persistently subjected to the contemporary imposition of mainly anachronistic moral constraints, that adversely affect their role as enlightened and creative moral agents, rendering them an unhappy and neglected minority. Moreover, they are clearly not insubstantial in terms of numbers and cultural importance, and their collective voice, in the twenty-first century, should not be denied on the basis of demoded and contentious moral concepts. The judicial application of allegedly 'objective morals' to censor or censure artworks is, in reality, a very subjective process. It frequently comprises simply uninformed, personal judicial determinations; and, equally lamentably, these are sometimes in a disturbingly transparent guise.

Part II

Art, Obscenity, Religion and the Law: Writings at the Turn of the Century

2

*When Art is Misunderstood: Obscene and Blasphemous Libel in 2000**

I INTRODUCTION

IN CONTEMPORARY ENGLISH law, the offences that regulate the interrelation of art and public morality law operate somewhat anomalously. For example, there is a specific defence of artistic merit to the charge of obscenity in section 4 of the Obscene Publications Act 1959,[1] but not to other public morality offences. This puzzling fact of legal inconsistency requires close scrutiny. The definition of art is a known difficulty for philosophers as well as lawyers, but it is clear that a body of opinion exists that to call something a work of art is not just to classify it, but also to say that it has a certain (esteemed) status. This is not an uncommon view and its adoption reinforces the need to protect art from unnecessary criminal control and punishment. In this analysis of the legal regulation of art, the term *art* is predominantly confined to non-motion visual art and creative writing and the author does not purport to consider in depth the notoriously difficult question 'what is art?', except implicitly. Nevertheless, it will be noticed that in the course of the general treatment of the art-public morality law relationship, some illumination of this difficulty will be offered; this illumination is designed to contribute in its own way to the greater 'definition of art' debate.

The rationales behind public morality offences vary. Unlike obscenity law, which has depravity and corruption as its target, blasphemy law protects the Christian God's image from vilification, and the remaining offences, which are examined closely below, protect the general public from grave offence, whether it be outrage or other adverse psychic effects from the presentation of pictorial or written indecent images. Joel Feinberg[2] argues cogently that the law should

* A precursor of this essay was published as 'Obscene and Blasphemous Libel: Misunderstanding Art' (2000) *Criminal Law Review* 652–60. The author's book, *The Legal Concept of Art* (Oxford, Hart Publishing, 1998) amplifies legal concerns related to those raised here.

[1] See below.

[2] J Feinberg, *The Moral Limits of Criminal Law: Offense to Others* (New York, Oxford University Press, 1985).

not treat *offence* as if it were as serious as *harm*, and he suggests that, if it is possible, modes of regulation such as injunctions or licensing procedures should be preferred to more draconian criminal law sanctions. Given that the purpose of the Obscene Publications Act 1959 is to prevent decent people from being corrupted as opposed to merely offended, the anomaly of the defence of artistic merit being available to the obscenity offence but not to other public morality law offences is even more marked. The Williams Committee Report,[3] on obscenity and film censorship, concluded that the risk of suppressing worthwhile creative art ruled out censorship of the written word but not the suppression of standard non-cognitive pornography. This was deemed to be unprotected by the variant on John Stuart Mill's argument from truth[4] that the Committee endorsed as the free speech justification to be adopted. Ronald Dworkin[5] has broadly condoned the Committee's conclusions, if not the arguments it employed. Without focussing on the details of this particular debate, it can nevertheless be confidently stated that it is now commonplace to envisage the accrual of truth as dependent on the legal enshrining of freedom of speech to its maximum possible limit.

This essay does not aim to reopen the art/pornography conceptual divide in the typical dichotomical way, but there are certain relevant things to be said about this area. It is argued by some that pornographic material has an adverse and harmful effect on those who are its consumers, or simply causes offence by foisting obscene or indecent displays on the unwitting or unimpressed. Some may think it morally justifiable for lewd images to be presented on the inside pages of a magazine but unjustifiable to promulgate licentiousness in posters, or on the Internet, more overtly and less discreetly in the public eye. Some may see different constraints to be necessary depending on whether the putatively offending item is literature or visual imagery. The protection of children is also correctly noted as a specific concern in this realm. But counter-considerations do exist. One view is that the availability of pornography of whatever type is a useful 'safety-valve', offering a sort of catharsis that helps prevent its consumers committing sex-related crimes. However, the alleged beneficial effects of pornography cannot be the subject of expert testimony in an obscenity trial. This was established in *DPP v Jordan*[6] where it was held that the public was not concerned with the relief of the sexually repressed. Some may argue that it is precisely pornography that currently requires a legal defence[7] now that anything that purports seriously to be art is often alleged to be on the whole protected. This essay will demonstrate, though, that English criminal law is for the most

[3] B Williams, *Report of the Committee on Obscenity and Film Censorship* (Cmnd 7772, 1979).

[4] See further, JS Mill, *On Liberty*, edited by G Himmelfarb (Harmondsworth, Penguin, 1974).

[5] R Dworkin, *A Matter of Principle* (Harvard, Harvard University Press, 1985).

[6] *DPP v Jordan* [1976] 3 All ER 775.

[7] On 30 November 1999, the Playboy Entertainment group told the US Supreme Court that a blanket ban on pornographic cable channels during the daylight hours breached the constitutional rights to free speech. See further, *The Daily Telegraph* (1 December 1999) 20.

part ideologically recalcitrant when it confronts new art at the cutting-edge of art development. Finally, although as intimated earlier, there is insufficient space here to do justice to the art/pornography conceptual distinction in a comprehensive way, it may be noted that whereas pornography is indubitably 'conative', art, whether creative literature or visual art, is not, if we take the definition of conation to be the exertion of the will that contemplation of images results in action.

II BACKCLOTH

There is a theme in English public morality law that comprises the prosecution of all art that sufficiently adversely affects certain moral scruples and sensibilities of the ordinary decent citizen. Traditionally, the two most prominent offences that encapsulate such policy are obscenity and blasphemy. On coming into force, the Obscene Publications Act 1959 was immediately confronted by DH Lawrence's *Lady Chatterley's Lover* as the first possible transgressor of its newly legally-established threshold of acceptable and unacceptable erotic portrayals.[8] Its publishers were found not guilty. Later, in *R v Lemon, R v Gay News Ltd*[9] a rare but successful prosecution for the violation of blasphemy law centred on a poem by James Kirkup, complete with illustration, that evoked images of homosexual behaviour with the body of Christ. Art, primarily in the sense of creative writing, therefore has a small but significant history of entanglement with the forces of legally-determined moral standards, a tendency that has only comparatively recently been dramatically revived by actions against non-motion visual art, as well as creative literature, in the last decade. Principally, these involve the fundamentalist religious uproar caused by the religiously iconoclastic work of novelist Salman Rushdie, and the bold, sensationalist, innovative art of Richard Gibson, utilising human flesh in a post-modern climate in which human organic material is now habitually drawn upon for artistic composition.[10] It is consonant with such developments that examination of the law-art relation is now particularly necessary, not least to ascertain whether the criminal law justly accommodates artistic initiatives that challenge accepted moral values or simply condemns them without attention to their unique ontology separate from the world of unspecialised literal facts.

[8] See further, CH Rolph, *The Trial of Lady Chatterley's Lover* (Penguin Books, 1961).

[9] *R v Lemon, R v Gay News Ltd* [1979] 2 WLR 281.

[10] For example, Helen Chadwick has frequently used human faeces in her art, and Andres Serrano has used urine, for *Piss Christ*, a controversial but unprosecuted work exhibited in the Saatchi collections (1991).

III THE OFFENCES

There are five art-relevant offences that require analysis, excluding race relations offences and seditious libel, which have a more incidental relation to art issues. First, the Obscene Publications Act 1959, s 1[11] proscribes publications that deprave and corrupt. Originally, obscenity was an ecclesiastical offence like blasphemy, and it retains in its basic character a clearly Christian element. Whether an item is obscene or not is a question for the jury, and expert evidence is not admissible on that issue. To deprave and corrupt connotes, albeit imprecisely, a *serious* illegal tendency, and is not equivalent to mere shock and disgust.[12] If an entity has a tendency to deprave and corrupt a significant proportion of its audience, the actual intention of its author is irrelevant. However, the Act provides in its section 4 a defence of 'public good':

> (1) Subject to subsection 1 (A) of this section a person shall not be convicted of an offence against section 2 of this Act if it proved that publication of the article in question is justified as being for the public good on the ground that it is in the interests of science, literature, art and learning, or of objects of general concern.

This ground can be established or negatived by the opinion of experts as to the item's artistic or other merit (section 4(2)).[13] The basic process is that the jury is directed to first consider whether an item is obscene within section 1; if not satisfied of that beyond reasonable doubt, they must acquit. However, if on the contrary, they are so satisfied, they should go on to consider whether, on a balance of probabilities, the publication of the item, though obscene, is for the public good. The onus of establishing the defence is on the accused.[14]

A cognate offence of obscene libel is blasphemous libel. Blasphemy is a common law offence proscribing the vilification of Christ and the essential tenets of Christianity. The intention of the publisher to publish is sufficient for a conviction if the jury decides that the libel published is to their minds blasphemous. The publisher need not even think, let alone intend, the material to be blasphemous.[15] Moreover, no defence of artistic or other merit is available. Another equally draconian common law offence relating to public morality has also been resurrected in recent years. This is the ancient crime of outraging public decency.[16] The jury simply ask themselves if an item outrages public decency,

[11] Section 1(1) provides: 'For the purposes of this Act an article shall be deemed to be obscene if its effect or (where the article comprises two or more distinct items) the effect of any one of its items is, if taken as a whole, such as to tend to deprave and corrupt persons who are likely, having regard to all relevant circumstances, to read, see or hear the matter contained or embodied in it.'

[12] *Martin Secker and Warburg* [1954] 2 All ER 683, 686 (per Stable J).

[13] Section 4(2) provides: 'It is hereby declared that the opinion of experts as to the literary, artistic, scientific or other merits of an article may be admitted in any proceeding under this Act either to establish or negative the said ground.'

[14] *Calder and Boyars Ltd* [1969] 1 QB 151.

[15] *Lemon* (n 9) 620.

[16] *See R v Gibson, R v Sylveire* [1990] 2 QB 619 [1990] 3 WLR 595.

and if they so decide the crime is permitted. Like blasphemy, it is a crime of virtual strict liability, with no artistic merit defence. This crime is partnered by the equally ancient common law offence of corrupting public morals, which has not featured in any case involving art, but which would also deny art a defence based on its intrinsic merit.

The final art-relevant crime examined in this article is that provided for by the Indecent Displays (Control) Act 1981. Section 1(1) prescribes that if any indecent matter is publically displayed, the person making the display and any person causing or permitting the display to be made, shall be guilty of an offence. However, the Act does not apply in relation to any matter included in a display of an art gallery or museum and visible only from within the gallery or museum. Art is therefore idiosyncratically defended here based exclusively on its physical context rather than its inherent merit. In addition, excluded from the operation of the Act are, first, displays that the public can go to see only on payment and, second, those displays preceded by a warning sign declaring no admittance to persons under 18 years of age.

IV THE RUSHDIE PROBLEMATIC

As is commonly known, Salman Rushdie is the author of a controversial novel entitled *The Satanic Verses*.[17] It won the Whitbread Prize for Literature in 1988 and has been translated into over 15 languages. It has been censored in all Muslim states and in India, China and South Africa.

On 13 March 1989, the Chief Metropolitan Magistrate refused to grant Abdul Hussain Choudhury summonses he had applied for against the novelist and his publishers, alleging the commission of the crimes of blasphemous and seditious libel. The magistrate based his decision on the grounds that blasphemy only pertained to the Christian religion and not to Islam, and that there was no attack on HM The Queen or the State to constitute seditious libel. An application for judicial review of this decision was promptly dismissed by the Divisional Court.[18] It supported the magistrate's finding that blasphemy related only to Christianity and that there was no incitement to violence against constituted authority to comprise seditious libel. It added that the European Convention on Human Rights (ECHR) did not require the law of blasphemy to be extended to other than the Christian religion. Strangely, it did not stress that in this case it was the exercise of the right of freedom of expression by Rushdie, rather than the free practice of religion, that was in fact jeopardised.

This case[19] reveals a lack of judicial awareness of the right to artistic expression and its theoretical basis. The Divisional Court stated that an attitude expressed in the medium of art is not necessarily prevented from being a blasphemous libel

[17] S Rushdie, *The Satanic Verses* (London, Viking Press, 1988)
[18] *R v Chief Metropolitan Stipendiary Magistrate, ex p Choudhury* [1990] 3 WLR 986.
[19] ibid.

simply because of its artistic context. However, this ignores the independence of created voices in art, and the autonomy of art as a specific cultural category, with its own symbolic methods and character distinct from 'real life' mechanisms with which, in the case of creative writing, for example, it has only an oblique relation because of its fictive dimension. The Court also failed to acknowledge that art is ambiguous because its appreciation includes an imaginative aspect on the part of the reader, and should be approached with an appropriate meditative attitude involving aesthetic psychic distance. When properly read, art can incite no 'real life' action other than the reader's psychic reaction to it in that aestheticised psychic personal environment. Moreover, the Court did not stress that the creation of art is long-established as a culturally worthy pursuit, and should not be condemned for an untutored inappropriate relation to it. This lacuna is probably explained by the present lack of an effective written constitutional right in England to free artistic expression which is a situation unlikely to alter despite the welcome coming into force of the Human Rights Act 1998, which guarantees, inter alia, freedom of expression in general, but not artistic expression in particular, in its incorporation of Article 10 of the ECHR.[20]

England is a democracy and not a priesthood-determined oligarchy, and the practice of religion and artistic practice are not irreconcilable in a democratic framework; what is democratically unworkable is any attempted silencing of art by a small religious lobby whose freedom to practice religion is unaffected by what is incorrectly seen as a competing artistic claim. Art is an option for a reader, not an imposition, and offers itself in a generous, non-constricting way. A court's ignoring of this specifically artistic character, and the laudable achievement inherent in it, together with the lack of an artistic merit defence, does art a great injustice. On a practical level, the virtual strict liability offence of blasphemy prohibits evidence of artistic intent being presented, thereby undermining the whole basis of art's singular and valuable distinctiveness to found a form of defence in itself. Within blasphemy's current structure, neither Islam nor art is held sacred, but it is clearly arguable that both should be, by the conceptual restructuring of the existing law, or its abolition. It is also evident that the protection of both art and a minority religion in England should be founded on a more comprehensive and subtle analysis than is currently revealed in legal practice. Ultimately, there is the difficult post-modern dilemma of accommodating the eclectic mix of sometimes conflicting values permeating various special-interest groups in contemporary England, and a simple solution is elusive. This does not mean, of course, that greater attention placed on exploring those value systems in an appropriately detailed way is fundamentally futile. On the contrary, it is a vital first step.

[20] See especially, the Human Right Act 1998, s 12.

V THE FOETUS EARRINGS

Richard Norman Gibson created an artwork called 'Human Earrings' which he exhibited in the Young Unknowns Gallery. The item comprised a model's head sculpture, each ear of which bore an earring made from a complete real human foetus. In *R v Gibson, R v Sylveire*,[21] the artist and the art gallery curator were found guilty of outraging public decency.

The Court of Appeal decided not to characterise the case as involving art. This was possible because there is no defence of public good on the ground of artistic merit appended to the ancient common law offence of outraging public decency. Such a defence would certainly have been available under the Obscene Publications Act 1959, a statute designed to protect worthy enterprises from criminal conviction.

Although prima facie Gibson's creations might appear distasteful, they bear the message that life is now so cheap that aborted foetuses can even be used as mere ornamentation in the superficial world of postmodernism. However, any such evidence of artistic intent was precluded in court by the virtual strict liability nature of the offence prosecuted. This was despite the fact that in 1964 the Solicitor-General had given an assurance[22] that the partner crime to outraging public decency, the crime of corrupting public morals, would not be charged to avoid the statutory defences contained in section 4 of the Obscene Publication Act 1959, including that based on artistic merit.

There is no hope of a fair defence for an artist and art gallery curator if no provision is made in the crime of outraging public decency for evidence based on the specific nature of art. The meaning of the piece is denuded of its intrinsic cultural significance in such circumstances, and the art exhibit becomes merely an outraging fact. If the item's artistic character had been recognised in this case, certain important factors could have been attended to by the Court in its defence. The Court could have noted, for example, that outrage cannot be achieved as a reaction to art unless the art is addressed without the appropriate distance necessary in an aesthetic attitude of mind, an attitude that can arguably be expected of not just art connoisseurs. It could have considered the argument that most people know that art can shock and that you often find art in an art gallery that you may choose to enter; it could also have reflected that an inappropriate reaction to his artwork is probably not something an artist should fairly have to consider, and that artistic intent is not usually castigated as base except in relatively unsophisticated environments. In this 'foetus earrings case', a reasonable member of the public was in effect caricatured as someone who, despite having entered an art gallery voluntarily, is incapable of reacting to art in the acknowledged way, even when it is blatantly exhibited as art in the traditional artistic

[21] *R v Gibson, R v Sylveire* (n 16).
[22] *Hansard*, HC Deb 1964, vol 695, col 1212.

situs of an art gallery. It is not self-evident that this standard of ignorance should be thus affirmed by a court of law.

VI THE 'SENSATION' EXHIBITION

Some exhibits in the 'Sensation' exhibition, which ran from 18 September to 28 December 1997, at the Royal Academy, epitomised the radicalisation of art at the end of the twentieth century. This extremism is partly explained by current artistic ambition to enter the glamorous media world via artistic sensationalism. Karel Appel's famous injunction that art must shock was utilised to the full in the 'Sensation' exhibition, and some observers thought it invited criminal sanctions for one or more of the offences concerning the preservation of public morality from sexual and sacrilegious indiscretions.

The particularly controversial works of that important exhibition are easily identified. Marcus Harvey's painting of the child-killer Myra Hindley, made with the cast of a child's handprint, outraged not only Winnie Johnson, mother of one of the Moors victims, who specifically exhorted the Royal Academy to withdraw the picture from its exhibition. However, there was no formal suggestion that the artist or art curators should be prosecuted either for obscenity under the 1959 Act or for the common law offence of outraging public decency. Another exhibit, comprising mannequins of children, devised, though not made, by brothers Jake and Dinos Chapman, also caused consternation. Some of the noses of the figures, all female, had been replaced by penises. The room they were in was barred to children, though it was not made clear on whose advice; but the vice squad had made demands to see the entire exhibition prior to its opening. The Chapmans' exhibit, being in a traditional art environment, would not infringe the Indecent Displays (Control) Act 1981, but would it deprave and corrupt? Would it outrage public decency? The answer to both questions would seem to have been decided in the negative by the vice squad as far as adult viewers were concerned.

A portrait in the exhibition by Chris Ofili,[23] of the Virgin Mary surrounded by explicit sexual photographs from hard-core pornographic magazines, upset many Catholics.[24] Was it blasphemous? It may be significant that blasphemy prosecution is founded on Anglican rather than Catholic religious sentiments and it is a reasonable assumption that this was one reason why Ofili's work escaped prosecution. More generally, the presence at the exhibition of warnings

[23] Winner of the Turner Prize 1998.

[24] In October 1999, the 'Sensation' exhibition opened in New York. New York Mayor, Mayor Giuliani, at a preview of the exhibition, reacted to Chris Ofili's work Virgin Mary by asserting that there is no right to government subsidy for desecrating someone else's religion. See further, *The Daily Telegraph* (24 September 1999)13. Australia's National Gallery cancelled its projected showing of 'Sensation' after the Australian Arts Minister received over 70 protest letters. See further, *The Daily Telegraph* (1 December 1999) 17.

that some of the artworks in 'Sensation' could be thought distasteful, and that parents should exercise their judgement in bringing children to the exhibition, must have contributed to satisfying the police that adequate protection of public morality had been accommodated so as to preclude the need for any prosecutions. The art lobby was therefore successful in preventing censorship at least as far as the adult audience was concerned (and few people convincingly argue that the psyches of children should go unprotected in such circumstances). However, it is instructive to compare the way the police handled the 'Sensation' exhibition with its treatment of Gibson and Sylveire in the foetus earrings case.[25] An ineluctable conclusion is that the difference in status of the exhibitions' respective organisers or the difference in status of the exhibitions' venues may have figured in police thinking; but perhaps for good reason. Police prosecution of personnel in the Royal Academy, the very core of the art establishment, and artists exhibited by it, might have inaugurated considerable protest at the lack of a guarantee of liberty of artistic expression in what for the moment in England remains an unwritten constitution of dubious efficacy in the protection of the rights of the artistically creative and their exhibitors.[26] The passing of the Human Rights Act 1998 may not assist them because current European human rights case law to be applied domestically confirms the legitimacy of operating a blasphemy law, for example, in Contracting States including the United Kingdom, in accordance with local moral standards within the States' 'margin of appreciation'. This is a consistent trend unlikely to be reversed in the course of the application of the 1998 Act.[27]

The question of blasphemy law's potential application to artworks can again be seen to arise at the millennium threshold with the showing of 'Heaven: An Exhibition That Will Break Your Heart'. One particularly provocative statue at this exhibition portrays the late Diana, Princess of Wales, as the Virgin Mary. The exhibition explores how cults based on the adoration of pop singers, royalty and fashion models are replacing the traditional subjects of Christian worship. Prosecution is unlikely to occur in relation to this exhibition, however, because there is an absence of the necessary vilification of Anglican religious icons to constitute blasphemy. Instead, it legitimately provokes by illustrating how the concept of the spiritually perfect has changed drastically in the current époque.[28]

[25] *Gibson, Sylveire* (n 16).

[26] Contrast the written constitutions of Germany and Austria, for example, which uphold the specific presumption that art is free: Article 5(3) of the German Basic Law and Article 17a of the Austrian Basic Law.

[27] *Wingrove v United Kingdom* [1997] 24 EHRR 1, consolidates previous European human rights case law in maintaining that a law of blasphemy clearly can be legitimately in force in Contracting States.

[28] In response to a preview of the exhibition, which ran from 1 December 1999 to 28 February 2000, at the Tate Gallery, Liverpool, the Bishop of Liverpool said that he had no objection to a challenging presentation of a secular paradise. See further, *The Sunday Telegraph*, (12 September 1999) 9.

VII CONCLUSIONS

Undifferentiated in criminal law as a specialised value distinct from other facts, art has had the power to complicate legal areas not attuned to its idiosyncrasies. In blasphemy law, this tendency is accentuated by a lack of attention to art's moral position in sacred religious texts that could otherwise have assisted the criminal law process of blasphemy's regulation. A popular view is that in its present form blasphemy law in England is demoded and should be abolished. What is certain is that its original spiritual purpose of preserving the perceived image of God has now been relegated to a position of little or no importance. The prevention of civil disorder is one of its prime secular objectives, and it is arguable that it is precisely the legal labelling of faiths worthy of protection from vilification that causes such disharmony in a religiously plural society. The simple answer would be to abolish blasphemy law and for the faithful to rely on God's influence alone to preserve divine reputation, if this is one of the deity's true priorities, which is obviously a matter of serious doubt. To resurrect the ancient crime of outraging public decency to condemn an artwork is also unjust, as well as anachronistic, given the paramountcy now of the Obscene Publication Act 1959 in that process, with its appropriate artistic merit defence that, arguably, should pertain in all obscenity-related laws. But even the 1959 Act does not remove the kernel of the problem, which is the degree to which art should be excused its occasional 'immorality', or be justified, without more, irrespective of it. Is art's very ontology sacred and immune from criminal investigation, or is art only safe from prosecution when displayed in the apposite context of a museum or gallery? It would appear, especially from the foetus earrings case, that the status of the locus of the artwork is particularly relevant in obscenity-related offences, and it seems that precisely where putative art is located is one practically viable basis for legal decision-making on whether something is or is not art. Whether this is theoretically justifiable from the standpoint of the understanding of what is or is not art is a matter of conjecture, but it is to be hoped that the non-prosecution of art in the morally controversial *Sensation* exhibition, on whatever basis, augurs a more just route of general respect for art by its restrictive, yet increasingly reluctant, public morality law opponent.

3

*The Uncultured God: The Triumph of Blasphemy Law over Art (2000)**

I INTRODUCTION

UNTIL VERY RECENTLY, blasphemy law was thought to be teetering on the brink of abolition if not desuetude at both national and international levels. It seemed to be inert and only ever revived or judicially referred to out of eccentric sentimentality[1] or for reasons of public order.[2] The last decade, however, has witnessed the resurrection of its domestic and European juridical profile. This has coincided with continued prolific legal interest in the law of freedom of expression. *Wingrove v United Kingdom*[3] is but the latest addition to a surprisingly fertile spate of blasphemy versus freedom of expression cases that have, notably, exclusively involved artistic media. Strangely, though, little attention has been paid to the conundrum of whether an artist can be realistically conceived as being capable of blaspheming via, for example, the characters in a film or creative prose in a novel. The emergence of art law as a specialism is now encouraging a more detailed approach to such questions: it emphasises, inter alia, art's distinctive ontology and context as highly relevant factors in cases where it is claimed that art is transgressing the law by violating paradigms the law has formed only when catering for purely factual rather than artistic circumstances (such as the necessity for aesthetic distance in a psychic response to an artwork). As a result, blasphemy law has become a more transversal category of much intellectual interest, accommodating not just strategic political problems such as the alleged anachronistic protection of a single faith in religiously plural societies but also the complexity generated by this art dimension that can no longer be disregarded as simply akin to literal statement or activity. In *Wingrove*, for example, these, and other challenging considerations, are central to the contemporary legal

* An earlier version of this essay (by this author) appeared as 'The Uncultured God: Blasphemy Law's Reprieve and the Art Matrix' (2000) *European Human Rights Law Review* 5, 512–21. It may be noted that blasphemy law in England was abrogated with effect from 2008.

[1] *R v Gott* [1922] 16 Cr App R 87.

[2] *Bowman v Secular Society Ltd* [1917] AC 406.

[3] *Wingrove v United Kingdom*, Report of the European Commission of Human Rights adopted on 10 January 1995; judgment of the European Court of Human Rights, 25 November 1996. Subsequent footnote references are to the Commission Report, and the Court's Judgment [1997] 24 EHRR 1.

conflict between blasphemy law and freedom of expression, which is the inconsistent and topical legal area this essay now examines.

II THE DOMESTIC CONTEXT

Before the appearance of Salman Rushdie's *The Satanic Verses*[4], blasphemy law was considered something of a dead letter in England. Prosecutions for blasphemy had been extremely exiguous for over 100 years, yet several attempts at its abolition had failed. It has been solely a common law offence since 1967[5] and there is no comprehensive definition of it. Legal certainty is jeopardised because, as the Law Commission in their Working Paper on blasphemy said, 'It is hardly an exaggeration to say that whether or not a publication is a blasphemous libel can only be judged *ex post facto*.'[6]

The generally perceived *actus reus* of the crime is the publication of anti-Christian matter which is not expressed in decent and temperate language but, rather, in the manner of offence, ridicule or vilification,[7] and the *mens rea* amounts to strict liability[8]: the defendant must know what words he is publishing but need neither intend nor realise that those words have the characteristics of a blasphemous publication.[9] Until the Rushdie debacle, the celebrated case was *R v Lemon, R v Gay News Ltd*,[10] in which the material complained of was a poem and accompanying illustration portraying a role for homosexual love in the body of the Christian tradition. Any artistic intent assumed for the pieces was subsumed under a finding of vilification. The mere fact of publication dispensed with the *mens rea*.

As suggested above, the legal profile of events prior to the latest case of *Wingrove*[11] could not be properly understood without due attention to the publication in 1988 of Salman Rushdie's fourth novel, *The Satanic Verses*. On 14 February 1989, the Iranian religious and political leader, Ayatollah Khomeini, issued a *fatwa* declaring that Rushdie and others connected with the publication of the book were thereby put under sentence of death under Muslim law. In England, considerable Muslim hostility to the book ensued, leading to an attempt to suppress it on the grounds of blasphemy against Islam. This action failed in *R v Chief Metropolitan Stipendiary Magistrate, ex p Choudhury*[12] primarily because it was held that blasphemy in England only pertained to the

[4] S Rushdie, *The Satanic Verses* (London, Viking Press, 1988)

[5] The Blasphemy Act 1697 was repealed by s 13, Sched 4, Part 1 of the Criminal Law Act 1967.

[6] Law Commission, *Offences against Religion and Public Worship* (Law Com No 79, 1981) para 6(1).

[7] Above, n 2.

[8] *R v Lemon, R v Gay News Ltd* [1979] 2 WLR 281.

[9] ibid.

[10] ibid.

[11] *Wingrove* (n 3).

[12] *R v Chief Metropolitan Stipendiary Magistrate, ex p Choudhury* [1990] 3 WLR 986.

Christian religion. The special place of the artist in producing allegedly blasphemous statements was ignored. No distinction was made between literary or artistic statements for artistic effect and nonartistic statements emergent from 'real life' political or religious belief. As we will see below, Nigel Wingrove's problems with blasphemy law, after his production of a film based on St Teresa of Avila, were confined to extra-legal bodies in the domestic context, but the Rushdie affair clearly lent an influential backcloth to national blasphemy adjudications of every order in that case.

III THE SATANIC VERSES

The controversy surrounding Salman Rushdie's *The Satanic Verses* unsurprisingly centred squarely on the Muslims reaction to the writer's novel. What is little emphasised, however, is that, far from being a discrete unit, Islam has produced a variety of differing voices on the subject, some much more liberal than others in terms of what should be condemned as blasphemous. One general Muslim complaint, though, was based on the tone and language of the novel. This was exacerbated by what was generally considered by Muslims to be the religiously 'turncoat' nature of the novelist himself. A purely Christian attack on Islam in a novel would not have provoked Muslim hostility to anything near the same degree of intolerance. It is also true to say that very few Muslims saw Rushdie's novel as insulated from condemnation by *fatwa* because it was (only) art. From their standpoint, the themes of fantasy and dream in Rushdie's book failed to excuse the author's artistic rather than politico-religious stance. This is unfortunate because Rushdie's major preoccupation throughout his writings is the very subjective nature of Man's creation of reality. Objectivelyconstrued Islam and art are thus particularly polarised in the Rushdie problematic. To estrange Rushdie even further from his one-time peers, it is quite possible that certain Muslims approached his novel relatively unfamiliar with this particular brand of Western creative writing, and thus simply misapprehended it and its peculiarly artistic social relevance and context.

IV THE EUROPEAN DOCTRINE

Obscenity law is cognate with blasphemy law, and, in *Muller v Switzerland*,[13] an established artist, and organisers of an exhibition of his artworks, were convicted under a Swiss obscenity law for publishing certain obscene articles, namely three 'crude' paintings, the content of which comprised subjects such as sodomy, fellatio and bestiality. The European Court of Human Rights (ECtHR)

[13] *Muller v Switzerland* E Ct HRR A 113 [1991] 13 EHRR 212.

referred to its earlier obscenity law judgment in *Handyside v United Kingdom*[14] and commented as follows:

> The applicant's conviction on the basis of Article 204 of the Swiss Criminal Code was intended to protect morals. Today, as at the time of the *Handyside* judgment, it is not possible to find in the legal and social orders of the Contracting States a uniform conception of morals.[15]

This statement ignores, of course, the fact that a liberal-moral European notion of immorality imposed on the Contracting States by the ECtHR would arguably be beneficial for upholding minority rights such as those of artists. The individual Contracting States may be habitually incapable of asserting other than an essentially parochial standard of morality, that may well be unduly static or backward-looking instead of developmentally progressive, out of line with the liberal evolution of, for example, contemporary continental metropolitan cultural ethics.

In the blasphemy context specifically, the European Commission of Human Rights affirmed the legitimacy of operating a national blasphemy law in *X and Y v United Kingdom*[16] (the *Gay News* case) though in *Choudhury v United Kingdom*[17] (the *Satanic Verses* case) the application, contending, inter alia, English law to be prejudicial against Islam under Articles 9[18] and 14[19] of the European Convention on Human Rights, was declared inadmissible by the Commission as manifestly ill-founded because Article 9 could not be interpreted as including a positive obligation on states to protect all religious sensibilities. As the complaint under Article 9[20] had been rejected as being incompatible *ratione materiae* with the provisions of the Convention, the complaint under Article 14[21] of the Convention also fell to be regarded as incompatible *ratione materiae* with the provisions of it within the meaning of Article 27(2).[22] This tendency of the

14 In *Handyside v United Kingdom* [1976] 1 EHRR 737, the Court formally permitted for the first time a certain margin of appreciation or discretion to the defendant state in its assessment of what the national public interest requires.

15 *Muller* (n 12) [35].

16 *X and Y v United Kingdom* [1983] EHRR 123.

17 *Choudhury v United Kingdom* [1991] 12 HRLJ 172.

18 Article 9 reads '1. Everyone has the right to freedom of thought, conscience and religion; this right includes freedom to change his religion or belief, and freedom, either alone or in community with others and in public or private, to manifest his religion or belief, in worship, teaching, practice and observance. 2. Freedom to manifest one's religion or beliefs shall be subject only to such limitations as are prescribed by law and are necessary in a democratic society in the interests of public safety, for the protection of public order, health or morals, or for the protection of the rights and freedoms of others.'

19 Article 14 reads 'The enjoyment of the rights and freedoms set forth in this Convention shall be secured without discrimination on any ground such as sex, race, colour, language, religion, political or other opinion, national or social origin, association with a national minority, property, birth or other status.'

20 See n 18.

21 See n 19.

22 Article 27(2) reads 'The Commission shall consider inadmissible any petition submitted under Article 25 which it considers incompatible with the provisions of the present Convention, manifestly ill-founded, or an abuse of the right of petition.'

Commission to support local law preserving endemic local interests then surprisingly forthrightly disappeared in *Otto-Preminger Institute v Austria*.[23]

In *Otto-Preminger*,[24] the applicant, Otto-Preminger-Institut Verein für audiovisuelle Mediengestaltung, was a private association based in Innsbruck. It directed an application against Austria to the Commission that concerned the prohibition against showing the film *Das Liebeskonzil* in the applicant association's cinema in Innsbruck on the grounds that its presentation would constitute the criminal offence of blasphemy. The film was seized and subsequently confiscated. The applicant association complained that such measures violated its right of freedom of expression as guaranteed by Article 10[25] of the Convention. The Commission declared the applicant association's complaint admissible. It considered that recourse to satirical artistic methods did not justify the imposition of a restriction on a work of art even if it deals with religion. The restrictions imposed were deemed disproportionate and unnecessary in a democratic society. The dissenting opinion of HG Schermers emphasised the importance of local tests: some communities are used to satire as a way of expression, others are not. Nevertheless, the majority accepted a broader European notion of what could morally prevail over a blasphemy charge in terms of freedom of expression. In its report, the Commission expressed the opinion that there was a breach of Article 10[26] by the seizure of the film (by nine votes to five) and by forfeiture of it (by 13 votes to one).[27] This decision was a significant landmark in the upholding of typical cosmopolitan postmodern values over more traditional local religious ones.

The ECtHR had other ideas.[28] In [55] of its judgment, the Court said:

> The Court cannot disregard the fact that the Roman Catholic religion is the religion of the overwhelming majority of Tyroleans . . . The Austrian authorities acted to ensure peace in that region . . . It is in the first place for the national authorities, who are better placed than the international judge, to assess the need for such a measure in the light of the situation obtaining locally at a given time.[29]

[23] Report of the European Commission of Human Rights adopted on 14 January 1993; judgment of the ECtHR of 20 September 1994. Subsequent footnote references are to the Commission Report, and the Court's judgment [1994] 19 EHRR 34.

[24] ibid.

[25] Article 10 reads '1. Everyone has the right to freedom of expression. This right shall include freedom to hold opinions and to receive and impart information and ideas without interference by public authority and regardless of frontiers. This article shall not prevent States from requiring the licensing of broadcasting, television or cinema enterprises. 2. The exercise of these freedoms, since it carries with it duties and responsibilities, may be subject to such formalities, conditions, restrictions or penalties as are prescribed by law and are necessary in a democratic society, in the interests of national security, territorial integrity or public safety, for the prevention of disorder or crime, for the protection of health or morals, for the protection of the reputation or rights of others, for preventing the disclosure of information received in confidence, or for maintaining the authority and impartiality of the judiciary.'

[26] ibid.

[27] See n 22, Commission Report, paras 82 and 83.

[28] *Otto-Preminger* judgment (n 23).

[29] ibid [56].

Before *Wingrove*,[30] this became the judgment that embodied the European human rights law on blasphemy despite its adoption of a local rather than supra-national perspective. Would the Commission in *Wingrove*[31] acquiesce to that prevailing judicial concept of what was illegitimate blasphemy, or would it espouse the dissenting opinion of Judges Palm, Pekkanen and Makarczyk in *Otto-Preminger*[32] that there was no point in guaranteeing freedom of expression only so long as it was used in accordance with (local moral) accepted opinion?[33] Would the Commission in *Wingrove*[34] aver that art could be expected, as well as permitted, to shock, or would it denude any art issue by concentrating only on the documented offence to certain religious people irrespective of the artistic medium of the message? Would the Court in *Wingrove*[35] subsequently agree with the Commission or would it, as in *Otto-Preminger*,[36] retain its own independent course on the blasphemy versus freedom of expression problem?

V WINGROVE FACTS AND THE COMMISSION REPORT

Wingrove[37] arose from the following circumstances. Nigel Wingrove produced an 18-minute video film treating the experiences of St Teresa of Avila, a sixteenth-century Carmelite nun who experienced ecstatic visions of Jesus Christ. The film was objected to by the British Board of Film Classification (BBFC) on the grounds that the treatment of an ersatz St Teresa's erotic experiences with a presented Christ figure comprised an unacceptable treatment of a sacred subject and would constitute an infringement of the criminal law of blasphemy if deliberated upon by a properly directed, reasonable jury. Accordingly, the BBFC refused to grant a certificate permitting the sale, hire or supply to the public of the said film, *Visions of Ecstasy*. On appeal to the Video Appeals Committee, the panel upheld the BBFC's decision by three votes to two. Consequently, Nigel Wingrove made an application to the Commission claiming a violation of the right of freedom of expression contrary to Article 10[38] of the European Convention on Human Rights. Article 10(1)[39] sets out the fundamental right to freedom of expression and Article 10(2)[40] indicates permitted state derogations from it in certain fixed circumstances, including in the interests of the protection of morals and the rights of others.

[30] *Wingrove* (n 3).
[31] ibid.
[32] *Otto-Preminger* (n 23).
[33] ibid.
[34] *Wingrove* (n 3).
[35] ibid.
[36] *Otto-Preminger* (n 23).
[37] *Wingrove* (n 3).
[38] See n 25.
[39] ibid.
[40] ibid.

The Commission concluded by 14 votes to two that there had been a violation of Article 10.[41] It reported that Wingrove's film was a video not a feature film and of unusually short length, and that its blasphemous parts were 'fleeting'.[42] It added that it was unlikely that members of the public would unintentionally find themselves viewing the video in the same way as they might walk into an art gallery or cinema, or browse through magazines. A person would have to make a conscious decision to view the applicant's video and it was unlikely that it would have been seen by anyone who was unaware of the film's probable subject matter.[43] The fact that certain Christians might be outraged by it did not in the Commission's opinion amount to a sufficiently compelling reason to prohibit its lawful supply. Moreover, the BBFC could have given the film an '18' certificate, thus limiting its viewing to people over that age. The Commission added that the refusal of the classification certificate for the film did not correspond to a pressing social need and considered that the interference with the applicant's freedom of expression was disproportionate to the aim pursued and could not be considered necessary in a democratic society within the meaning of Article 10(2).[44] The case was then referred to the Court for its judgment.

A The Court's Judgment

The applicant's right to freedom of expression was clearly violated and this was not disputed. The question for the Court was whether such violation was justified under Article 10(2)[45] or was an unwarranted violation of Article 10.[46] The Court first had to decide if the interference with Nigel Wingrove's exercise of freedom of expression was 'prescribed by law'. It pronounced that English blasphemy law could not be said to not afford adequate protection against arbitrary interference, so was therefore prescribed by law: there was no general uncertainty or disagreement as to the definition of what constituted blasphemy, and the Court added that, with appropriate legal advice, the applicant could have reasonably foreseen that certain scenes in the film could fall within the scope of the English blasphemy offence.[47] The Court then affirmed the 'legitimacy of the aim' pursued by the censors: the fact that blasphemy law operative in England only protected the Christian faith, and did not treat all religions on an equal footing, did not detract from that legitimacy. Moreover, the aim of the interference, the Court pronounced, was fully consonant with the aims of Article 9[48]

[41] *Wingrove* (n 3).
[42] ibid. Commission Report, para 66.
[43] ibid, para 67.
[44] See n 25.
[45] ibid.
[46] ibid.
[47] *Wingrove* judgment (n 3) [43].
[48] See n 18.

of the Convention. The Court then considered whether the precise censoring interference was 'necessary'. It noted that blasphemy laws were still in force in various European countries, and, though rarely applied, could not be adjudged to be unnecessary in a democratic society. In addition, whereas there was little room for restriction of political speech and questions of public interest, a wider 'margin of appreciation' was generally available to states in relation to matters liable to offend intimate personal convictions in the sphere of religion or morals. The Court further held that national authorities were in a better position to define these requirements, and rule on the necessity of a restriction, than an international judiciary.[49] Its conclusion was that the national authorities' margin of appreciation had not been overstepped and there had accordingly been no violation of Article 10[50]: the reasons given to justify the interference could not be said to be arbitrary or excessive.

B Appraisal of the Judgment

Wingrove[51] is an important case for many reasons. First, it confirms that operating a blasphemy law is a legally valid choice for any state under the Court's jurisdiction. The Court disclaimed its entitlement to 'Europeanise' the notion of blasphemy, leaving the concept and its practical ambit to be interpreted at a local level. This is arguably a dereliction of duty because one principal role of the Court is to provide a useful supranational solution for Contracting States' observance whenever appropriate. It is particularly important in the case of a legally ambiguous term like blasphemy to determine its precise import. Although in *Wingrove*[52] the Court admitted that the definition of blasphemy was elusive,[53] it nevertheless said, somewhat disingenuously, that there was no disagreement over its definition.[54] But it is difficult to agree or disagree about the definition of a concept that goes so unclarified at both national and international levels. Secondly, *Wingrove*[55] is important because it implicitly upholds freedom of religion over freedom of expression even though the freedom of religion encapsulated in Article 9[56] of the Convention does not extend to protection from challenge to religious stereotypes because in such a challenge there is no detraction from freedom of religious practice. Censorship, though, *ipso facto* curtails freedom of expression. Thirdly, *Wingrove*[57] displays the limited prag-

[49] *Wingrove* judgment (n 3) [63]. This echoes the Court's view as expressed in *Otto-Preminger* judgment (n 23) [56].
[50] See n 25.
[51] *Wingrove* (n 3).
[52] ibid.
[53] *Wingrove* judgment [42].
[54] ibid [43].
[55] *Wingrove* (n 3).
[56] See n 18.
[57] *Wingrove* (n 3).

matism of the Court: it said that the material in Wingrove's video, once on the market, could be copied, lent, rented, sold and viewed in different homes. In these circumstances, the Court held, it was not unreasonable for the national authorities to consider that the film could have reached a public to whom it would have caused offence. However, as the Commission had pointed out in the same case, one simply could not view it unintentionally.[58]

In other matters, too, the Commission and the Court have been at loggerheads. In both *Wingrove*[59] and *Otto-Preminger*,[60] the two human rights bodies have categorically disagreed as to the case result. In both cases, the Court has reversed the Commission's decision, in both cases upholding blasphemy law as a necessary constraint on freedom of expression on the respective facts of those cases. Unlike the Commission, in both cases the Court has upheld rights consonant with, but not included within, Article 9[61] of the Convention, over freedom of expression embodied in Article 10. This is particularly lamentable in view of the following observations.

VI OVERVIEW

In the United Kingdom, the Law Commission[62] advised that the deficiencies of the law of blasphemy are so serious and fundamental that it ought not to remain as it is and that no measure short of abolition would be adequate to deal with such defects. Not least amongst the deficiencies is the lack of appreciation of the modus operandi of artistic intentions and forms; which have only a specialist oblique relation to life, unlike a literal defaming of God: if in blasphemy law it is the mode of the allegedly blaspheming utterance that results in prosecution, as in English law, careful legal attention should be paid to the specific mode or medium of art, which has its own ontological cultural mechanisms aside from 'real life' modes of expression. Moreover, as British campaigners against blasphemy laws have long pointed out, civilised society has collapsed neither in the United States of America, which protects free speech under the first amendment obviating the possibility of blasphemy actions, nor in France, Sweden, Denmark or Norway, which have all abolished blasphemy laws. Significantly, the particular *Wingrove*[63] ruling came on the same day as the Lord Chancellor, Lord Mackay of Clashfern, represented the United Kingdom Government in a visit to the ECtHR: he wanted to impress on it the need for Contracting States to be able to manage their own affairs in accordance with national character, traditions, religious beliefs and moral standards. In addition, although the Court

[58] ibid, Commission Report, para 67.
[59] *Wingrove* (n 3).
[60] *Otto-Preminger* (n 23).
[61] See n 18.
[62] Law Commission Report (Law Com No 145, 1985).
[63] *Wingrove* (n 3).

and the United Kingdom's present unwritten constitution both purport to uphold freedom of expression, the preference for upholding blasphemy law over it not only permits the silencing of artistic enterprise in favour of galvanising religious belief, but disfavours art, which is more universally participated in, in favour of what is in practice a small censoring lobby which happens to be religious in its justification.[64] This problem is compounded in English blasphemy law by making all publishers of a blasphemous libel virtually strictly liable. Finally, highly secularised justifications are given for the upholding of blasphemy law, such as the need to preserve civil order, whereas if attention were paid to the spiritual origins of the offence, one might discern a creative God in favour of human artistic creativity over a needless protection of His own reputation, criticism of which He is doubtless amply able to accommodate in all His wise omniscience. Such now merely contingent intellectual considerations are yet to be voiced in Strasbourg and secularised blasphemy law has gained a new lease of life at the conceptually unlikely expense of freedom of expression in its artistic form.[65]

VII REFORM

Within the domestic context, section 12 of the United Kingdom's Human Rights Act 1998, now in force, provides that where a court is considering granting relief for the right to respect for private life (protected by Article 8 of the European Convention on Human Rights), it must have 'particular regard' to the right to freedom of expression if such a decision might affect the exercise of this right.[66] However, it is unclear how the right to freedom of thought, conscience and religion (in section 13 of the Human Rights Act 1998) and freedom of expression (in section 12 of that Act) will interact in a blasphemy context. The Strasbourg institutions, though, inexplicably tend to give priority to the Convention's former freedom over other rights with which it may conflict.[67]

There is a persuasive argument that in egalitarian postmodernism the law of blasphemy should be extended to all religions and be protective of atheistic and agnostic ideologies as well: blasphemy law may be indispensably required to safeguard the conduct of inter-religious discourse. However, it seems to me that the arguments for the abolition of blasphemy law are nearly overwhelming, irrespective of the opposing emphasis on the need for blasphemy law, for equable, rational

[64] See further, Paul Kearns, 'Art, Freedom and the Christian Law of England' (1994) 1 *Maastricht Journal of European and Comparative Law* 307.

[65] A sculpture by Bernini, 'Santa Teresa in Ecstasy', was first displayed in public in l651, provoking the comment in a contemporary pamphlet that a pure virgin had been prostituted. Modern scholarship has since proclaimed the sculpture as being amongst the most important artistic creations of its period.

[66] Note, in particular, ss 12(1) and 12(4).

[67] See further, DJ Harris, M O'Boyle and C Warbrick, *Law of the European Convention on Human Rights* 2nd edn (Oxford, Oxford University Press, 2009) 356–60.

religious interaction conducive to public peace in a religiously-diversified common culture. To this end, the views of Anthony Bradney seem to this author the most powerful.[68] Bradney points out that 'one of Lon Fuller's eight ways to fail to make law is to draft a law which is so obscure that neither ordinary citizen nor trained lawyer can understand what the law commands or forbids'.[69]

The present law of blasphemy, Bradney argues, is an example of precisely such a failure: there is difficulty in identifying the communities, religious or otherwise, which are to be protected; there is a problem in trying to divide up religious icons amongst the various religious communities; and linked to this is the problem that religious icons are also cultural goods having value for everyone.[70] Additionally, what boundaries, if any, map out the various religious and non-religious territories? Is there a compelling correlation between blasphemy and heresy? In what sense is a creative artist specially removed from the ordinary blasphemer? Yet more pertinent questions are inspired by Bradney's stance. Freedom of speech follows naturally from the fact of human life: should this freedom be curtailed on the basis of protecting a more societally-developed countervailing 'faith'? Should not new thought be communicable, in the name of freedom of self-expression and the value in increasing the store of human knowledge, even to the discomfort of those who believe something contrary, a discomfort which is merely a psychic opposition rather than a practical hindrance to maintaining and expressing one's own belief? Is it not the case that a faith embodying enough inherent truth should be strong enough to counteract conceptual opposition because of its own intrinsic truth content, without the need to resort to law to bolster its tenets?

These are just some of the questions raised by those sceptical of the justifications for a law of blasphemy. To this author, their good sense seems unanswerable by any opposing lobby. The debate nevertheless continues largely because of the conflict between thought on the one hand and belief on the other, but also because, in a very religiously plural society such as that of the United Kingdom, optimal practical solutions to potential and real religious conflict, with or without blasphemy law, are on the whole elusive. It is nevertheless hoped that this essay has demonstrated that art, at least, should be in its own specialist sphere sacrosanct, immune to the reach of blasphemy law that has only ever been designed to remedy more literal alleged harms.

[68] See further, Anthony Bradney, *Religions, Rights and Laws* (Leicester, Leicester University Press, 1993) Ch 5.

[69] ibid 92.

[70] ibid 93.

4

*Postmodern Art: A Reflection on Western Legal Paradigms in 2000**

> There will always be skylark; even a few nightingales. But arts are not only the human equivalent of the song of singing birds.[1]

I INTRODUCTION

OBSCENITY LAWS AND other related public morality laws regulate activities and facts that contravene certain legally-decided imperative moral values. They are an example of state paternalism to keep public moral standards healthy. It is usually only incidentally that art is caught by laws designed for such purpose and, in general, public morality laws disregard the cultural distinctiveness of art as a factor in its legal-moral assessment.

The aim of this essay is to present a specialised survey of key decisions in the legal regulation of art in England, primarily, but also in contemporary America and Europe, when governed by European human rights law upholding freedom of (artistic) expression. As 'art', the author includes here novels, poetry, photographs and film. Its legal regulation obviously does not occur in a vacuum. The prevailing societal mood inevitably colours the shaping and application of moral laws. So does the type of art produced in any given period. The historical era covered by this article is technically known as postmodernism,[2] and we must establish first its discernible basic trends so that the legal regulation of art is understood in the context of that period's prevailing social and cultural mores. Equally necessary is a critique of what 'obscene' art may embrace – is there legal proscription of just 'obscene' art, and what is obscenity? Is there legal determination of what legitimate erotic art is and what is unacceptable pornography? Are specialised legal tests used to proscribe the varying entities that violate a societal notion of basic moral standards?

* A precursor of this essay (by this author) appeared as 'Public Morality Laws and the Creation and Appreciation of Art: The Postmodern Western Experience' in PLC Torremans (ed), *Legal Convergence in the Enlarged Europe of the New Millennium* (Kluwer International, 2000) 143–60.

[1] Dore Ashton (ed), *Twentieth Century Artists on Art* (New York, Pantheon Books, 1985) 150.

[2] See further, F Jameson, *Postmodernism, Or, The Cultural Logic of Late Capitalism* (London, Verso, 1991).

From this grounding, the essay proceeds to consider specific instances of the infringement of public-moral laws by art. The paradigms chosen are those which have been the most controversial. They include the battles between DH Lawrence, the novelist and poet, and public morality laws, notably the English Obscene Publications Act 1959; the notorious foetus earrings sculpture of Richard Gibson that violated the English 'outraging of public decency' common law offence; the victimisation of Salman Rushdie for producing *The Satanic Verses*[3] and that work's alleged blasphemy; the allegedly blasphemous film by Nigel Wingrove exploring the ecstatic visions of a putative St Teresa of Avila in sensual union with a presented Christ figure; the morally provocative 1997 art exhibition in the English Royal Academy aptly named 'Sensation'; and, finally, the legal brouhaha surrounding the homo-erotic, and other 'disturbing' photographs of American Robert Mapplethorpe. Together, these instances of art's real and potential entanglement with public morality laws are scrutinised to try to establish whether any particular themes of confrontation emerge, and whether legal measures to regulate art production, and exhibition are necessary, and if so, whether such measures are efficacious. If Karel Appel[4] was correct in his statement that 'art must shock', a tension may exist between art's habitual method of operating and more conservative legal mechanisms. It can be argued that a robust public can face anything art produces with equanimity, in which case law's tussle with morally controversial art is fundamentally unnecessary. On the other hand, it may be said that art should not be privileged with exemption from the purview of public morality laws simply because art has been traditionally perceived as of particular cultural worth. The radicalisation of art in late postmodernism may cry out for censure in a metropolitan code that treats the famous and the infamous as equal messengers, both capable of achieving stardom through shock tactics, irrespective of moral or immoral content. In the end, art might defy rationale, and confuse legal strictures by its transcending ambiguity, insulated from logical comprehension. This essay aims to test such hypotheses and to ascertain the reality of the art-law interface in the legal setting.

II POSTMODERNISM

Modernism is the term that has been used for the period 1890–1940, permitting thereafter the contingent term 'postmodernism' for the subsequent period. Postmodernism has a variety of sociologically-determinable traits, not merely in terms of art development but also in terms of public consciousness, that, inter alia, shape law that reflects that consciousness. Law is an agent of the past and evolves more slowly in its processes that most other societal units, such as,

[3] S Rushdie, *The Satanic Verses* (London, Viking Press, 1988)

[4] A painter of the Cobra movement, formed in 1948 by a group of artists from Copenhagen, Brussels and Amsterdam. The movement rejected the abstraction of post-war European painting, considering it lifeless and too passive.

for example, art and fashion. Because of essentially conservative tradition, the likelihood is that law sometimes has difficulty in dealing with phenomena that are not neatly a priori, especially in the realm of allegedly objective 'goods' or evils. Of particular concern to a legal system is the threat to order and the continuity of that order. Postmodernism's espousal of the meaninglessness of all higher truths and the purported parity of attitudes irrespective of status rest uneasily with a legal sense of hierarchy. An obsession with cosmetic/surface images also alienates postmodernism from ready legal acceptance; and the postmodernist devaluing of the Christian God, in particular, undermines the foundation on which English law, for example, is built. The lack of one cohesive moral framework in postmodernism promotes nihilism on the part of citizens, who are further undermined by the rise of technological depersonalisation. The emergence of political correctness imposes a totalitarian application to formal and informal language, much as envisaged by George Orwell,[5] and there is little that is 'native' to postmodernism because of civic and personal eclecticism characteristic of this era that so demonstrably lacks a 'zeitgeist'.[6] Inhabited by people who are de-centred, impressionable and quick to change stimulus,[7] the postmodern period is antithetical to the solid longevity of law and its atavistic values. Other characteristics of postmodernism include its metropolitan focus, habitual sexual promiscuity amongst the young, and indifference to matters of justice and principle. In such an environment, art prospers whereas law is invaded.

So it is against this postmodernist backcloth that we witness the attempted legal control of a somewhat anarchic ethos that produces radical, possibly moral-free art. The inherent *value* in art per se tends to be ignored in favour of an egalitarian ethic of cultural equality where cartoons, for example, are as revered as old masters, under a broadened concept of art that threatens to lose its implicit value credential.

In postmodern art, a membrane of simulacra blurs the underlying real, and objective reality is endlessly subjectivised. Law tries to monitor such precarious realities but is itself overwhelmed by increasing layers of bureaucratisation. The artificial threatens to become the thing itself, and a means often lacks a concerted end. What particularly confutes a legal regime is the popular cry to reinforce equivalence of entities, everyone having a compelling claim to equal significance, the culprit as much as the law-enforcer. Such an environment replicates no strata of historical values, upholds no tested traditions, and perpetuates no natural respect. Law is at sea in a mass of converging externalised realities, given voice by those who manipulate the plasticity of the era.

[5] Especially in his novels *1984* (London, Secker and Warburg, 1949) and *Animal Farm* (London, Secker and Warburg, 1945).

[6] A neat term for prevailing world trends in contemporary thought.

[7] Via a lack of solid 'Weltanschauung' or life view.

III OBSCENITY

Let us now examine one moral taboo the law traditionally monitors, ie obscenity. First, it is not self-evident what 'obscenity' is, and it is arguable that obscenity can only result from a non-artistic experience. This is because only when an item is reacted to in an aesthetic context can art result. Obscenity results from seeing the object out of context. In the aulic setting of law, art charged with being obscene is seen doubly out of context.

These observations arise from the truth that the art experience is not a passive experience. The active psychic participation of an audience co-creates it. Art results from engagement, and the particular type of engagement that results from the appropriate aesthetic psychic attitude. The pornographic legacy is the release of a physical impulse, whereas the art context and result is always meditative.

In view of these truths, it is remarkable that the English law, for example, has not provided a special exemption for erotic art that rests on its artistic character, and its necessarily calm receipt. Instead, art is defended from an obscenity charge by providing it in England with a defence to justify it. There is no recognition that sexually explicit art is legitimate simply because of its natural ontology. Art does not need a defence; it needs a champion to point out its inherent goodness as a spiritually-created item for sober contemplation.

It is not the entire Christian West that is appalled by erotic stimuli outside an artistic context. Ilona Staller was a hard-core pornography star and this did not stop her being elected to the Italian Parliament. In France, President Mitterand had various mistresses without incurring the treatment President Clinton has had to endure simply because of extra-marital affairs (to which his wife and daughter are now reconciled). It is a peculiarly Anglo-American attitude to condemn people for their sexual relations to the extent that they lose office as well as self-esteem. Although art should be, and theoretically is, insulated from condemnation as obscene based on its very method of being, its intrinsic 'art' quality, 'real life' scenarios reveal that sexual publicity endangers livelihoods. This is a lamentable consequence of Anglo-American cultural immaturity, displaying a sex obsession akin to that of a pubescent schoolboy.

The distinction between English and American law in curbing obscenity rests on a constitutional difference. In America freedom of speech is upheld, but obscenity is not deemed to be 'speech'. In England, freedom of expression is only implicit and not invoked as a right in court. This position changes to one akin to that in America (and that under the European Convention on Human Rights (ECHR), which is its model) with the coming into force of the Human Rights Act 1998. Then, a constitutional level of protection for artistic expression is codified in England. Whether art is exempted from obscenity charges when that arises is a matter for pessimism based on the American analogy. Artistic expression also lacks adequate protection under the ECHR when its content violates 'local' (ie 'national') standards. In all these mentioned instances, there is no presumption that art, whatever its content, is free.[8] This absolutist stance is unpopular because of its extremity and because its appeal is not universal.

Artistic products of contemporary England, such as those of Damien Hirst,[9] do not always bear the natural insignia of art, and could be confused with artifice, such is their apparently contrived art quality based on a visual ordinariness or functionality. It is arguable moreover, that art which reflects violence, such as Hirst's dead animal art, is more 'obscene' than art which reflects sexual events. In France, the elevation of violence to a place of obscenity restriction is complete, whereas in England and America it is the prurience factor that still in effect determines the hypostasis of the basic obscenity law rules.

It seems strange that the portrayal of a legal act, ie that of sexual intercourse, is condemned in England and America when sufficiently explicit, whereas the private acts themselves whether heterosexual or homosexual, are not proscribed.[10] Contrast that position with that of violence in films: such violence in 'real life' would constitute various legal assaults up to the point of murder. Nevertheless, it is sex that is the Anglo-American bugbear and it is this factor that we witness being repeatedly prosecuted under obscenity or obscenity-allied, legislation. Sadly, a more appropriate legislative practice criminalising violent images as obscene does not find general favour with Anglo-American law-makers although it is based on common sense.

As far as art is concerned, its imagery is usually[11] redeemed in England if it is of artistic merit[12] even though obscene, and in America the constitutional standards of obscenity in practice relaxes when art is in the legal spotlight, as seen in *Roth v United States*.[13] Nevertheless, avant-garde art may yet present such moral 'outrages' according to conventional sexual tastes that both England and American mechanisms will still spring into place to censor and condemn the most errant art.

[8] The Austrian Constitution is a rare example of a system that upholds the presumption that art is free.

[9] One of the artists of the Young British Artists movement.

[10] Except in certain specialised cases which remain anachronistic anomalies.

[11] Most prosecutions come under the Obscene Publications Act 1959 which provides a defence of artistic merit (see n 12). On rarer occasions, the common law offence of 'outraging public decency' is utilised, which provides no such defence.

[12] Section 4 of the Obscene Publication Act 1959 provides: '(1) A person shall not be convicted of an offence against Section 2 of this Act, and an order of forfeiture shall not be made under the foregoing section, if it is proved that publication of the article in question is justified as being for the public good on art or learning, or other objects of general concern. (2) It is hereby declared that the opinion of experts as to the literary, artistic, scientific or other merits of an article may be admitted in any proceedings under this Act either to establish or to negative the said ground.'

[13] *Roth v United States* (1957) 354 US 476, 1 L ED 2d 1498, 77 S Ct 134, reh den 355 US 852, 2 L Ed 2d 60, 78 S Ct 8.

IV LADY CHATTERLEY AND DH LAWRENCE

DH Lawrence is now established as one of England's finest writers but during his lifetime his moral reputation, as gleaned from his creative products, was that of a maverick. This was perhaps ineluctable if we see the artist's role as at the forefront of moral insight, with antennae to discern shifts in the surrounding moral cosmos that would naturally go against the moral status quo because it was developmental. Lawrence's brushes with the law ranged from 1915 to 1964 and were all alleged violations of public morality law suppressing certain presentations of sex.

Under Lord Campbell's Obscene Publications Act 1857, 1011 copies of Lawrence's beautiful book *The Rainbow*[14] were destroyed in law's inherently perfunctory manner. His main morally iconoclastic work, *Lady Chatterley's Lover*[15], received very poor reviews but did not face legal hurdles immediately. This was because the book was first published privately in Florence, in 1928, and only an insignificant number percolated through the English customs barriers. Lawrence's poetry was not as fortunate. In 1929, his anthology *Pansies*[16] was seized by the (English) Post Office. When 14 of the poems were withdrawn from the collection, the Director of Public Prosecutions was sufficiently satisfied to not take further steps. At the same time, the introduction to Lawrence's volume of paintings was also seized but no legal action was thought necessary. In 1930, Lawrence wrote *A Propos of Lady Chatterley's Lover*[17] in which he addressed obscenity issues head on. Sadly, this piece of literature did not focus on the law; otherwise Lawrence could have used it to help defend him against his later prosecutions.

The novelist is in a very difficult, if not impossible, position when the law dictates that art, 'even art' must not transgress society's established moral outlook, however difficult that consciousness is to evaluate. It is precisely one of the novelist's vocations to throw new light on moral matters so his problem is intrinsic and ontological: how can he do this without seeming to willfully transgress society's existing moral benchmarks? In the eyes of the law, the novelist's vocation appears to involve precisely that. It is a matter of different hermeneutics being used: art starts from a standpoint of psychic adventure and creation, law starts from the standpoint of social security and moral preservation.

The legal position was personified in England by Justice Byrne, the presiding judge in the case when *Lady Chatterley's Lover* was prosecuted for obscenity under the then Obscene Publications Act 1959.[18] The new Act provided for experts to be called to assist the jury, but Justice Byrne clearly despised their use.

[14] DH Lawrence, *The Rainbow* (New York, B.W. Heubsch, 1915)
[15] DH Lawrence, *Lady Chatterley's Lover* (London, Penguin Group, 2011)
[16] DH Lawrence, *Pansies* (London, Martin Secker, 1930)
[17] DH Lawrence, *A Propos of Lady Chatterley's Lover* (London, Penguin Group, 2006)
[18] See further, CH Rolph, *The Trial of Lady Chatterley* (London, Penguin Books, 1961).

The way to assess the book, according to the judge, was in a non-specialist way, so that the ordinary decent citizen's reaction to the book could be gauged, not that of an art critic. More seriously, he misdirected the jury on the balance probabilities requirement, and asserted that, although he acknowledged Lawrence as one of the greatest writers of the twentieth century, the trial was about morality not aesthetic taste, and that society's morality, despite being nebulous and insusceptible to scientific assessment, could be 'harmed' by books like *Lady Chatterley's Lover*. In urging the jury to read the book dispassionately, and not to compare it with other books, the judge attempted to remove the metaphorical spectacles that are specifically imperative to appreciating a literary work of art, and arguably necessary to co-create it, ie by the interplay of the reader and text.

Justice Byrne ignored the novel's details and was disgusted by Lawrence's brand of artistic realism – for him 'dirty' language was redeemable only for scientific and not artistic purposes. As if it were a blasphemy trial, Justice Byrne highlighted the 'sacred' importance of marriage and strongly implied that Lawrence's message was pro promiscuity and adultery. The judge had no comprehension of art's unique place in the sociological scheme, confusing it with literal speech and arguments. He also constructed his own concept of legitimate sex as one which is borne only of 'affection'.

Mercifully for Lawrence, the jury had other ideas and returned a 'not guilty' verdict, vindicating the book, its author, its publishers and its expert assessors. This result heralded a new wave of sexual 'morality' for which the 1960s is now famous. A virtually parallel American trial reached the same conclusion as the English one, though its process was much different, not least because the American trial was founded, for constitutional reasons, on the issue of freedom not morality. In the West, Canada also joined the Anglo-American contingent in saving the book from the thump of an uncivilised fist. Postmodern mentalities embraced the creative urge.

V THE FOETUS EARRINGS AND GIBSON AND SYLVEIRE

In England, in January 1989, Richard Norman Gibson, an artist, and Peter Sylveire, a curator, were found guilty of 'outraging public decency', a little-used common law offence that complements the Obscene Publications Act 1959. They were acquitted on a second count alleging a public nuisance. Gibson was fined £500 or 28 days' imprisonment in default; Sylveire was fined £350 with 21 days' imprisonment in default. They had been audacious enough to create and exhibit, respectively, an artwork using real human flesh. The facts are gruesome.

Number 82, The Cut, London SE1 is the 'Young Unknowns' art gallery where Sylveire exhibited art by Gibson including, inter alia, the 'Human Earrings': this particular exhibit constituted a model's head, from each ear of which was hanging an earring made from a real human foetus of three and half months gestation. Before the exhibition opened, the police arrived, and Gibson and Sylveire were astonished that it appeared that they had done something 'wrong'. They were charged accordingly and, in due course, they were convicted. They appealed against the conviction.[19]

The English Court of Appeal dismissed their appeal, giving the following grounds articulated by Chief Justice Lord Lane: that the offence of 'outraging public decency' did not illegitimately overlap with that of 'obscene' publication under the 1959 Act;[20] that no *mens rea* of intention or recklessness needed to be proved;[21] and that no particular attention needed to be drawn to the offending exhibit to satisfy any publicity factor.[22]

In its judgment, the Court ignored the whole 'art' issue. This is no important omission for those concerned about the arts in general. It is explained by the fact that only under the Obscene Publications Act 1959 is a defence of public good based on artistic merit available: the common law crime of outraging public decency contains no such safety net, and whether or not an object is characterised as 'art' is immaterial in the context of that crime. Strangely, the Court relied on the blasphemy case of *R v Lemon, R v Gay News Ltd*[23] as its main authority, whereas *Knuller (Publishing, Printing and Promotions) Ltd v Director of Public Prosecutions*,[24] a case which specifically focused on outraging public decency, was treated less centrally. This is significant because *Knuller* involved much more liberal reasoning than *Lemon*, with an emphasis on tolerance towards minorities, whatever they happen to be, including, feasibly, artists as such a group. The Lords spoke of 'liberty of the citizen' in *Knuller*, whereas in *Lemon* the accused was condemned outright for the publication of an irreligious poem and accompanying illustration. So, to pursue the harsh and puritanical route of *Lemon*, the Court in *Gibson, Sylveire* de-emphasised the crime of outraging public decency's leading authority *Knuller*, choosing instead to apply the censoring attitude of the only contingently-related *Lemon* case. *Knuller's* dominant message of freedom was entirely bypassed, amounting to a dereliction of primary duty by the Court in *Gibson, Sylveire*, which failed, for whatever reason, to apply *Knuller* directly, in favour rather of *Lemon*, on the main facts and issues of the case, for which the *Knuller* reasoning was conspicuously relevant, authoritative and compelling.

19 *R v Gibson, R v Sylveire* [1990] 2 QB 619; [1990] 3 WLR 595.

20 Since there was no suggestion that anyone was likely to be corrupted by the exhibiting of the earrings, the prosecution for the existing common law offence of outraging public decency was not precluded by s 2(4) of the 1959 Act.

21 Since the object of the common law offence of 'outraging public decency' was to protect the public from feelings of outrage by such exhibitions, there was no requirement for the prosecution to prove that the person charged had an intention to outrage or appreciated the risk of such outrage and determined nevertheless to run the risk.

22 There was no requirement that the (second) appellant, Sylveire, should have drawn particular attention to the exhibit before he could be convicted.

23 *R v Lemon, R v Gay News Ltd* [1979] AC 617, [1979] 1 All ER 898, [1979] 2 WLR 281.

24 *Knuller (Publishing, Printing and Promotions) Ltd v Director of Public Prosecutions* [1973] AC 435, [1972] 2 All ER 898, [1972] 3 WLR 143.

The obviously unjust path judicially taken in the foetus earrings case highlights a lack of understanding of art by the judiciary in general. Even where such understanding exists, respect for art is usually absent. What seems to be particularly judicially-lacking is an awareness of art's central cultural importance. If the Court in *Gibson, Sylveire* had recognised this, it may have entertained a different analysis of the case's indubitably distasteful facts. Instead of being a case based on an offensive act of abusing aborted human beings, the Court should have stopped to reflect, as one should with any artwork, and asked itself *why* the exhibit was so comprised. It may then have considered that art, by virtue of its intrinsic essence, *can* be shocking. Some maintain that for something to be art, it *must* shock. An enlightened court would see that if members of the public enter an art gallery, they can expect to be shocked (in the psychic sense of aesthetic, contemplative, art-contextual reflex to art *qua* art). *Outrage* cannot result unless an artwork is approached incorrectly (ie without the art-focused attitude). A wrong attitude to his art can hardly be considered the fault of the artist. This is a corollary of the established acceptance of the distinctively artistic *modus operandi*. An artist is at the core of the art mechanism and cannot be expected to stand on the outside of it, when implicitly in its heart, in order to oversee or anticipate ignorant reactions to his artwork. The art-appreciative dimension of members of the public should preclude inappropriate responses to art, but it seems that this facility is not universally activated, probably due to a lacuna in art-appreciating education. Again, it is not up to the artist to provide such education. Considering all the facts, what prevails as an overall impression is that judge and jury should not be unaware of the way art differs from other facts, but are. We cannot punish an artist for other people's ignorance.

VI THE SATANIC VERSES AND SALMAN RUSHDIE

In March 1989, Abdul Hussain Choudhury sought summonses against the novelist Salman Rushdie, alleging blasphemous and seditious libel at common law, accomplished apparently by the publication of *The Satanic Verses*, a novel that infuriated many Muslims. The quest was met with refusal by the Chief Metropolitan Magistrate sitting at Bow Street Magistrates' Court, London, even though the novel had been banned in all Muslim states, China, India and South Africa. Mr Choudhury subsequently sought to quash the magistrate's decision by an order of *certiorari*, and to direct him to issue the summonses by an order of *mandamus*. The Divisional Court dismissed the application, stating that the English common law offence of blasphemy was restricted to a scurrilous vilification of the Christian religion, and did not apply to Islam. The Court also held that, with respect to seditious libel, that there was no incitement to violence against constituted authority though the book had, inter alia, allegedly promoted hostility and ill will among different classes of Her Majesty

The Queen's subjects, and caused the breakdown of British-Iranian diplomatic relations.

What interests us in this case[25] is the implicit English legal acceptance of the view that art *can* be blasphemous, even though prosecution was unsuccessful in this particular instance. The Divisional Court disclosed its opinion that an attitude expressed in the medium of art, in this case a novel, is not necessarily prevented from being a blasphemous libel just because of its artistic quality, viz, simply because the statement is put into the mouth of a character, even a disreputable character, in a novel. This stance ignores the ontologically-implicit autonomy of voices in art, and the autonomy of art as a distinct, acknowledged, independent cultural category. If a publication is couched in decent and temperate language, under current English law it cannot constitute blasphemy in the legal sense. Are not artistic statements in a novel in an inherently orderly, or indeed hermetic, environment? Art offers itself in this context and cannot impose itself. It is passive, ready to be activated only by a reader's will to read it. This is hardly stereotypically legally obnoxious. One artistic attitude, moreover, is that once artwork is written, it ceases to belong to the writer and belongs, rather, to a now impossible exercise to discern an author's own everyday beliefs from his voice and message in a novel, where the latter are implicitly 'artified'. From sacred texts, we glean nothing about how we are specifically to deal with art that contains allegedly offensive irreligious images or messages.

What the Rushdie scenario shows us, notably in this context of *R v Chief Metropolitan Stipendiary Magistrate ex p Choudhury*,[26] is that the power of the artistic word is received as if it were as or more powerful than a simple literal statement. Art and power are not usually mentioned in the same breath, even if, for example, art and money are. So our creative writers have a particular responsibility in the postmodern world, where art as a sub-set of societal interests can gain pre-eminence. What seems to have been jettisoned *en route* is art's traditional (only) *symbolic* relation to life, and with this we are losing the associations of art with magic and mystique, and other processes much more subliminal than those of fact, which deny a literal comprehension. This is the legacy of a world which is now always on the edge of its seat, highly politicised and strait-jacketed by movements such as that of political correctness, which doubtless had laudable origins. The Western metropolis is the seat of that world and the fabric is rich, eclectic and volatile, with few obvious hierarchies and fewer 'normal' standards. What products will outlast this protean age?

VII ST TERESA OF AVILA AND NIGEL WINGROVE

St Teresa of Avila was a sixteenth-century Carmelite nun who experienced intense, ecstatic encounters with Christ, while Englishman Nigel Wingrove

[25] *R v Chief Metropolitan Stipendiary Magistrate, ex p Choudhury* [1991] 1 QB 429.
[26] ibid.

made an 18-minute video film on her story. The British Board of Film Classification refused to give a certificate permitting the sale of the film, which Wingrove had entitled 'Visions of Ecstasy', on the ground that the film comprised an unacceptable treatment of a sacred subject and would contravene English blasphemy law. With an appeal to the Video Appeals Committee having failed, Wingrove applied to the European Commission of Human Rights claiming a violation of his right to freedom of expression as set out in Article 10 of the European Convention on Human Rights. Article 10, paragraph 1[27] contains the fundamental right to freedom of expression provision and Article 10, paragraph 2[28] sets out permitted state derogations from it in certain given circumstances, including in the interests of the protection of morals and the rights of others. The Commission concluded by 14 votes to two that there had been a violation of Article 10 and set out its reasons: any blasphemous parts of the film were fleeting; a conscious decision would have to be made to watch the video; and there was no pressing social need for a classification certificate request. The case was then referred to the European Court of Human Rights (ECtHR).[29]

The ECtHR reached a different result from that of the Commission – the interference with Wingrove's exercise of freedom of expression was prescribed by law: the censors had pursued a legitimate aim; the precise interference with Wingrove's right of freedom of expression could not be judged unnecessary; the national authorities' margin of appreciation had not been overstepped, and such a margin was wider in the sphere of morals than in the context of political speech.

The Court clearly declined to 'Europeanise' the concept of blasphemy which is not helpful when a role of the Court is to provide a supra-national solution in the field of rights. Moreover, it was disingenuous of the Court to uphold that the law of blasphemy was sufficiently unambiguous so as not to be unjustly uncertain and prescribed by law. There is constant disagreement about what constitutes blasphemy for legal purposes.

The judgment of the ECtHR in the *Wingrove v United Kingdom* case is disappointing to those in favour of free expression in the motion arts. It is arguably anachronistic to favour religious values over artistic ones, given the religious and non-religious plurality of belief now harboured in the postmodern state. The judgment is clearly unprogressive and of appeal only to the religiously dogmatic of illiberal frame of mind. Moreover, in no way did Wingrove's film interfere with the practice of religion, and it is clearly tenable that preoccupation with

[27] Article 10, para 1, reads: 'Everyone has the right to freedom of expression. This right shall include freedom to hold opinions and to receive and impart information and ideas without interference by public authority and regardless of frontiers. This Article shall not prevent States from requiring the licensing of broadcasting, television or cinema enterprises.'

[28] Article 10, para 2, reads: 'The exercise of these freedoms, since it carries with it duties and responsibilities, may be subject to such formalities, conditions, restrictions or penalties as are prescribed by law and are necessary in a democratic society, in the interests of national security, territorial integrity or public safety, for the prevention of disorder or crime, for the protection of health or morals, for the protection of the reputation or rights of others, for preventing the disclosure of information received in confidence, or for maintaining the authority and impartiality of the judiciary.'

[29] *Wingrove v United Kingdom* [1997] 24 EHRR 1-119, July 1997, Part 1.

the reputation of the Christian God was a very minor aspect of societal concern in the 1990s. In the *Wingrove* case, the ECtHR pandered to the enforcement of considerable archaic, religious, formal exactitude at the expense of creative, dynamic, artistic and precious expression, in tune with the mores of the current European époque.

VIII THE 'SENSATION' EXHIBITION

From 18 September to 28 December 1997, an invigorating art exhibition took place at the Royal Academy, Burlington Houses, London. Entitled 'Sensation' it included works by various highly avant-garde artists including Damien Hirst, famous for art incorporating 'blood and gore'. Various members of the public objected to some of the exhibits in 'Sensation' on the grounds that, in differing ways, they were simply 'offensive'. Perhaps the aphorism 'Art must shock' could be modified in the current era to 'Art must offend' such is the multitude of morally-confrontational artworks produced in contemporary circles.

The most strikingly controversial exhibit at 'Sensation' was Marcus Harvey's painting of Myra Hindley – made from child-sized handprints. Myra Hindley is a notorious murderer of children and the juxtaposition here of her face, and part of a child's anatomy creating it, seems to capitalise on the horror of Hindley's reviling deeds, though the *precise* cause of offence to others of such an arrangement remains somewhat conceptually elusive. The mere fact that Hindley was being 'celebrated' in art was probably the underlying, distressing catalyst at the time.

Another artist, Chris Ofili, presented the Virgin Mary in a cascade of hard-core pornography; and Jake and Dinos Chapman also caused upset with an exhibit in which some of the 'noses' of the female figures were replaced by penises. No criminal charges were brought against these artists, probably because the vice squad had monitored the exhibition prior to its opening. As a consequence, the Chapmans' exhibit, for example, was barred to children at a pre-emptive stage. The Myra Hindley painting escaped being charged with (i) outraging public decency, to which no defence of artistic merit is attached, and (ii) obscene publication, to which a defence of artistic merit is attached. For obscenity in (ii) the item has to tend to 'deprave and corrupt' and it is difficult to see how the Hindley painting could effect such processes, any more than it could inculcate outrage per se. The exhibit was nevertheless clearly distasteful in the minds of some. An examination of artistic intent, involving an interview with the artist concerned, could have helped to ascertain if there was a clearly non-criminal intention but in outraging public decency, and producing obscenities in the legal sense, such intention is overlooked until, in the obscenity context, it is scrutinised as part of the statutory artistic merit defence. Chris Ofili's pornography-adored Virgin Mary could be considered blasphemous by Catholics, in particular, but since the English common law offence of blasphemy is based on

Anglican sentiment, any blasphemy charge would probably fail. There is no evidence, however, that such action was even considered at a formal level, and it may well be that potential litigants would be intimidated by the Royal Academy's implicit approval of the works in 'Sensation'. In one way, it is very encouraging that artistic freedom was not interfered with even in the face of such moral iconoclasm, signalling, perhaps, a demise in prosecution fervour in such circumstances, with the implicit acknowledgement that there are more serious crimes to investigate than those alleged to emanate from art. After all, art is only obliquely relevant to real-life discord.

IX 'THE PERFECT MOMENT' AND ROBERT MAPPLETHORPE

Amongst other productions, the late American art photographer Robert Mapplethorpe constructed 'The Perfect Moment', an exhibition of photographs that contained a selection of his works on homo-erotic themes. In view of this content, guidelines of a substantive nature were issued by Congress on what the National Endowment for Art (NEA) could fund. Behind this stop was Senator Jesse Helms. There was banning of funding for art enterprises including 'obscene materials'. Such prohibitions naturally have an impact on the artistic quality assessment of projects that are submitted for consideration for public funding by the NEA: there must be a content appraisal that ignores the quality of forbidden works. It is clearly arguable that 'decency clauses' contravene the first Amendment's guarantee of freedom of speech ('speech' has an extended meaning including all artistic expression, excluding obscenity, which is regarded as not being speech). There will always be art of questionable taste and the categorising of 'obscenity' as non-speech threatens to embrace many controversial works that arguably do not come into the obscenity class, but are merely experimental with moral themes. This stems from the ineluctable difficulty of defining 'obscenity'. In Mapplethorpe's case, the chosen subject-matter was not designed to instigate depravity and, like all art, is simply incapable of conation, ie exercising the will that an idea results in action. Such specialist analysis of art is, of course, ignored by Congress.

In late 1997, the English police confiscated a book of photographs by Mapplethorpe from the library of the University of Central England. The University's Vice-Chancellor was threatened with criminal prosecution under the Obscene Publications Act 1959. In late 1998, the book was returned to the University library when the Vice-Chancellor signed a receipt. The Vice-Chancellor observed that the Crown Prosecution Service found only two homosexual pictures contrary to the Act, when some heterosexual ones were comparably disturbing. He concluded that there is in that service an element of homophobia. He also concluded that there was doubt that 'any material in this day and age can be regarded as obscene by virtue of its likelihood to deprave or corrupt' because such a concept belongs to a value system that was probably outdated even when the Act was passed. The Vice-Chancellor's message was that a welcome repercussion of his Mapplethorpe experience would be the removal of the Act from the statute book.[30]

X CONCLUSION

A disturbing facet of Western media publicity is an unhealthy preoccupation with sexual matters. This is particularly the case in the context of politics, where sex 'scandals' in England and America have jeopardised or terminated the careers of certain politicians. This reveals an immature moral fabric inherent in Anglo-American values, almost pathologically sexually obsessional. This deflects attention from more important, truly moral concerns such as lack of professional integrity pertinent to the post occupied. The private life of a professional man is *ipso facto* private. It should not concern others unless it reveals hypocrisy or illegality. In the context of art, it is astonishing that artistic 'sinnlichekeit'[31] is straitjacketed by an uncompromising puritanical legal ethic that deeroticises not only, then, 'real-life' sexual 'indiscretions', but also those presented quite morally legitimately in the critically-acknowledged contained operation of art. It is only art-ignorance that permits art to be conceived of as a moral threat, and it is highly unsophisticated to equate one's psychic reaction to art with that to 'real life' scenarios (not forgetting that reactions to sexual events in 'real life' are, of course, also wholly disproportionately exaggerated, not least by the English tabloid press). Art is inherently immune to self-corruption, as well as totally un-corrupting of its audience, unless mistaken for fact. Art is ontologically insulated from immorality: it is those who react to art inappropriately who import a moral filth that contaminates what they experience. The creativity implicit in art means it is inherently un-damaging. True art cannot damage psyches, and possesses no will factor to try to achieve destruction in any way except in the aesthetic capsule of art appreciation in the artistic dimension, which is itself rare, and confined to the motion arts. Art is the soul's answer to the denial of transcendence in the human condition.

None of the legal paradigms examined in this article involved the pre-censorship of art creation content. Nothing so totaliarian would be permitted in democracies. What needs to happen is the next stage, ie the removal of impediments to artistic *publication* even in controversial spheres. This may be seen as presuming the success of art education in training audiences to treat art as art. But even without that success, art should not be the victim of others' ignorance. There is the proviso, of course, that protection of children is naturally imperative, and some art can only be comprehended by adults. Nothing must compromise that peremptory norm.

[30] The Vice-Chancellor, Peter Knight, expressed his views in various fora, but the precise information here was gleaned from the Times Higher Education Supplement, 9 October 1998, p 16.

[31] This particularly appropriate and evocative German term equates approximately with the English noun 'sensibility'.

An artist's manifesto is often unknown even to herself: art can involve mysterious effects, and the conscious act of art creation does not always find as partner the product produced as consciously artistically envisaged. This is a characteristic of art which remains largely ignored when allegedly transgressive art comes before a criminal court. Inherent in art is the possibility of 'mystique'. Law tends not to relish such impressionistic uncertainty of idea and form or positively appreciate the (artistic) effect of a marked sensibility. It should do so when art is in the legal arena, because it has defence implications in its essentially non-criminal ambience.

The specific clashes between law and art that this essay has traced, reveal different types of injustice. In the case of DH Lawrence, there was a life-long tension between erotic sensibility and the moral structures the law imposed. The durability of his literary appeal signals that the triumph was ultimately his. This has the side-effect of making legal restraint seem unqualifiedly trivial. Gibson's foetus earrings introduce a very typically fin-de-siècle problem, when art reaches its ultimate boundary with fact. Here we perceive the clamp of the law eradicating artistic intention as a factor in the legal process. It is draconian and unforgiving, and very unthinking: no intellectual enlightenment penetrates the court-room. Salman Rushdie's *The Satanic Verses* is the product of a dare-devil, un-reverential and mischievous, polytheistic world, with artistic rebellion against a sacred object. Nigel Wingrove's 'Visions of Ecstasy' is not shy to show the human side of a martyr. This work's condemnation shows revulsion for such an exposition when the preferred image of the subject is of a personified ideal. The 'Sensation' exhibition reveals the overwhelming iconoclasm of mainly artistic youth, and its vibrant lack of deference to established socio-moral canons epitomises rather predictably the view of the artist as a Romantic rebel, of artistic youth, and its vibrant lack of deference to established socio-moral canons synergy as conspiratorial. Mapplethorpe is the extreme artist anti-Christ, if treated from a very fundamentalist Christian hermeneutical stance. From a very liberal one, he embodies Christ's implicit passion for freedom of expression: turned like the tables of the money-lenders in the courtyard of the temple, the photographer eclipses our rational senses in angry demonstration, evoking new energies, and desperate for the sanctity of dynamic ideas. As Carl André has said, 'art is not like a chemical formula but like a chemical reaction'.[32] Is art meeting law conflagration?

There is a danger that the law-art relation can be caricatured as permanent antithesis: sense against sensibility, reason against emotion, rule against spark. It is hoped that this assessment of the more subtle aspects of this ontological divide will engender deeper consideration of a much-ignored art-law problematic, with dramatic implications for personal and professional freedom, for integrity and truth.[33]

[32] See n 2, 189.
[33] See further, P Kearns, *The Legal Concept of Art* (Oxford, Hart Publishing, 1998).

5

*Obscenity Law and the Creative Writer: The Case of DH Lawrence**

I INTRODUCTION

THIS ESSAY EXAMINES the legal history of DH Lawrence's encounters with obscenity law from 1951 to 1964, centred on the trials of his novel *Lady Chatterley's Lover*.

Obscenity, so difficult to define, is a feature of legal focus in all national legal systems concerned with the uploading of public morality. In accordance with the facts, the author of the essay has chosen a comparative law approach, referring to the legal treatment of *Lady Chatterley's Lover* in France, the United States of America, Canada, Japan and India, in addition to espousing the more conventional approach of analysis of the English trial. The result arguably offers a more holistic impression of how Lawrence's novel was tackled by obscenity law.

As a consequence of his conflicts with public morality laws, Lawrence became very interested in censorship and wrote very intelligently on the subject. If one has a Romantic view of the artistic process, this positive repercussion may be regarded as a form of 'beauty out of strife'.

II INTERNATIONAL INVOLVEMENTS

The subject of DH Lawrence's difficulties with obscenity laws became very topical on 30 November 1996. Japan, a country where pornography was freely available for the first time in 46 years, condoned the publication of an uncensored version of *Lady Chatterley's Lover*.[1] The Shinchosha publishing house provided a full Japanese translation of Lawrence's classic, including passages still officially banned. In 1950, the Japanese Supreme Court had found a complete Japanese translation of the author's book obscene and ordered about 80 pages of love scenes to be deleted. 1996 seems remote from 1915 to 1964 when a variety of Lawrence's works were persistently plagued by public morality laws, most notably in England.

* A variation on this essay appeared in (1998) 22 *Columbia VLA Journal of Law and the Arts* 2, 525–31.

[1] '"Chatterley" to Bare all in Japan' *The Independent* (London, 12 November 1996) 12.

In accordance with the judgment of Sir John Dickinson at Bow Street, London, on 13 March 1915, 1011 copies of Lawrence's *The Rainbow* were destroyed under Lord Campbell's Obscene Publications Act of 1857.[2] Published privately in Florence, Italy, in 1928, his *Lady Chatterley's Lover* received vehemently antagonistic English reviews, but since only a few copies percolated through the customs barriers and there was no-one in England to prosecute, the hostility was confined to the world of literary debate. Instead, Lawrence's poetry was a victim: in January 1929, the English Post Office seized the manuscript of his anthology *Pansies* and very shortly afterwards the introduction to his paintings.[3] Fortunately for the author, there were no legal proceedings when Lawrence's publishers, Martin Secker, complied with the Director of Public Prosecutions' recommendation that 14 of the poems be omitted. In July of the same year, a folio of Blake was allegedly amongst works seized in a police raid of the Warren Galleries' exhibition of Lawrence's pictures, and, on 8 August, 13 of them were the object of a police application for a destruction order. Before a magistrate's court,[4] the defendants promised to close the exhibition: five guineas in costs were awarded against them and the case was dismissed.

Lawrence very much resented the legal hounding. This is unsurprising. A man of culture such as Lawrence would not expect the intrusion of the hostile mechanism of legal prosecution when he is evidently a creator of fine literature rather than an anonymous merchant of pornography. It is also arguably a great indictment of law's priorities and a conspicuous insult to what may be called 'special personalities'[5] to hinder or blight the progress of their genius for the sake of what could be perceived as law's less elevated objects. In a society where good literature is lauded, it seems ironic that acknowledged exponents of it should be thwarted by an establishment sense of morality that has, in Lawrence's own case, so little practical effect except his own worry and concomitant bitterness which contrasts so markedly in worth with the cultural and aesthetic joy good literature endlessly gives. From the lover of literature's standpoint, how many would in practice be harmed by, for example, Lawrence's 14 indicated poems, in comparison to how may benefit from having a complete picture of the creative product of an English literary hero? In Lawrence's case, he was to be especially gifted in his own lifetime so it is not merely with the benefit of hindsight that such an argument can be successfully posted. Retrospectivity naturally adds to the weight of the evidence in the sense that we now know the further revered literary works Lawrence was to create subsequent to his prosecutions. In 1930, in his *A Propos of Lady Chatterley's Lover*, Lawrence addressed the obscenity issue by stating that it is a creative piece;[6] if it treated legal matters it may have been influential in

[2] DH Lawrence, *The Rainbow* (New York, B.W. Heubsch, 1915)

[3] DH Lawrence, *Pansies* (London, Martin Secker, 1930)

[4] Marlborough Street Magistrates Court, Mr Mead, an octogenarian, presiding.

[5] A term used by Professor Aleksander Peczenik at the 'Workshop on Narrative Coherence and Legal Interpretation', European University Institute, 13 October 1987.

[6] DH Lawrence, *A Propos to Lady Chatterley's Lover* (London, Penguin Group, 2006)

defending the novel in later prosecutions (1959 in America, 1960 in England). Sadly, Lawrence was then no longer alive to defend it.

In France, *Lady Chatterley's Lover* had a smoother passage than in America and England, with the Titus edition merely filed there in the early 1930s.[7] It was not prosecuted then, or subsequently, in France. In the early 1950s, Japan's high courts had no consistent approach to artistic merit's role in the determination of obscenity but took a strong concerted line against the novel. On 26 April 1951, Nagoya High Court pronounced: 'Obscene literature and drawings are those which tend to mislead the general public in their just understanding of sexual life and to corrupt good morals, and their artistic merits shall not be taken into consideration when judging their obscenity.'[8] On 10 December 1952, Tokyo High Court predicated:

> Literature . . . deals with the problems of men in their social lives. It must abide by the conditions which form and maintain social order . . . It [cannot] . . . neglect these conditions. Such conditions bring about a certain limit to the manner in which literature can express itself . . . However, there can be a case in which the artistic character of literature attenuates and sublimates sexual impulse created by sexual description in certain passages, or in which the persuasive of the philosophy or the idea of literature, does away with the character of obscenity.[9]

The Japanese Supreme Court concluded in finding *Lady Chatterley's Lover* obscene despite full recognition of its artistic worth:

> Art and obscenity are concepts which belong to two separate, distinct dimensions; and it cannot be said that they cannot exist side by side . . . [T]he obscene nature of the work cannot be denied solely for the reason that the work in question is artistic literature . . . No matter how supreme the quality of art may be, it does not necessarily wipe out the stigma of obscenity. Art, even art, does not have the special privilege of presenting obscene matters to the public. Be he an artist or a literary man, he may not violate the duty imposed upon the general public, the duty of respecting the feeling of shame and humility and the law predicated upon morality.[10]

In America, two years later, there was another protracted story. The first trial of the novel was within the Post Office Department and the presiding judicial officer was Charles D Ablard.[11] He decided only that he was not going to decide and the case of Lady Chatterley was referred to Postmaster General Summerfield for a final departmental decision. That decision went unambiguously against the book:

[7] Paris, 1930 and 1932.

[8] Quoted in the comparative law appendix of Norman St John-Stevas, *Obscenity and the Law* (London, Secker and Warburg, 1956) 254–55.

[9] ibid 255.

[10] *Koyama v State*, 11 J Sup Ct Crim 997 (1957), quoted in John Henry Merryman and Albert E Elsen, *Law Ethics and the Visual Arts*, 3rd edn (Pennsylvania, Pennsylvania University Press, 1987) 487.

[11] Although part of the legislative and judicial powers. For practical purposes the department trials are the same as those in ordinary courts.

> The contemporary community standards are not such that this book should be allowed to be transmitted in the mails.
>
> The book is replete with descriptions in minute detail of sexual acts engaged in or discussed by the book's principal characters. These descriptions utilize filthy, offensive and degrading words and terms. Any literary merit the book may have is far outweighed by the pornographic and smutty passages and words, so that the book, taken as a whole, is an obscene and filthy work . . .[12]

However, in the federal courts, this decision was reversed, with Judge Bryan of the District Court for the Southern District of New York attentive to the language's relevance to plot and character development and espousing the view that any isolated obscene passages did not submerge the presiding theme. On appeal by the Government, Judges Clark, Waterman and Moore affirmed in favour of the book. In the principal opinion, Judge Clark differentiated such a work from hard core pornography that lacks character or plot development, emphasising purely physical action. Interestingly, Judge Clark followed Judge Bryan in a view of the book as as much polemic as novel. He looked to the author's purpose for the achievement of which he considered any 'smutty' passages integral and appreciated the moving emotions of the descriptions treating sex. There was no further government appeal to the Supreme Court and no more prosecutions by enforcement officials of any of the states.

III THE ENGLISH SITUATION AND ITS WIDER REPERCUSSIONS

In England, the novel met with a very antagonistic judge, Justice Byrne. In his summing up,[13] he was squarely against the jury basing its views on those of experts, an approach which patently undermined the whole rationale behind the statutory right to call them. Justice Byrne's stance towards *Lady Chatterley's Lover* was that of a proud non-specialist and he wished the jury to approach the text with similar minds, unenlightened about only academically-appreciated elements such as the writer's purpose. He wanted the jury to react as their normal selves (presumed by him to be uninformed about art); he wanted them to put the work out of its appropriate artistic context; he wanted the jury to eschew the sophisticated appraisals of critics close to what he perceived to be Lawrence's ignoble cause. The sense behind such a stance was doubtless considered by many as perfectly legitimate and professional if highly antipathetic to art: the judge's role is to protect the whole of society and society is not synonymous with the world of art; the 'man in the street', when exposed to the book in a library or book-shop context, would not have the benefit of experts to enlighten him or her about the true purpose of the text's allegedly obscene passages. However, it is not so certain that Justice Byrne's adverse treatment of the

[12] Charles Rembar, *The End of Obscenity* (London, Andre Deutsch Ltd, 1968) 117.

[13] See also CH Rolph, *The Trial of Lady Chatterley* (London, Penguin Books, 1961) 225–35.

issue of literary merit as a defence was beyond criticism as a matter of justice being seen to be done.

The first day of Justice Byrne's summing up in the trial of *Lady Chatterley's Lover* was on 1 November 1960 and was not uncontroversial. The judge told the jury that they were exercising their minds not about questions of taste but about moral standards: the question was whether the novel was immoral, not whether they happened to like it. He also opined that the sense that morality is fundamental to the well-being of the community must prevail over the desire for self-expression. Because morality defies definition, it might beg the question how one can ever know in advance what jeopardises it, but Justice Byrne was enured against such abstracted considerations. He also told the jury that the novel was to be read 'dispassionately' (even though the ontology of the art form requires a reaction to it of an emotional, as well as of a purely cerebral or logical, dimension[14]). Justice Byrne also said of the critics called to give evidence that 'nobody, of course, for one moment questions the honesty of their opinions'. His implication is that their honesty is their only virtue. The judge also displayed no real interest in the novel's details saying, for example, 'living with her husband in this dreary place of Wragby, I think it was called'. Strangely, he has a better memory for the completeness of the descriptions of sexual intercourse, though this could be explained by the fact that the focus of the trial was obscenity, which therefore required greater attention. Justice Byrne explained the 'public good' defence to the jury: if the jury is satisfied that it is an obscene book, they are then to go on to consider the further question, he says, 'have the defendants established the probability that the merits of the book as a novel are so high that they outbalance the obscenity, so that its publication is for the public good?'[15] In law, the defendants only had to establish that on the balance of probabilities their case was the stronger. The judicial use of 'so high' is misleading for it suggests merit has to dramatically outweigh obscenity, whereas it only has to outweigh it. Although Justice Byrne acknowledged that all the witnesses subscribed to the fact that *Lady Chatterley's Lover* was a book of literary merit and that Lawrence was one of the great authors of the twentieth century, he asserted that the jury was to consider the book by itself rather than in comparative relation to other books. In the course of ascertainment of obscene quality, it would seem profitable to compare the text in issue with other books of a similar genre so as to decide the threshold of condemnation.

[14] Roman Ingarden (1893–1970), the major contributor of Husserlian strict phenomenology to aesthetics and literary theory up to today, considers relating to a work 'in a more or less emotional way', a significant aspect of the reading process. See Roman Lngarden, *The Cognition of the Literary Work of Art* 6, Ruth Ann Crowley and Kenneth R Olson trans (Evanston, Illinois, Northwestern University Press, 1973). Note, too, the crucial role of the reader in the production of meaning in critical deconstructionist theory derived from the work of Jacques Derrida. See Christopher Norris, *Deconstruction: Theory and Practice* (London, Methuen, 1982).

[15] Rolph (n 13) 223. The reader may more generally note that my critique of this judgment necessarily revisits, in this more specialised context, that provided in my contemporary overview at 25–26 above.

The second day of Justice Byrne's summing up in the trial was on 2 November 1960. Here, the judge espoused a strictly legal concept of marriage which differs from the concept of marriage in creative literature, which tends to be less rigid. For example, in Virgil's *The Aeneid*, Book four,[16] the 'marriage' of Dido and Aeneas occurs spontaneously when they are hunting in the mountains. Justice Byrne emphasised promiscuity and adultery as the prime legal factors, whereas obscenity and any countervailing exonerating merit should have been the focus. The judge was clearly against artistic realism: he did not approve of Lawrence using words as a gamekeeper might use them; he also said, incorrectly, that the 'dirty' language could be redeemed only if its purpose was scientific rather than artistic. In response to Dame Rebecca West's testimony for the defence, Justice Byrne intoned: 'That was her view, for what it is worth.' He was similarly dismissive of the notion that sex could be thrilling as much as affectionate, and doubted whether the sexual passages were treated on a 'holy' basis, and whether a couple's union in a non-legal sense could have 'sacred' importance. One might have been forgiven for thinking it was a blasphemy trial.

Despite Justice Byrne's eristic efforts, the verdict in the trial was not guilty. This was a triumph for art and a defeat for literalism: the jury had appreciated the artistic order of *Lady Chatterley's Lover* and had dismissed the judge's literal attitude of taking the offending passages out of their appropriate artistic context. For the lawyer who specialises in obscenity law, it is frustrating that we will never know more precise details of the verdict: was the book simply not obscene or obscene but justified? But this is a less momentous omission than is the fact of Lawrence's unqualified legal victory.

This paralleled the American trial, and it is fascinating how such different trials produced the same result. In America, the defence called two witnesses; in England it called 35. The American witnesses were presented as established critics, qualified to testify expertly on literary matters. They were people called to supply evidence that would help the court decide whether the book had value. Although this was also a function of the English witnesses, they were not so confined. The latter included, in addition to literary critics, four clergymen and one witness whose qualifications were that she was young, bright, female and a Roman Catholic – qualifications useful in many walks of life other than to testify on literary merit.[17] Some of the English witnesses testified on ethics as much as literature and seem to have been called to attribute respectability to the novel rather than literary merit: the defending clergymen impliedly challenged Justice Byrne's views of the moral demands of Christian England. The presence of famous witnesses, such as a television personality, was perhaps intended to give a certain status to the book, incongruous though it might otherwise seem. In contrast, *Lady Chatterley's Lover* was defended in America because it presented a view on a sub-

[16] A central book of Virgil's *The Aeneid*, beginning with Queen Dido agonising in her love for Aeneas and ending in her suicide.

[17] Rembar (n 12) 153 (in the chapter entitled 'Lady Chatterley: Postscript').

ject rather than on the premise that it actually promoted morality.[18] The American witnesses were strictly literary and were restricted at the trial to this role.

The American trial of *Lady Chatterley's Lover* was based on the issue of freedom, the British one on morality, courtesy of the United States Constitution and the English anti-obscenity statute which, respectively, fostered such priorities. In the English trial two members of Parliament, Norman St John-Stevas and Roy Jenkins, were called to testify that their Obscene Publications Act (1959) was not designed to apply to the novel on trial. Strictly speaking this was a constitutional error because when a statute has been passed, the legislators' job is done; for some of them to re-appear in a court context to say what their Act was meant to say makes Parliament seem unreliable and inconclusive in its statute-making. It also blurs legislative and judicial functions.

The English attack was on the person of Lady Chatterley not on the novel.[19] The judge considered her actions immoral and treated them as if from life (whilst at the same time disapproving of artistic realism). In America, however, the courts declared that a writer must be free to portray any kind of character. 'If she were a professional prostitute', Judge Bryan said, 'it wouldn't make any difference'.[20] Whereas in England there was a jury but nothing beyond the jury's verdict, in America there was an acquittal and no appeal. In both jurisdictions, the legal issue for the experts was whether the novel was redeemed because it was creative literature communicating worthy ideas. However, the Obscene Publications Act (1959) need not have been used by the English witnesses as connecting the right to publish with the moral colour of the publication. It is arguable that the fixation on morality in the English trial regrettably obscured the more important oriflamme of freedom.[21] But at least in England and America *Lady Chatterley's Lover* did go free, as it did in Canada, in 1962, before the Supreme Court there.[22] India[23] and Japan, however, suppressed the work.[24] It would seem though, as we approach the twenty-first century, that certain Eastern jurisdictions, notably Japan, are now habituated to the idea of freedom of expression for artistic media.

[18] ibid 157.

[19] ibid 155.

[20] ibid.

[21] ibid.

[22] *Regina v Brodie*, 32 DLR 2d 507, 529 (1962).

[23] *Ranji Udeshi v Maharashtra Times* (London), 20 August 1964.

[24] This result is surprising, particularly in the case of India, given the open exhibition of the erotic intrinsic to Hindu culture, for example, and the factually just reputation of the Christian West as the more habitual censors.

Part III

Later Developments and Writing on Art, Obscenity, Religion and the Law

6

*The Decline of Obscenity Law: A 2007 Perspective**

I INTRODUCTION

IT IS TIMELY to examine the efficacy of the law enshrined in obscene and blasphemous libel because of the recent occurrence of a host of morally controversial, and potentially illegal, writings, art exhibitions, and television programmes in England that have all gone unprosecuted, despite the manifest and varied displays of indignation and dismay shown by certain individuals and groups, notably faith groups, in our culturally-eclectic nation. This essay reveals the historical lack of conceptual and practical integrity in these unduly complex libels and charts some topical instances when the laws of obscene and blasphemous libel could have been the basis for successful prosecutions in the last seven years[1] in England, but, seemingly inexplicably, were rarely adverted to and never utilised. It will be argued that this situation militates against their continuing survival as merely vestigial elements of English law. In short, the essence of obscene libel is a tendency on the part of a 'published' article to deprave and corrupt, while blasphemous libel is committed by any scurrilous vilification of the Christian religion, including its principal iconic figures. There are other lesser, sometimes parallel, offences of a similar nature that will also, in due course, be examined here. Most emphasis, however, is placed on obscenity, since this is the principal criminal libel even though, arguably, it is blasphemy that has been the subject of the most volatile controversy in the English contemporary media. The true underlying purpose of these two libels, which are sometimes used in a complementary way, has never been completely certain, which is remarkable in itself; and, with respect to content, the *mens rea* components have been draconian because they approximate to strict liability. It will be argued here that it is only anachronistically that these paternalistic measures can be justified and developed in the slightly chauvinistic terms of preserving the

* The author wishes to express his thanks to Professor Andrew Sanders for his valuable comments on an earlier draft of this essay, that formed a variation on the instant text as 'The Ineluctable Decline of Obscene Libel: Exculpation and Abolition' (2007) *Criminal Law Review* 667–76.

[1] In 2000, the author recorded the state of the law at the time and the facts caught by it. See further, Paul Kearns, 'Obscene and Blasphemous Libel: Misunderstanding Art' (2000) *Criminal Law Review* 652.

intrinsic calm and stability of our country, an argument the secular reasoning of which is antithetical to blasphemy's putative religious hypostasis, and which ignores the presence in English law of other adequate safeguards specifically designed as public order measures.[2]

II BASIC ANOMALIES

A Obscene Libel and Parallel or Similar Crimes

The fundamental law relating to obscenity is now statutory and, accordingly, the Obscene Publications Act 1959 provides a legal test for it:

> For the purposes of this Act an article shall be deemed to be obscene if its effect or (where the article comprises two or more distinct items) the effect of any one of its items is, if taken as a whole, such as to tend to deprave and corrupt persons who are likely, having regard to all relevant circumstances, to read, see or hear the matter contained or embodied in it.

Although this provision is commendably clear on its face, there are nevertheless difficulties associated with it. The first thing to notice is that the statutory definition of obscenity differs from its ordinary meaning, which can be rendered as synonymous with colloquial adjectives such as disgusting or filthy. The term in ordinary usage can also have a sexual dimension that approximates to lascivious or lewd. The statutory definition, however, suggests a grave immorality which may have its root in the times when obscenity was an ecclesiastical offence akin to blasphemy. The legal sense of obscenity was once confined to sexual immorality whereas in more recent times it has been rather artificially extended to cover the favourable presentation of drug-taking[3] and acts that incite violence.[4] The consequence is that it is difficult to predict what further unpleasant portrayals will be found to come under 'obscenity' as a now burgeoning legal term of art: in view of the current hostility to smoking tobacco,[5] that exercise might soon be legally subsumed under the obscenity label. In addition, juries are now put in a very complicated position conceptually when it comes to deliberating on what is legally obscene. They have to evaluate the strength of the conjunctive terms 'deprave and corrupt' using the filter of what they consider ordinary decent people's standards and they have to be able to distinguish between what might only mildly lead someone morally astray, on the one hand, and what is sufficiently serious to be depraving and corrupting on the other. It is their unenviable prerogative to infer accurately prevailing public-moral standards and to engage in subtle distinctions bearing on the actual moral weight of

[2] Notably under the Public Order Act 1936.

[3] See further, *John Calder (Publications) Ltd v Powell* [1965] 1 QB 509, [1965] 1 All ER 159.

[4] *DPP v AB and C Chewing Gum Ltd* [1968] 1 QB 159, [1967] 2 All ER 504.

[5] From 1 July 2007, smoking was banned in public places in England. See also, 'Tom can hit Jerry with an axe but Ofcom won't let him smoke' *The Daily Telegraph* (22 August 2006).

certain allegedly, morally damaging materials. Judges, of course, may assist juries with their directions concerning these tasks but have done so in notoriously contrasting ways, some assuming a liberal position, for example, and others not. Further, the question always remains as to whom the law is supposed to be protecting from depravity and corruption and the necessary content and size of such a group. The jury has to speculate on these matters and that again renders the law dangerously uncertain and open to misapplication.

The *mens rea* of the obscenity offence is also unclear and controversial. It is certain, though, that the actual intention of the author of a work is irrelevant. This causes particular difficulty when art or literature is alleged to be obscene because the specialised intention of artists and creative writers goes unconsidered, even though it is essential to the basic ontology of artistic creativity, including its product.[6] The law strictly says that if an article has a tendency to deprave a significant proportion of the readership, it does not matter how pure or noble the author's intention may have been, the article produced is obscene.[7] However, because the offence of obscenity has existed at both common law and statutory levels, the ascertainment of the *mens rea* requirement can become a somewhat complex process. At common law, the case of *Hicklin*[8] is traditionally cited as authority for the proposition that no *mens rea* is required for the crime of obscenity. Nevertheless, on a strict interpretation of the judicial rationale in the case, *Hicklin*[9] is considered better authority for the proposition that if the defendant publishes that which he knows will have a tendency to deprave and corrupt, it is no defence that he did so with the best of motives. Additional complication arises from the dubious judicial pronouncements in other common law cases. In *De Montalk*,[10] for example, it was held that intention was to be inferred from the act of publication. Later, in *Penguin Books*,[11] Justice Byrne held, in addition, that if the defendant publishes an article that is obscene, the inference that he intends to deprave and corrupt is irrebuttable. However, adopting such a stance today would appear to be inconsistent with section 8 of the Criminal Justice Act 1967 that prescribes:

> A court or jury in determining whether a person has committed an offence, (a) shall not be bound to infer that he intended or foresaw a result of his actions by reason only of its being a natural and probable consequence of those actions; but (b) shall decide whether he did intend or foresee that result by reference to all the evidence drawing such inferences from the evidence as appear proper in the circumstances.

In subsequent cases based on the Obscene Publications Act 1959, the confusion from the common law cases is palpable. Most judges deliberating on obscenity

[6] Judges rarely acknowledge that art is a specialised cultural value that demands discrete treatment when laws of a more general nature are applied to it. See n 2.

[7] *Calder and Boyars Ltd* [1969] 1 QB 151, 168.

[8] *Hicklin* (1868) LR 3 QB 360.

[9] ibid.

[10] *De Montalk* (1932) 23 Cr App Rep 182.

[11] See CH Rolph, *The Trial of Lady Chatterley* (Penguin Books, 1961) 234.

under the Act are content to say that although obscenity is a matter of strict liability under the Act, this was not the case before the Act, and, accordingly, an intention to deprave and corrupt in those days had to be established. It was not the intention of Parliament to revise the common law and it could be that the Act has inadvertently restricted the requirement of *mens rea* in the manner of Justice Byrne. This leaves us with the straightforward result that obscenity is indeed a crime of strict liability, but it is a conclusion ascertained alarmingly circuitously. This would not matter unduly except that the 1959 Act did not explicitly abolish common law obscene libel. Rather, in section 2(4), it provided that:

> A person publishing an article shall not be proceeded against for an offence at common law consisting of the publication of any matter contained or embodied in the article where it is of the essence of the offence that the matter is obscene.

A mercifully clear interpretation of this law would be that all proceedings regarding obscene publications per se should be brought under the Act. However, unfortunately, that subsection has not been subsequently interpreted in that way. In *Shaw*,[12] for example, the common law crimes of conspiracy to corrupt public morals (a common law offence) and obscenity (a statutory offence) were conflated, with the hybrid consequence that there had been the publication of an obscene article at common law. This causes problems for legal certainty in relation to the operation of the defence to obscenity in section 4 of the 1959 Act, particularly when the rule that any extant related common law measure should not be activated to evade that statutory defence now exists.

Section 4 of the Obscene Publications Act 1959, as amended by the Criminal Law Act 1977, provides a defence of 'public good' as follows:

> (1) Subject to subsection (1A) of this section a person shall not be convicted of an offence against section 2 of this Act . . . if it is proved that publication of the article in question is justified as being for the public good on the ground that it is in the interests of science, literature, art or learning, or of other objects of general concern.
>
> (2) It is hereby declared that the opinion of experts as to the literary, artistic, scientific or other merits of an article may be admitted in any proceedings under this Act either to establish or negative the said ground.

At a practical level, this defence provides another exacting process for a jury. First, the jury should be directed to consider whether an article is obscene. If not satisfied of this beyond reasonable doubt, they must acquit; but if so satisfied, they must go on to consider whether, on a balance of probabilities, the publication of the article, though deemed by them obscene, is for the public good. It is unclear whether they must assess counteraction of the article's obscene quality with its meritorious aspects or whether they must weigh up all good and bad factors together, and then, as a result of this synthesis, derive a

[12] *Shaw* [1962] AC 220, [1961] 2 All ER 446.

conclusion one way or another. This does not assist clarity or consistency in the law. In addition, an archaic rule pertains to the defence: expert evidence is inadmissible to support a defence under section 4 if it is to the effect that pornography is psychologically beneficial to those who are 'sexually repressed, perverted or deviant', in that it relieves their sexual frustrations and, accordingly, diverts them from anti-social sexual activities.[13] This prejudice against the alleged value of pornography in certain instances removes the possibility of raising key scientific evidence that is now habitually used in other circumstances. Also, oddly, under the Act, it is still not permissible to adduce evidence that other books which are comparably obscene to the one in issue are in free circulation in society.[14] Nevertheless, evidence relating to other books, somewhat inconsistently, may now be adduced to ascertain the 'climate of literature' when trying to establish the literary merit of the book in issue under section 4.[15] The anomaly is exacerbated by the comparably unusual rule that literary intention can be relevant to the question of literary merit[16] but not to the question of basic *mens rea*. Further problems arise from the inapplicability of the defence to obscenity-related common law crimes. In relation to the common law crime of corrupting public morals, the Solicitor-General issued a warning in Parliament[17] that the prosecution of that crime should not be used to circumvent the statutory defence in the 1959 Act; but in the case of *Gibson*,[18] the cognate offence of outraging public decency[19] was prosecuted, probably disingenuously, to avoid the availability to the defendants of an artistic merit defence. This antinomy is unjustifiable.

It is clear that the notions of depravity and corruption in obscene libel are habitually used conjunctively but can be used interchangeably, and that they are legally perceived as somewhat extreme states, implicitly graver than the (mere) 'corruption of public morals' at common law. However, it remains unclear how depravity and corruption in obscene libel, on the one hand, and the crime of corrupting public morals, on the other, can be usefully distinguished for prosecution purposes. Similarly, the distinction between obscene libel and outraging public decency is far from clear-cut. It can be argued that outraging public decency does not necessarily cause depravity and corruption and that the offences are accordingly adequately distinguishable. This argument is conceptually neat and hence quite seductive. However, it is very difficult to cite an actual

[13] See further, *DPP v Jordan* [1976] 3 All ER 775.

[14] See further, *Reiter* [1954] 2 QB 16, [1954] 1 All ER 741.

[15] See *Elliott* [1996] 1 Cr App Rep 432, 435, [1996] Crim LR 264.

[16] See further n 11.

[17] 3 June 1964. See further, Paul Kearns, *The Legal Concept of Art* (Oxford, Hart Publishing, 1998) 34.

[18] *Gibson* [1991] 1 All ER 439, [1990] Crim LR 738.

[19] The common law offence of outraging public decency is unsatisfactorily defined and it is unsurprising that the Law Commission recommended its abolition as far back as 1976 (Law Commission, *Conspiracy and Criminal Law Reform* (Law Com No 76, 1976), para. 3.143. See further, Professor David Ormerod, 'Case and Comment, Act of Outraging Public Decency' (2006) *Criminal Law Review* 993.

circumstance when the given offensive item will cause the one type of reaction or effect rather than the other. This practical hurdle threatens the consistency of legal decision-making in this area. Resolution of the problem is, sadly, not assisted by the ongoing controversy as to the precise character of audience that should be legally deemed to be the one likely to be adversely affected. A fortiori, the exact impact of an allegedly immoral influence on a given individual involves a highly subjective assessment that is difficult to generalise from, and difficult to quantify in terms of a communally-relevant gravity.

B Blasphemous Libel

A cognate offence of obscene libel is blasphemous libel, which is now exclusively a common law crime and which is in its own way anomalous and problematic. Originally, this ancient offence was committed simply by denying the truth of the Christian religion, which was tantamount to a heresy charge. Now that we live in a religiously plural society, it is impractical to have an offence with these ecclesiastically absolutist, monotheistic, solely Christian roots. However, through the centuries, the offence grew to be rather more complex and its justification more secular. The essence of the offence became a supposed tendency to shake the fabric of society generally.[20] This reasoning was gradually supplemented by the added requirement that the expression of this tendency had to be scurrilous rather than decent and temperate, thus legitimising even controversial religious debate conducted in a peaceable manner. Because it is unlikely now that religious argument of a type anticipated at the time of the offence's origins will inevitably cause a breach of the peace or civil strife, the subsistence of the offence of blasphemy in modern and postmodern times appears anachronistic. And yet, as late as 1979, a blasphemy prosecution occurred after a gap of over 50 years. This was *R v Lemon, R v Gay News Ltd*,[21] and it arose from the appearance in the magazine *Gay News* of a poem by James Kirkup, which included a description of homosexual activity with the body of the dead Christ and an accompanying illustration. There was no proof of provocation to violence, as required by the House of Lords in the earlier 1917 case of *Bowman v Secular Society Ltd*.[22] Instead, the prosecution was successful based on a less strict test, which appears to be a religious version of the test for the common law offence of outraging public decency. It is as follows: a publication is blasphemous if it is couched in indecent or offensive terms likely to shock and outrage the feelings of the general body of Christians in the community. *Lemon*[23] thus resurrected the ancient thrust of the offence which did not require

[20] In the earlier cases, in particular, judges tended to slightly melodramatise the deleterious effects of alleged immoral influences.

[21] *R v Lemon, R v Gay News Ltd* [1979] 2 WLR 281.

[22] *Bowman v Secular Society Ltd* [1917] AC 406.

[23] *Lemon* (n 21).

either an intemperate or unpeaceable utterance to secure a conviction. This is lamentable not just because it is highly retrograde. Because the offending item comprised a poem plus illustration, it could at least loosely be said to constitute creative literature, plus artwork. However, there is no provision in the common law of blasphemy for a defence of literary or artistic merit. In addition, the publication *Gay News* is habitually read only by gay or bisexual people. This is the 'community' which was addressed, ie a specialised one not the 'Christian' community at large. Moreover, the question can be put as to whether fiction or visual art can ever be blasphemous since art is an oblique, symbolic medium that does not produce literal utterance. This latter point acquires relevance again in the 1990 case of *R v Chief Metropolitan Stipendiary Magistrate, ex p Choudhury*.[24] In this case, Mr Choudhury, offended by Salman Rushdie's novel *The Satanic Verses*,[25] sought summonses against the novelist and his publisher alleging blasphemous and seditious libel. The magistrate and, subsequently, the Divisional Court, denied such summonses on the grounds that blasphemy could only be committed in relation to the Christian religion and sedition could not be legally made out either on the facts. The courts did not consider, however, another interesting apparent flaw in the attempted prosecution. The alleged blasphemy in the novel occurred in dream sequences so were far removed from simple literal utterance, and it is arguable that the mode of presentation of the utterance, being artistic, should take the publication outside the bounds of legally-formulated blasphemy because of art's unique, culturally-distinct, ontological form. This is not the only way in which the case is intellectually dissatisfying. Christ is revered in Islam as a prophet, though not as the Messiah, but an insult to Islam can also be an insult to the image of Christ as respected in Islam, and thus blasphemous. Such a converse consideration could have been used to found a more convincing challenge to a book such as Rushdie's by appealing to the necessarily Christian slant of the offence.

III EXONERATION

The classic situation when obscenity and related laws have been applied in the past is when there have been explicit sexual presentations that prosecutors have considered too graphic. Such approaches have been greatly relaxed in recent years. In the summer of 2000, for example, the British Board of Film Classification agreed to liberalise its R18 pornographic video classification to allow more explicit scenes, though child pornography and bestiality remained outlawed.[26] In November 2002, it was agreed to allow hardcore pornography

[24] *R v Chief Metropolitan Stipendiary Magistrate, ex p Choudhury* [1990] 3 WLR 986.

[25] S Rushdie, *The Satanic Verses* (London, Viking Press, 1988)

[26] See further, Colin Munro, 'Sex, Law and Videotape: The R18 Category' (2006) *Criminal Law Review* 957. The way is now clear to replace antiquated provisions on obscene publications with an offence tailored to current, more robust standards of public tolerance of obscene images. For a lucid

inside British jails after prisoners mounted a successful challenge to its denial based on the Human Rights Act 1998.[27] These events highlight the fact that the overall understated public policy aim now is to proscribe only the most extreme cases of alleged public immorality and to implicitly condone many acts that would once have readily attracted the state's use of traditional obscenity and obscenity-related laws. In recent years, the moral debate about obscene, corrupting or outraging entities has veered away from the acceptability of those elements in art and has instead addressed the issue of the now general acceptability of uncensored pornography for adults and whether that extreme material should still be proscribed as being morally deleterious in its effects. In England, as in France,[28] it is now the portrayal of violence that is considered a greater evil, together with presentations that concern bestiality or explicitly or implicitly threaten children, such as those which might appear to exonerate the behaviour of paedophiles in one way or another. Nevertheless, there have been several instances in England when the police could have activated, but omitted to activate, our now virtually dormant public morality laws, notably in the sphere of the arts. Whatever the apparent merits on the facts, refusal to engage these atavistic provisions in the following general circumstances could have seriously undermined their central constitutional role.

The most sensational example probably comprises the public exhibitions and television shows that brought 'anatomical art' by Gunther Von Hagens to the attention of the British public in 2002. These operations on corpses dramatically questioned the common conception of the sanctity of the dead body, and brought explicit autopsies to English living rooms, and were undoubtedly in very dubious taste. The legal machinery to protect the English public from such spectacles was probably the offence of outraging public decency since this appears more conceptually fitting than crimes relating to the corruption of morals, but at all times prosecution remained hypothetical despite the fact that many were grossly offended by being exposed to these excoriations. In the same year, a stuffed mutant animal, which comprised of a sheep's head attached to the body of a Saint Bernard dog, appeared in the Royal Academy's 'Summer Exhibition' which upset many animal activists. Such art is now, however, somewhat common. In 2003, the most sexually explicit show ever to appear in London theatre occurred in the form of *XXX*. At no stage were public morality

commentary on contemporary reform, see further, Jacob Rowbottom, 'Obscenity Laws and the Internet: Targeting the Supply and Demand' (2006) *Criminal Law Review* 97. The Home Office has recommended a new, distinct offence of possessing 'explicit pornography containing actual scenes or realistic depictions of': intercourse or oral sex with an animal; sexual interference with a human corpse; serious violence in a sexual context; and serious sexual violence. See further, 'Consultation: On the Possession of Extreme Pornographic Material' (Scottish Executive and Home Office, 2005).

[27] See *The Sunday Telegraph* (10 November 2002) 6. The prisoners cited Article 10 of the European Convention on Human Rights which guarantees the right of free expression, and its obverse, the right to freedom of information.

[28] The relevant part of the relatively new French penal code entered into force on 1 March 1994. The old code Article 283 became Article 227-24 of the newer code. Because of this correspondence, case law based on the old Article 283 is still justiciable.

laws invoked to curb its blatant presentations of uncensored video sex. Also in 2003, Channel 4 broadcasted a picture of a Chinese performance artist eating a dead baby. The Independent Television Commission said that the programme was 'contrary to good taste and decency' but there was no prosecution. Channel 4 refused to accept the judgment of the Commission, insisting that the shocking images fulfilled its remit to 'take on challenging subjects and explore cultural boundaries'.[29] In the same year, live sodomy was controversially legally tolerated on the stage of the National Theatre in Mark Ravenhill's crudely and provocatively entitled *Shopping and Fucking*. Again, the obscenity and obscenity-related laws were not drawn upon to curtail the potential offence given.

In 2004, Mel Gibson's film *The Passion of the Christ* presented images of mutilation and gore, and was vilified as being anti-Semitic (despite the logical argument that to be true to the Gospels it had to be). There was never a legal attempt to censor the film or prosecute the director. No English law prohibits inspiration from an authentic ancient source, despite possible objections to its religious bias from a more egalitarian postmodern perspective. Later in that year, a play by Gurpreet Kaur Bhatti called *Behzti* caused huge offence and outrage, mainly to Sikhs. It portrays rape, abuse and murder in a Sikh temple. The play's showing remained legally unchallenged despite civil unrest, and blasphemy law was not invoked as it only protects the Christian religion. Mainstream films such as *Ai No Corrida*, *Romance*, *Baise-Moi*, and *Intimacy* have allegedly now made the distinction between art and pornography meaningless, and the 2005 film *9 Songs*, which included 35minutes of unsimulated sex, was unprecedented in its sexual candour. Also in 2005, *Jerry Springer: The Opera* enraged many Christians. However, the BBC Director General would not bow to extremist religious groups like Christian Voice, an organisation that claimed the programme was blasphemous.[30] In the same year, Damien Hirst's exhibition 'Stations of the Cross' also upset certain Christians in its evident flagrant irreverence, and religious objections were also expressed in relation to a Michele Coxon sculpture at Shrewsbury Abbey, Shropshire: the object was made of crushed animal bones to show the suffering felt by Christ but was misinterpreted as depicting his body rotting after being crucified. In 2006, John Cameron Mitchell's film *Shortbus* caused moral concern because of its explicit scenes of unsimulated sexual relationships, but no legal action against the film was ever even suggested. Many mainstream novels are also now considered more explicit than standard pornography, such as *The Sexual Life of Catherine M* by Catherine Millet,[31] *Politics* by Adam Thirlwell,[32] *I Am Charlotte Simmons* by Tom Wolfe,[33] and the most recent works of Melissa P and Jane Juska. These,

[29] See further, 'Reprimand over C4 Cannibal Art', *The Guardian* (11 March 2003) 9.

[30] The Christian pressure group lost an attempt to have Mark Thompson, the Director General of the BBC, charged with blasphemy for broadcasting the programme. See *The Daily Telegraph*, (16 January 2007) 2.

[31] C Millet, *The Sexual Life of Catherine M* (New York, Grove Press, 2002) (A Hunter trans)

[32] A Thirlwell, *Politics* (London, Jonathan Cape Ltd, 2003)

[33] T Wolfe, *I Am Charlotte Simmons*, (New York, Farrar, Straus and Grioux, 2004)

like the above-mentioned films, have all avoided legal censure in the form of obscenity and related laws. Since these escape sanctions, it becomes clear that obscenity laws and their ilk have now become at least demoded when it comes to monitoring the allegedly immoral in the realm of the arts. In practice, though not in theory, such controversial events have been effectively if not expressly exculpated, and reveal the acute extent to which the police are reluctant to instigate legal actions based on public-moral laws, reflecting by omission our very libertine state's now habitual indifference to enforcing morally paternalistic measures that nevertheless still have an established, if now dormant, constitutional function.

IV CONCLUSIONS: DESUETUDE AND ABROGATION

In 1998, Susan SM Edwards[34] examined the contemporary application of obscenity law by police, prosecutors and the courts, and presented the lay findings of the first national study ever conducted into pornography trials in the Crown Court in England and Wales. The findings demonstrated that only five cases within a six-month period were fully considered by a jury. Moreover, since only one conviction resulted in a sentence of more than six months' imprisonment, she concluded that the Crown Court jurisdiction, at least for this index offence, was virtually obsolete. The study, of course, also reflects the desuetude of the statutory offence of obscenity and its vestigial common law counterpart at a more general level, and, on this ground alone, it is difficult to justify obscenity law's retention in English law. But there are also other objections to the maintenance of this law which strongly suggest its abrogation. The 1959 Obscene Publications Act's own terms are somewhat inept: the archaic 'deprave and corrupt' test is no longer realistic as an appropriate measure for determining obscenity, and the defence of 'public good' it provides for was primed for abolition when the ill-fated Obscenity Bill of 1999 included its legal deletion. The jury's highly conceptual role in balancing an article's obscene content with various types of cultural merit, as an antidote to the obscenity, is almost designed to cause confusion, and the overlapping of obscene libel with cognate offences such as the common law offence of corrupting public morals render the area juridically precarious, inconsistent and unclear prosecutorially and substantively. Another objection to the statutory offence of obscene libel is that, like the majority of its related offences, it is in effect a strict liability measure when the often complex cultural nature of the objects of its application suggests close analysis of the originator's intentions regarding the creation and publication of the article in question. There seems no good reason to maintain or revive obscene libel and its associated offences when their single and combined effect

[34] See further, Susan SM Edwards, 'On the Contemporary Application of the Obscene Publications Act 1959' (1998) *Criminal Law Review* 843.

is an unduly complex mechanism whose infrequency of usage also dictates its abolition. A fortiori, the redundancy of this convoluted obscenity matrix is clearly exacerbated by the fact that nowadays, as previously illustrated, so many potentially legally-obscene phenomena go unnoticed or ignored and implicitly exonerated. It is easy to see that there is an expedience-based, if not obviously ethical, argument that only a law to prohibit obscenity *in extremis* is strictly required in a contemporary context.[35]

Prosecutions for blasphemy have been conspicuously infrequent for over 100years, but this consistent lack of prosecution has not assisted attempts to abolish it, despite the evidence that in practice Christianity's vigour precludes the necessity for protection of this kind. There are also, of course, other powerful indicia that militate against blasphemy's role as a continuing but sociologically-debilitated legal-moral watchdog in English society. The foremost argument now against the retention of a blasphemy law must be the apparent unjustifiability of protecting only Christianity from vilification when the English nation is increasingly religiously and conscientiously[36] plural. However, extending blasphemy law to cover all religious beliefs would not be a successful step because of the universal inability to define the practical ambit of concepts like 'religion', and because some alleged religions, such as Satanism, clearly appear inherently odious, and undeserving of religious protection on the basis of their undeniably pernicious tenets. The projection of blasphemy law to cover all religions might also result in a proliferation of inter-faith blasphemy prosecutions that would be intellectually fascinating but extremely difficult to administer and resolve. Instead, the Law Commission,[37] by a majority, has recommended that blasphemy law should be abolished, thereby removing any complaint that English law practises, as a matter of policy, a chauvinistic inequality regarding conscientious and religious belief. The recent amending of public order legislation,[38] in the main to accommodate Muslims, may have been all that was required to encourage fair justice, implicitly alleviating the burden of maintaining at least the blasphemy element of a precarious construct of dilapidated public-moral laws that are conceptually, structurally, and practically fit for eradication.

[35] Such a law might well be that advocated by the Home Office. See further, n 26.

[36] Atheism and agnosticism, as well as non-Christian religions, go unprotected under the current law.

[37] Law Commission, *Offences against Religion and Public Worship* (Law Com No 145, 1985).

[38] The Racial and Religious Hatred Act 2006. On incitement to religious hatred, see further, Paul Kearns, 'The Occlusion of Opinion: Incitement to Religious Hatred' (2005) *Amicus Curiae* 59, 20 and Essay 8 of the present work.

7

The End of Blasphemy Law: A 2008 Perspective[1]

I INTRODUCTION

THE SOCIOLOGIST MAX Weber observed that the ultimately possible attitudes to life are irreconcilable, and hence their struggle can never be brought to a final conclusion. Nevertheless, blasphemy law, which has been a venerable offence for several centuries in English law, and which has durably protected Christian values, has now been repealed, practically irretrievably, because it is allegedly demoded in both policy and principle. The law abrogating blasphemy law is section 79 of the Criminal Justice and Immigration Act 2008, which received Royal Assent on 8 May 2008. Section 153(2)(d) of that Act provides for its provisions to come into force two months after Royal Assent. At the time of writing, this enforcement date has only very recently been reached.

Although blasphemy law has now been rendered obsolete, it was once a key plank in the English criminal law which has been much-influenced by Christianity. Moreover, blasphemy law has acted in the past as a law of constitutional importance for the enforcement of public morality, recognising Christ as the *Kulturheros* of western civilisation, and protecting his image and theosophy accordingly. In affording him and his religious creed particular iconic protection, the law in effect attempted to insulate his reputation and beliefs from defamation. With the passage of time, only ill-tempered or scurrilous attacks on Christ's image and teachings formed the *actus reus* of the crime, but the *mens rea* of the offence was always minimal, and a matter of strict liability: it was never required that the intention to blaspheme was necessary for the offence to be committed. All that was required for a conviction was that Christ and his religion had in fact been vilified by the defendant in an unseemly way. The reasons for prohibiting blasphemy eventually became secularised and blasphemy law was used to keep public order primarily, highlighting again the requirement that the criticism of Christianity needed to be other than sober for the offence to be properly constituted. It is also significant that, throughout its history, blasphemy law's protection was claimed to relate to Anglicanism alone, so the Virgin Mary, for example, as a Catholic symbol, argu-

[1] A precursor of this essay by this author appeared as 'The End of Blasphemy Law' (2008) *Amicus Curiae: The Journal for the Society for Advanced Legal Studies* 76, 25–27.

ably fell outside its terms. However, this theological point is neither certain nor compelling because in 'high church' Anglicanism the Virgin plays a very crucial part in everyday worship. What is indisputable, though, is that the law of blasphemy adversely affected freedom of expression throughout its progress in England, hence why the Americans refused to use it, since it would have infringed the right to free speech enshrined in the First Amendment, a provision that to them has itself acquired almost religious significance. In England, blasphemy law has now been superseded, in effect, by incitement to religious hatred, in 2006 legislation that came into force on 1 October 2007, namely the Racial and Religious Hatred Act. Muslims had never been protected under the Public Order Act 1936 because this legislation extended only to races, so religious minorities were denied parity of protection. The 2006 Act has filled this lacuna but, like blasphemy law, is still, in the minds of some, an undue restriction on free speech. There is also always the intractable legal problem of how to define a 'religion' for protection purposes. The shift in protective priorities is more important than it might at first appear and will be referred to in this short essay after the elaboration of the historical significance of blasphemy law is complete.

II BRIEF ANALYSIS OF BLASPHEMY LAW IN THE UK

Such was once the importance of the Christian religion in England that it was from early times illegal to produce blasphemous statements, orally or in writing. Blasphemy included the denial of the truth of the Christian religion, the Bible, the Book of Common Prayer or the existence of the Christian God. Protecting undifferentiated 'society' from any event of blasphemy was to ensure the internal tranquility of the kingdom as much as to prevent the tainting of the image of Christ. It was supposed that the whole of society would lose its basic integrity if blasphemy were permitted but it was also acknowledged that decorous formal discourse on the fundamentals of any religion could not constitute the offence. The law was aimed at the riotous mode or even potential of the utterance. Civil disorder today is unlikely to result from blasphemy relating to the Christian religion but it is important to note that anti-Islamic utterances could easily lead to breaches of the peace in contemporary England, so the law has recently evolved in a different way to accommodate Muslims, as specified above.

Somewhat unconscionably, when the traditional blasphemy offence became utilised in more modern times, in the case of *R v Lemon, R v Gay News Ltd*,[2] for example, illegal blasphemy was deemed to result in accordance with a much less violence-based rationale, attenuating one implicit reason for the offence that rested on the projected ill-defined but probable volatile and hostile reaction to the blasphemous statement. In the aforementioned case, an allegedly

[2] *R v Lemon, R v Gay News Ltd* [1979] AC 617.

blasphemous poem plus illustration in the newspaper *Gay News* was the target of prosecution at the instigation of family-values campaigner, the late Mary Whitehouse. The prosecution succeeded based on the offensiveness of the material, and it was never suggested that that material had to provoke violence to come within the ambit of blasphemy law, which was an unwelcome step for those concerned about the human right of free speech. The contentious material in *Lemon* had been published in a newspaper for gay and bisexual people but the House of Lords ignored the fact that its selective context was relevant. It also failed to investigate the intentions behind the material which could be described as 'art'. It simply applied strict liability. This is out of tandem with the postmodern emphasis on respecting all sub-sets of society, including artists and writers. It took the law back to the values of its mediaeval roots. There had, moreover, been no blasphemy prosecution for over 60 years before the *Lemon* imbroglio.

The law was to be tested again in more recent times in the case of *Chief Metropolitan Stipendiary Magistrate, ex p Choudhury*,[3] which can be referred to as the 'Rushdie case'. A summons was sought against Salman Rushdie and his publishers for an alleged blasphemous libel, inter alia, by the publication of Rushdie's novel *The Satanic Verses*. A summons was refused at both first instance and Divisional Court levels. Both courts concurred in stating that blasphemy law only applied to the protection of the Christian religion and could not be extended to protect Islam. This was evidently in ignorance of the pertinent hierological consideration that Christ is recognised as a prophet (if not the Messiah) in Islam. In addition, neither court considered the culturally specialised position of art (a novel) in the blasphemy context, and other relevant questions. Is it possible to blaspheme through characters in a work of art or does blasphemy law only apply to literal, as opposed to symbolic, fictive statements? In a religiously-plural society, can a law protecting only one religion be fair and justifiable? Should blasphemy law be a strict liability offence or should it, for example, include an assessment of whether Rushdie, or any other creative writer in a similar position, knew the probable effect of his words, even though their locus was a solely artistic context? In 1985, the Law Commission had recommended that blasphemy law should be abolished. The two commissioners against such a radical step *simpliciter* suggested that blasphemy law should be replaced by a new offence designed to proscribe any acts that were deemed to outrage religious feelings. The Racial and Religious Hatred Act 2006 broadly amounts to implementing the salient part of their proposals. Regarding the majority decision, it has taken until July 2008 to remove blasphemy law from the common law as the Law Commission instructed in the mid-1980s. This delay is no shock; neither is the ultimate abrogation: blasphemy law has been only rarely prosecuted in England, and, when it was eventually repealed, its state was anachronistic, and moderately vestigial.

[3] *R v Chief Metropolitan Stipendiary Magistrate, ex p Choudhury* [1990] 3 WLR 986.

III UK BLASPHEMY LAW IN AN INTERNATIONAL CONTEXT

Blasphemy has appeared as a central issue before the European Court of Human Rights. Although the cases involving the United Kingdom directly are few, they are seminally significant. The European Commission of Human Rights affirmed the legitimacy of operating a national blasphemy law in *X and Y v United Kingdom*,[4] which was the international extension of the *Lemon* case. It did so even though the elements of such offences are usually relatively unclear, the use of such crimes haphazard, and the results of their application inconsistent. In *Choudhury v United Kingdom*,[5] which was the international extension of the Rushdie case, the application contending that English law was prejudicial against Islam was declared inadmissible by the Commission as manifestly ill-founded because there was no positive obligation on states, under European Convention on Human Rights law, to protect all religious sensibilities. These cases are interesting because, by using its margin of appreciation, the Strasbourg organs of the Convention have allowed the Contracting States to apply their own blasphemy laws without Convention review of a thorough kind, which is arguably a dereliction of duty. Instead of revising unsatisfactory blasphemy law in a proactive way, the Strasbourg organs have been content to give the local states a free rein, and no remedial assistance, even with such an opaque and sometimes arbitrarily-applied law. It is unusual for the Convention, as a 'living instrument', to be developmentally behind national initiatives regarding such law, since the duty of the Convention organs that apply it is to secure decisions that are in harmony with the prevailing current social, moral and political consciousness of the people it is meant to protect. There is now the anomaly that blasphemy law has been abolished in the United Kingdom but is still very much extant in European Convention jurisprudential doctrine. In the United Kingdom case of *Wingrove v United Kingdom*,[6] which was adjudicated upon by the European Court of Human Rights, and which resulted in Nigel Wingrove failing in his attempt to reverse a local decision that had found his video-film, *Visions of Ecstasy*, potentially blasphemous, the international Court's decision was to simply reaffirm without appropriate analysis the local refusal to give the video-film a certificate, so that the consequence that it could not be distributed and shown remained insubstantially reviewed. It also appears that, paradoxically, the organs of the Convention, notably the Court, now have a less liberal approach to artistic freedom than the United Kingdom itself, whose decisions the Convention organs are conscientiously bound to reappraise, and test for legitimacy, in relation to the fundamental rights that those organs are specifically designed to protect.

[4] *X and Y v United Kingdom* [1983] EHRR 123.

[5] *Choudhury v United Kingdom* [1991] 12 HRLJ 172.

[6] *Wingrove v United Kingdom* [1997] 24 EHRR 1.

IV SOME CONCLUDING OBSERVATIONS

Historically, the operation of blasphemy law in England preserved a reverence for the sociologically-indigenous, if not completely native, Anglican religious culture in England, centred on widespread, and nearly uniform, Christian belief. In the era of postmodernism, the pre-eminence of such endemic spiritual values in the United Kingdom has been reduced in part following a gradual political reappraisal of our now religiously-diverse national society. A central concern has focused on the vibrant faith of Muslims, and the need for the protection of Islam from vilification. Emphasis has thus shifted from one God to another, and the preservation of law and order in a religiously-plural society has featured strongly as a motivating factor in bringing about the Racial and Religious Hatred Act 2006 primarily to protect Muslims. Some commentators of a conservative disposition resent the displacement of Christianity for another faith as a matter of political and legal priority. However, this recalcitrant approach does not accommodate the importance of realpolitik. Faced with a potentially volatile situation given the stark reality of terrorism, it is perhaps politically, and thereafter legally, wise to try to peaceably accommodate a possibly inflammatory confrontation between more traditional Christianity-based religious values and those that are somewhat alien to a number of United Kingdom citizens but which are strongly adhered to and strenuously vocalised by a religious minority. There is arguably a sensible sacrifice of the Christian dominance in British affairs for the promotion of a more eclectic social reality with various forms of personal religious identification. However, this tendency has been promoted by the Blairite fostering of multi-culturalism and its logical partner political correctness, both of which have been founded on sociological misassumptions, and which have contributed to the suppression of free speech, a democratic value which the organs applying the European Convention on Human Rights purport to uphold as cardinal. What Christian conservatives now discern in contemporary Britain is the lessening of one religion's legal support in favour of another's, even though it is far from axiomatic that one faith's religious rights or freedoms should increasingly prevail over any other's, or prevail over the right to free speech. They would contend that such dramatic though stealthily incremental changes should be brought about in a politically overt and very well-reasoned way to the total satisfaction of all members of the national community. Nevertheless, our legal policy-makers are obliged to take an ideologically-neutral, pragmatic and syncretic course regarding a lamentably complex and controversial matrix of virtually irreconcilable competing interests; and, as Isiah Berlin opined, the world that we encounter in ordinary experience is one in which we are faced by choices equally absolute, the realisation of some of which must inevitably mean the sacrifice of others.

8

*Incitement to Religious Hatred and its Effects on Free Speech**

I HISTORICAL ANALYSIS[1]

AT THE TIME of writing, incitement to religious hatred, which will still feasibly become a new crime, is still in its incipient stages of development, and was first proposed by the former Home Secretary David Blunkett as part of his more general legal reform plans. The central idea behind the offence is that it would supersede the ancient offence of blasphemous libel and simultaneously supplement the existing public order offence of incitement to racial hatred. One policy reason for instituting this new offence rests on the surprising reality that Muslims are currently unprotected under the laws relating to the protection of public order because they are deemed by the existing legal wisdom to comprise a religious rather than a racial group. They are thus unprotected under the crime of incitement to racial hatred because they do not constitute a race, and, in addition, go unprotected under the extant blasphemy law because blasphemy in the United Kingdom only protects the Christian religion from vilification, more particularly Anglicanism. A new crime of incitement to religious hatred would arguably remedy the adverse position of Muslims in our multi-cultural society by providing a new offence protecting religious groups, particularly minorities, which would co-extensively lead to the concomitant, automatic repeal of our now outmoded blasphemy law which anachronistically protects only Christianity in our contemporary postmodern, religiously-plural, national-social environment. The new crime would also, naturally, have the advantage over blasphemy law of protecting other small religious minority groups. The price for this innovative reform appears to some the sacrifice of freedom of expression in the United Kingdom. This fear is sadly enhanced by the opaque image of incitement to religious hatred as far as the public is concerned. The constituent elements of the proposed new offence have not been sufficiently

* A precursor of this essay, by this author, appeared as 'The Occlusion of Opinion: Incitement to Religious Hatred' (2005) *Amicus Curiae: Journal of the Society of Advanced Legal Studies* 59, 20–23. That article was translated into German to be included in Thomas Schirrmacher, Thomas Zimmermanns (eds), *'Ein Maulkorb fur Christen?', Studies in Religious Freedom* (Bonn, VKW, 2005) vol 10.

[1] This section was written in 2005, prior to the Racial and Religious Hatred Act 2006.

transparent to satisfy critics that a draconian limit on free speech is not going to be indirectly achieved.

A Charting the History of the Debate

The evolution of the proposed new law has been somewhat haphazard. On 7 July 2004, a fresh attempt to outlaw acts of religious hatred was made by Mr Blunkett because an earlier directly-comparable change in the law had been abandoned in 2001 after claims that it would be unworkable. The 2004 initiative framed the law in terms of a criminal offence of inciting hatred against groups or individuals on the grounds of their beliefs. This would carry a maximum seven-year prison sentence. The earlier 2001 proposal was conceived as part of anti-terrorist legislation and had been denounced as an attack on free speech, prompting fears from Rowan Atkinson and other comedians that they could be prosecuted for lampooning religious figures. It provided no definition of 'religious belief' or of 'religion', and even by 2004 many ministers still believed that such a law was unnecessary. The harshest critics said that the planned legislation in both 2001 and 2004 would prove divisive and impractical, and was being offered as 'a sop' to the Muslim community, which was allegedly feeling vulnerable after the terrorist attacks of September 11.

However, in reality Muslims have been pressing for an incitement law for many years. As alluded to above, unlike Sikhs and Jews, for example, Muslims are not covered by racial hatred laws, and a Lords select committee comparatively recently opined that the same standards of protection should be afforded to all religions. But past governments have taken the view that most cases of incitement against Muslims could be dealt with by existing laws. Tough penalties do exist for religiously-motivated aggravated assaults, but with only a handful of resultant convictions. Despite this paucity, it has been persistently argued that freedom of speech and expression should only be curtailed when there is a likelihood and intention to threaten public order. Such advocates think it inappropriate to punish those who merely offend others' religious sensibilities. By 2004, Mr Blunkett was ready to affirm that the offence would be designed to deal with those who deliberately stir up dissension and hate and not those who criticise beliefs with which they disagree. The then Government believed it possible to make such a distinction in law; it also believed that the new offence could be used against fundamentalist Islamist preachers, as well as protecting Muslims from attacks. On 6 July 2004, a meeting of EU interior ministers, chaired by Mr Blunkett at Hassop Hall, Derbyshire, agreed that militant Islamic groups should face a ban across Europe to help combat the threat from Al-Qa'eda. Otto Schily, Germany's interior minister, called for a common approach towards groups that constitute 'a threat to society', including restrictions on freedom of association. One fundamentalist organisation had been banned in Germany because it's 'objectives did not tally with our constitution', he said. Schily continued, 'It won't do if the same thing is not then banned in a neighbouring country. We have to act in harmony.' From a British perspective, Britain operates a proscription list containing the names of several Islamist organisations, including Al-Qa'eda. It is illegal to support a group on the list, raise funds for it or attend its meetings. Under the German proposal, any group banned in one country would be proscribed in the rest of the EU. The summit agreed the need to harmonise police, counter-terrorism and border control measures to stifle support for fundamentalists.

In the light of anti-terrorist rhetoric, inciting religious hatred as a crime could be viewed as a counter-measure, inviting political activists against Britain's better interests to chant their aggressive creeds. For this and other reasons, by 8 December 2004, David Blunkett faced a growing revolt over plans to make incitement to religious hatred an offence. On 7 December 2004, MPs from all parties denounced the measure, which has been condemned by legal experts, Christians, secular organisations, writers, and, as previously mentioned, comedians. To appease the measure's critics, Mr Blunkett then tried to set out the circumstances in which the law could be used. He asserted that the offence would not criminalise material that just stirs up ridicule, prejudice, dislike, contempt or anger or which simply causes offence. He urged that a person who does not intend to stir up hatred is not guilty if he or she does not know that their words, behaviour, written material, recording or programmes were threatening, abusive or insulting. Moreover, he pointed out that the medley of envisaged associated offences on the religious incitement theme would not apply to anything that takes place in one's own home. To prevent misuse through private prosecutions, all prosecutions would require the consent of the Attorney General.

The critics were not impressed, not least because, with the lack of a definition in the putative offence of the word 'religion', the wording of the crime contemplated was still too loose, and thus represented a clear threat to free speech. David Davis, the then Shadow Home Secretary, said: 'This legislation will curb freedom of speech without any benefit being realised. Evil ideas should be met with challenge. The best remedy for evil ideas is more speech not less.' Labour backbenchers also lined up to criticise the Bill as Liberal Democrats warned that it was likely to be rejected in both the Commons and the Lords. Jon Owen Jones, Labour MP for Cardiff Central, said: 'Some of us are very concerned about legislating about religious belief. There is a real danger that if one looks at religious tracts one will find many reasons in this Bill to prosecute people for their religious beliefs.' Robert Marshall-Andrews, Labour MP for Medway, said: 'I have very grave doubts as to whether it should be criminal, as opposed to merely socially unacceptable, to incite hatred against someone because of what we do; and religion is what we do and not what we are.' However, as WB Yeats, the late Irish poet, might proffer, 'Who can tell the dancer from the dance?'. This quotation usefully points us to the central underlying problem with the proposed new offence, *viz* that its very object is ambiguous, and too conceptually indistinct to be legislated on successfully, let alone to everyone's factual satisfaction.

B Further Considerations

Apart from such observations by politicians, there are several other germane factors and arguments that contribute to the debate on incitement to religious hatred's legal, conceptual and practical viability. Mr Blunkett envisaged that the proposed law would cover both hatred *of* a particular religion and hatred arising *from* a religion. Because of this, it may be difficult to ascertain who is being religiously intolerant in a confrontation between two proponents of different belief systems, such as a conservative Anglican and a homosexual rights campaigner. It is also arguable that the policy emphasis in any liberal society should centre on policing action and not policing thought, on crime and not controlling minds. And yet in the era of strict political correctness, it is unsurprising if lamentable that the focus of governmental control sometimes has individual psyches rather than actual devious practice as its target. Some argue that it is simply not the business of government to determine ethical issues connected with the often long-held belief of individuals; and it is very difficult to establish when the legitimate expression of fundamentally incompatible faiths carries over into incitement to 'religious hatred'. Others are cynical about exactly why Mr Blunkett slipped into the Serious Organised Crime and Police Bill measures extending to cover a religious form of hatred. As stated previously, whereas mono-ethnic 'faith groups', such as Jews and Sikhs, are already protected by laws against racial incitement, that law does not currently cover multi-ethnic 'faith groups' such as Muslims. The cynical maintain that the religious incitement measure is an attempt by New Labour to claw back Muslim support that was squandered through the war in Iraq.

According to some, the proposed law will inhibit religious debate and stifle legitimate criticism of religious groups including, ironically, general objections to religious practice on the whole, on the grounds that it causes unnecessary inter-personal and inter-group hostility. In view of such observations, it might have been prudent and helpful to insert into the relevant Bill a section that unequivocally states that scholarly open debate on religion and matters consequential to religious belief and practice should be fostered in schools, colleges and universities. Such open exchange was the very keystone of Periclean Athens, which forms the basis of the modern democratic ideal. Surely, such interaction in the public arena must be preferable to the present proposal, which one feels can only provoke and promote prejudiced opinion in clandestine ghettos. On 5 March 2005, the then Minister for Racial Equality said in a letter to *The Times* newspaper that the same routine arguments as those offered against the proposed new crime of stirring up religious hatred had been offered in debates since the 1960s against provisions on incitement to racial hatred. This is not completely so, because a person cannot choose his or her race, but is free to choose a religion. The Minister also said that the new law would not proscribe criticism of religious beliefs; but if one criticises a person's religious beliefs by saying they are barbaric, cruel, superstitious, intolerant and anti-social, one can plausibly be accused of stirring up hatred against that person. Practical problems also arise in connection with the proposed offence. It will fall to the Police to make the initial decision to investigate an allegation, arrest suspects and seize property. A legitimate query is whether the Government plans to train the Police in the nuances of comparative theology.

The proposed legislation is sometimes justified by the perceived necessity to tackle 'extremists', such as those involved in the 2001 domestic riots. However, the Government has so far failed to provide a single specific example of any words or behaviour which could not be prosecuted under existing law and which could and should be prosecuted under the proposed new law. What constitutes 'incitement' is a matter of subjective opinion, and any judicial decisions where the notoriously subjective area of religion is in issue are arguably destined to be commensurately subjective. The matter is further complicated by the character of the alleged incitement. Salman Rushdie's novel, *The Satanic Verses*[2], is a work of fiction that could hypothetically be caught by the terms of the proposed new law as stirring up hatred against Islam. But what about freedom of artistic expression, which is culturally and ontologically distinct as a process, and only relates to any alleged offensiveness obliquely, since art is symbolic not literal? It is arguable that, in some respects, a law against religious hatred is, in effect, an invitation to commit it. It incites each faith to take offence, and ensures that the most zealous can make the most trouble. Criminalising incitement to religious hatred could increase intolerance and hatred if used by different groups as a weapon against each other, cause the deterioration of good relations between different groups and hinder the enforcement of law and order. If the Government is really interested in 'strength in diversity', community cohesion and race equality, the optimal route is probably to allow people to express their religious beliefs freely and without fear. Moreover, there are lessons to be learnt from abroad. On 18 December 2004, in Victoria, Australia, two Christian clerics were convicted of violating the Racial and Religious Tolerance Act 2004. The facts were as follows. Two months after the statute's enactment, Daniel Scot and Pastor Danny Nalliah conducted a Melbourne seminar on Islam. As a matter of concrete fact, Daniel was born in Pakistan, is an authority in Islamic studies, and translates the Koran from the Arabic. Three Australian converts to Islam attended the seminar and took notes. Not long afterwards, the Islamic Council of Victoria made a formal complaint of vilification against them. The scholars were subsequently found guilty of violating the new law, in part because they read passages from the Koran that the complainants claimed vilified them.

[2] S Rushdie, *The Satanic Verses* (London, Viking Press, 1988)

C Additional Observations

Freedom of speech and expression, as fashioned in the West, includes the right to offend. One example of tolerating alleged offences is quite striking, and unfortunately ironic, and demonstrates that it is not only Muslims who can be affronted in accordance with their religious sensibilities. According to Randhir Singh Bains, it is the right to offend that has so far prevented Hindus from formulating a dispute over a verse in the Koran (Verse 39, Chapter 8) that urges 'Muslims to make war on idol-worshippers (Hindus) until idolatry is no more and Allah's religion reigns supreme'. Should a law against incitement to religious hatred be enacted, however, Hindus would be free from such self-imposed constraints, and would be perfectly within their legal and moral rights to insist that such apparently 'offensive' verses, which could be construed as illegal under the proposed new law, should be expunged from the Koran. Unlikely and undesirable though this may be, it raises very serious concerns of an inter-faith confrontational problematic that could escalate under a new law of incitement to religious hatred. But the immediate example shifts attention away from, and arguably detracts from, the relevance of the particularly Muslim dilemma in the context of the proposed new law. All religious groups experience the contempt for, ignorance of, and lack of interest in religious belief and practice in contemporary, largely secular Britain, but it weighs particularly heavily on Muslims, whose international community is desperately economically deprived (70 per cent of Pakistani and Bangladeshi children live in poverty), and increasingly adversely affected by anti-terrorist legislation. Very sadly, the proposed law of incitement to religious hatred would not lead to an increased respect for Islam because the law as currently framed is such a potential curtailment of free speech, the right that the West upholds as the cardinal right. Nevertheless, a comparable law could and should be enacted which at least protects the Muslim way of life in a similar way to the one that safeguards the security of Jewish and Sikh communities in Britain without seeming to compromise freedom of opinion. Not addressing the very particular Muslim plight is a recipe for perpetuating Muslim dissatisfaction with a British sense of justice that so cruelly neglects the necessities of Islam, a lacuna in social duty which could ultimately lead to Britain's ineluctable, more precarious detriment in the wider world. As Iqbal Sacranie so cogently said,

> Muslims in Britain do not seek to create an enclave or a parallel culture. They want to be respected as British. That is what they are. And the government that sees and treats them as such, by criminalising offences directed specifically at them, is a government that understands its obligations.[3]

[3] Sir Iqbal Sacranie served as Secretary General of the Muslim Council of Britain (MCB). See, further, The London Gazette (Supplement) no 57665 at 1, 11 June 2005.

Nevertheless, on 17 May 2005, Don Horrocks, head of public affairs at the Evangelical Alliance, said, 'We still consider that this legislation is likely to undermine freedom of speech, damage community relations, and usher in a new climate of illiberalism and repression.' Despite this, the current Home Secretary, Charles Clarke, maintains, at the time of writing, that the Government will use the Parliament Act, if necessary, to force through an Incitement to Religious Hatred Bill, thereby overcoming the already proven opposition of the House of Lords. This is not necessarily wise, because, as the Lords contend, the measure will clearly inescapably compromise free speech in one way or another. The envisaged law will preclude open debate on serious issues, including religion, in favour of a potentially lethal gagging device of Orwellian prediction and dimension, palpably unwelcome and unworkable in any true democracy of western inspiration.

If a crime to stir up racial hatred does exist, the question may be asked whether there should be an extension of that offence to cover incitement to *religious* hatred. The expression of hatred of religious groups causes profound psychological injury of a similar level to that caused by the expression of racial enmity. However, different religions have different degrees of tolerance regarding their reaction to, for example, artistic or literary modes of abuse of their respective religions. In the United Kingdom, where freedom of expression is a positive right, it would be highly unlikely that the Christian community would react violently to emotive criticism of their faith (in contrast to, for example, a Muslim reaction to an antagonistic portrayal of their religion or religious icons, especially by an alleged apostate, as in the Salman Rushdie scenario). It is also arguable that there should be no legally obligatory measure to achieve respect for a given belief or set of beliefs. Freedom of expression sometimes legitimately includes the dissemination of concepts that shock and disturb, including via artistic media.

II A SHORT 2013 POSTSCRIPT TO THE 2006 ACT

The offence of stirring up racial hatred was introduced by section 6 of the Race Relations Act 1965 in order to curb provocative and inflammatory racist expression. This has now been complemented by the Racial and Religious Hatred Act 2006, which provides for a cognate crime of incitement to religious hatred. Prosecutions for the offences of stirring up racial or religious hatred under the Act can only be brought with the consent of the Attorney-General, which has so far been relatively sparingly granted. Although satirising religious doctrines might be found offensive to traditional believers, such an action would not be likely to stir up *hatred* against such believers. An example can be given of Monty Python's 1979 comedy film, *The Life of Brian*, which certain Christians or Jews could be easily offended by, but which could not feasibly be construed as inculcating actual hatred towards them. The 2006 provisions accordingly include a specific defence for freedom of expression, but religious belief is very broadly defined, which could potentially lead to a wide range of prosecutions. However, such breadth affords a great degree of discretion to the courts, which could rule out poorly justified claims of alleged incitement. Nevertheless, despite assurances from the Joint Committee on Human Rights, some commentators, notably creative writers and comedians, consider that the 2006 legislation presents a serious threat to freedom of expression, including freedom of artistic expression. This standpoint is supported by the fact that for many years a blasphemy law was extant in England that was never considered by the European Court of Human Rights to be incompatible with, for example, artistic freedom, or free speech in general. It remains to be seen whether the 2006 legislation will be used against the initial publishers of provocative images or whether it will be reserved for when there are unduly extreme *reactions* to allegedly offensive, sometimes artistic, material. There can be no clear predictions about this in a religiously pluralistic society, where religious fundamentalists reside with more liberal religious believers, agnostics, and atheists; or the simply religiously indifferent who form quite a large sector of the current national citizenry. Whatever the domestic significance of the Act, it is a successful development internationally, because it facilitates our international compliance with the International Covenant on Civil and Political Rights, a move that was significantly overdue.

Part IV

Highly Topical Legal Issues on the Regulation of Artistic Freedom

9

The Contemporary Rights of Artists in England, France and the USA (2013)[1]

I INTRODUCTION

ARTISTS' RIGHTS ARE a rare topic in legal scholarship, and it is a common proposition that art and law are clearly poles apart in terms of their basic ontologies and associated cultural infrastructures. Artists are not renowned for their business acumen, and it is not just a romantic notion that artists are usually oblivious to the law and their rights. Copyright inheres in created objects automatically, right from the moment of their physical manifestation, and artists are therefore saved the trouble of formally registering their central intellectual property right courtesy of this deliberately helpful and paternalistic gesture on the part of the law. In other respects, it is arguable that although artists who achieve some popular acclaim are frequently lauded for their creativity, they are habitually denied financial benefits commensurate with such encomium. In the postmodern environment, this is not the case with multi-millionaire artists such as Damien Hirst, but it certainly was the case with earlier artists such as Van Gogh, who famously sold only one painting during his lifetime, and who would now be considerably wealthier given the extravagant sums now paid for his works. Why acknowledged art ultimately possesses significant fiscal worth as well as social allure is a matter of debate, but as a matter of popular sociology[2] it is sometimes alleged that artistic creation is understood

[1] A shorter precursor of part of this essay, on a narrower theme, appeared in print as 'The Neglected Minority: The Penurious Human Rights of Artists' in Reza Banakar (ed), *Rights in Context* (Farnham, Ashgate, 2010) 83–96. A different analysis of the subject of this essay will appear in the law journal *Art, Antiquity and Law* in 2013: at the time of writing, the publishing editor does not know in which precise issue it will fall. Its title is 'A Hidden Minority: A Comparative Analysis of the Rights of Artists in England, France and the USA'. In the essay, UK law is to be understood as also covered by the term 'English law', where that is appropriate and accurate. When UK law specifically is examined, as in the context of copyright, the text is explicit about it. Because the essay aims to be wide-ranging, certain minor details have had to be sacrificed for reasons of space. The author has nevertheless endeavoured to methodically itemise as much relevant ground as is feasible in a work of this nature, which seeks to provide a comprehensive critique of artists' rights (for the first time in legal scholarship) in three jurisdictions. The footnoting herein is relatively light, in accordance with the required professional style of the associated law journal, which must be adhered to.

[2] On this subject, see generally, Jean Duvignaud, *The Sociology of Art* (London, Paladin, 1972). The notion of art's enigmatic power is common to many of the world's cultures, notably in those

in terms of some kind of magical process, which consequently attracts great attention. To pursue sociological assumptions further, it is also commonplace to generalise about the personal nature of artists as a distinct breed. They are alleged to be unconventional creatures living on a higher plane of reality than ordinary folk, an image that rehabilitates them in the eyes of society, which might otherwise protest about their radical individualism. This almost surreal mystique acts as an excuse for the liberties artists tend to take, and justifies them ontologically as having a common essence housing all manner of peculiarity, that is fortuitously offset by a sort of charismatic, intangible, transcendent power.

So how does law accommodate these intractable eccentrics? In the world of rights, artists' general legal interests are bifurcated but are not then neatly congregated within the two separate streams. However, some generalisations can be made. The first set of relevant rights fall into the broad category of freedom of artistic expression; the second set of artists' rights exist in the law of intellectual property. Following a Hohfeldian classification of rights, the first set are liberty rights, and the second set are claim rights. The first set concern artistic choice of subject matter, the second artists' economic interests in their products. The central investigation of this essay is whether artists' liberty rights in the form of human rights are adequately legally protected, and whether existing intellectual property rights are sufficient to provide for artists' needs. Liberty of artistic expression is protected in provisions sometimes within national constitutions or national laws lower in the domestic hierarchy, and sometimes within international human rights treaties. Contrastingly, artists' intellectual property interests are more straightforwardly preserved within a wide ambit of usually only national copyright laws. Ideologically and practically, a basic conflict can arise between the prevention of copying others' work and artistic liberty, a tension which is somewhat inevitable. However, there is a correlation in Western thought between genuine creativity and the presence of originality, so few artists aim in their practices to borrow from others' work in fashioning their own art, though some artworks, notably collages, involve a collation of preconstituted materials that may contain others' art.

In the broader scheme of things, art attracts legal attention infrequently, and the human and other rights of artists, as adverted to above, are seldom grouped together as a specific homogeneous body. It may not then be surprising that this essay encompasses the first detailed critique of artists' rights *simpliciter*. By way of contrast, much academic attention has been focused on the law of intellectual property, which, as well as affording basic copyright protection to artistic works, includes what are termed 'moral rights', and a right comparable to a moral right, namely the 'droit de suite' (the artist's resale right). All these rights exist for authors of original works, and, as previously mentioned, have been the subject

connected with Hinduism. Moreover, the overpowering reverence of art that makes enthusiasts feel weak when faced with the particular object of their 'worship' has been popular enough as a phenomenon to warrant a special label in art history, ie the 'Stendhal Syndrome'.

of much careful analysis by copyright lawyers. In this specialised area, artists' rights are clearly prescribed in many legal jurisdictions. However, in other legal subject areas, notably the law of human rights, artists' rights are comparatively under-researched and indistinct. Accordingly, another principal broad object of this essay is an examination of the specialised juridification of art issues in the context of freedom of expression, and the degree to which artists' rights are identified and effectively protected in that legal sphere. The classic scenario here involves the confrontation between artistic freedom and the legal, often constitutional, enforcement of morality; sometimes, though, artistic creativity can also be claimed to be illegal if seditious. This essay therefore in part involves an analysis of the interaction of art with the laws of obscenity and blasphemy, together with sedition. This can be succinctly characterised as the relationship between artistic freedom and certain libel laws (which will also involve referring briefly to the law of defamation so as to be an holistic study of art's treatment within the collective law of libel). A key feature of this theme is art's heteronomous position when placed in a legal arena, and the way this conflicts with the philosophically recognised autonomy of art ontologically, and as a cultural phenomenon in society. Another central concern here is the determination of the quality of the appropriate legal skill of courts to deal with the specialised character of art when art is engaged by the legal process. This will involve an assessment, for the purposes of rights discourse in particular, of the efficacy of the judicialisation of art in terms of juridical fairness to art, as identified in relevant legal judgments. Attention must also be paid to the era in which the art-law relationship occurs because in classical and mediaeval times, art was a rule-based activity. The then strict canons of the artistic process meant that art was comparatively recognisable once produced, in accordance with its own methodological strictures. Contrastingly, in the postmodern époque,[3] art is identified merely by what can be termed self-legitimation. In essence, the current position is that all practising artists need to do for the identification of their vocation is to proclaim themselves artists, and their product art, so that society is then obliged to be infinitely flexible regarding the definition of who is a bona fide artist, and what, definitionally, constitutes art. As far as the law is concerned, this position is unsatisfactory because law relies heavily on conceptual certainties to render clear and consistent justice. The ambiguity of art in the postmodern era confounds law's more stable internal points of reference and the efficiency of its habitual operation. This in part explains what we will discover to be a judicial reluctance to acknowledge artists' human rights, in particular, within a reciprocal dialogue of understanding, which supplements a judicial tendency to non-engagement with habitual as well as complex artistic terms of reference, that find themselves usually unwelcome within law's definitive and incisive mechanism for categorical, binary,

[3] See further, Fredric Jameson, *Postmodernism* (London, Verso, 1991). Postmodernism acquires its name because, chronologically, it follows Modernism. Characteristics of postmodern art include the presence of simulacra, the tendency to eclecticism, and the lack of affirmations of native or endemic values in favour of neo-classical motifs.

unequivocal dispute resolution. This phenomenon is compounded by an antagonism between art's prospective, usually avant-garde, *modus operandi*, and law's reflex to the past, including its systemic use of precedents.

II THE HUMAN RIGHTS OF ARTISTS

A The Legal Positions in England, France and the USA

In England, art is sometimes the object of prosecution for obscenity. Under the Obscene Publications Act 1959, the relevant legal test is whether the publication has a tendency to deprave and corrupt. It amounts to being a strict liability offence. If a jury is satisfied that the tendency exists, there is a conviction. However, if the object under legal scrutiny is art or literature, for example, a defence of artistic or literary merit for the public good is available under the 1959 Act's section 4. If that defence is successfully made out, it cancels the obscenity, and the creative work is exonerated. This happened in the first major case under the 1959 legislation involving DH Lawrence's novel, *Lady Chatterley's Lover*.[4] This case of 1960 is representative of most judicial attitudes in this context. The judge in the *Chatterley* case was Justice Byrne, who was aggressively antagonistic towards the novel because of its erotic qualities and 'immoral' messages. He treated the novel as if it were ordinary prose rather than a work of fiction and imagination. He treated its details as literal fact. He was dismissive of the expert witnesses who had come to court to defend the novel as having artistic merit, evidence explicitly provided for as relevant under the 1959 Act. He displayed virtually no knowledge of this genre of creative writing and was blinkered by his obsession with the immoral nature of the storyline. There was no suggestion in his judgment condemning the novel that artists/creative writers had a unique mode of working that entailed creating *oeuvres* that had only an oblique and symbolic relationship to real-life matters. Moreover, no judicial cognisance was taken of the argument that such people have a right to express what they wish in the artistic realm, and that the societal recognition of their culturally distinct role underlines their indisputable value. Fortunately for the novel's publishers, the jury ignored Justice Byrne's hostility to art and found in their favour. This artistic triumph was achieved despite the absence of judicial attention to the relevance of a right to free speech. The situation could be different today courtesy of the Human Rights Act 1998, which came into force in

[4] See further, Paul Kearns, 'Obscenity Law and the Creative Writer: The Case of D.H. Lawrence' (1998) 22 *Columbia-VLA Journal of Law and the Arts* 4, 525. Lawrence's life was peppered with intrusions of legal censorship regarding his visual as well as literary art, particularly in the UK. Lawrence wrote *Lady Chatterley's Lover* (London, Penguin Group, 2011) in Villa Cimbrone, Ravello, Italy, where he was free from such legal-moral constraints. The liberating effect of Italy on English people was famously captured by the novelist EM Forster in *A Room with a View*, a novel set in Florence, Italy.

2000. That legislation ensures that a relevant rights-based approach is to be entertained, if not always expected, in such circumstances.

In the later English case of *R v Lemon, R v Gay News Ltd,*[5] another morality related offence threatened artistic freedom. At the instigation of the late Mary Whitehouse, a poem and accompanying illustration, which had featured in the journal *Gay News*, was prosecuted for blasphemy. The items allegedly vilified the Christian religion by the depiction of homosexual interference with Christ's dead body. The offence was again one of virtually strict liability. Again no mention was made of freedom of artistic expression. The question was simply put to the jury if these publications were blasphemous. The jury held that they were. No investigation of artistic intent was involved. No judicial attempt was made to appreciate the artistic relevance of the artworks for a gay or bisexual readership. The case was insulated from art-pertinent concerns by the strict application of draconian censorship. Artists' rights were again ignored and the House of Lords was blithely impervious to their relevance.

In 1989, a summons was sought to charge the award-winning novelist Salman Rushdie with, inter alia, blasphemous libel, in relation to certain passages in his novel *The Satanic Verses* which could be classified as anti-Islamic. The Court of First Instance refused the application and had its decision affirmed by the English Divisional Court.[6] Both courts based their decisions on the fact that in England the crime of blasphemy pertained only to the Christian religion, the inference being that the novel was only potentially blasphemous in the eyes of Muslims as an affront to Islam, a matter to which the courts held English blasphemy law to be indifferent. This stance ignored the relevance of Christ as a prophet (though not the Messiah) in Islamic religious doctrine. No mention was made at either court level of *The Satanic Verses* being a work of the creative imagination. No question was raised as to whether an artistic statement, in contradistinction to a literal one, could ever be literally blasphemous. Again, notions such as artists' rights were kept extrinsic to the legal proceedings.

In the same year, 1989, the artist Richard Gibson was prosecuted for outraging public decency, a little-used English offence at common law.[7] This visual artist had constructed a model's head, on the ears of which were earrings made out of real human foetuses. Unlike under the 1959 obscenity legislation, no artistic merit defence could be obtained to counteract outraging public decency. By the police's utilisation of this particular offence of strict liability, there was therefore no way that the artist could convey to the Court artistic intentions that could feasibly redeem him. Gibson could have been self-consciously lamenting in his art the lack of respect for human life to the degree of it being used as mere ornament, for example. However, art matters were excluded from the jury's purview, and the jury found against Gibson forthwith. The lack of availability of artistic

[5] *R v Lemon, R v Gay News Ltd* [1979] AC 617, [1979] 1 All ER 898, [1979] 2 WLR 281.
[6] *R v Chief Metropolitan Stipendiary Magistrate, ex p Choudhury* [1990] 3 WLR 986.
[7] *R v Gibson, R v Sylveire* [1990] 2 QB 619, [1990] 3 WLR 595.

discourse in the courtroom precluded freedom of artistic expression to be aired as a relevant juridical concern in the case. Again, an artist was condemned by a jury that remained ignorant about the *modus operandi* of his creative vocation and profession. It is clearly arguable that such crucial detail should be provided by the judge, if the trial is to be fair, and publicly perceived to be fair.

In France, the approximate equivalent to our obscenity law is *l'outrage aux bonnes moeurs*.[8] Historically, this law has been used to suppress obscenities but from the mid-nineteenth century, after the famous cases involving Flaubert and Baudelaire, no art has been legally challenged as immoral. Art is viewed in France as an *oeuvre d'esprit* (a work of the mind or spirit) and is now elevated above the possible constraints of censorship. One exception relates to violent films; another is based on the uncontested need for the protection of children. Sexual representations in art for adults go unprosecuted. This is unsurprising since so much highly explicit pornography is freely available on the Internet, which has none of the dignity and aesthetic allure that art possesses. The French intellectual legal approach is very satisfactory to the minds of art-appreciating individuals. It escapes criticism for not differentiating between art and literal facts, and obviates the need for the provision of legal defences for artists whose work is morally controversial. There is no law against blasphemy in France.

In the United States of America, the legal stance adopted is formalistic. All obscenity falls outside the protection of the First Amendment, which protects freedom of expression. A constitutional standard operates to determine whether something is or is not obscene.[9]Art which has 'serious artistic value' is deemed not to be obscene.[10] As with 'artistic merit' in English obscenity law, 'serious artistic value' is very difficult to evaluate, and the legal task of such evaluation cannot fail to be executed subjectively. This clearly clashes with the general legal principle that judges are not legally permitted to be arbiters of taste. In copyright law, this hurdle is overcome to some degree by the legal search for the presence of the more objectively determinable quality of 'artistic character' as the legal litmus test for what is or is not an 'artistic work'. This approach could be adopted and modified profitably in the context of obscenity law: all works of objectively apparent artistic character could be insulated against prosecution for immorality on the basis of their inclusion in an objective artistic category

[8] The 'outraging' of good morals. A comparable law in England is outraging public decency, which is ancient, and which rests uneasily with the 1959 Act on obscene publications as a measure of contemporary application. An irregularity emergent from the archaic offence's current prosecution is based on the fact that outraging public decency can be used, arguably wrongly, to circumvent s 4 of the 1959 Act's artistic merit defence to an obscenity charge, even though this is clearly legally antinomic. The two offences, used as alternatives, should not be allowed to so overlap to the detriment of the protection of artists under s 4. The practical impact of this was shown in July 2008 when a private prosecution for outraging public decency was launched against the Baltic Centre for Contemporary Art in Gateshead, in relation to a Terence Koh statue exhibited there, which comprised a sexually provocative representation of Christ. No artistic merit defence could be utilised by the gallery.

[9] *Roth v US* 354 US 476, 1 L Ed 2d 1498, 77 S Ct 134 (1957).

[10] *Miller v California* 413 US 15 (1973).

that is beyond the strictures of moral concern based simply on a definition of the character of art as legally amoral. In America, there is no blasphemy law because that would be contrary to the First Amendment. Removing all art from the constraint of obscenity laws would also be consonant with the spirit of the First Amendment.

As well as concerns about obscene and blasphemous libel and their detrimental effects on artistic creativity and freedom, there is also a debate, most prevalent in the USA, about whether an artwork could, in theory, or in practice, or in both, defame. For example, if fictional characters in a novel are based on real-life models and those fictional characters are full of vices, to what degree is this circumstance of legal relevance to the real-life models if readers identify the notorious fictional characters with them? In such circumstances, could the real-life models (individually) bring successful actions against the novelist for defamation? This legal and factual conundrum is resolved in the defamation law of the United States of America by the use of a doctrine known as 'defamation by fiction'. This is very complex and its effects on artists' rights is readily apparent: writers of fiction often draw on real-life characters as the raw material for artistic inspiration; it is arguable that to do otherwise would be to present artistically just useless fantasies instead of instructive commentaries on real-life matters. In brief, the law in this area should be governed by the concept of malice. It is submitted that it must be demonstrated by the plaintiff that the creative artist bore ill will towards him in so unpleasantly fictionally characterising him in his novel. In more succinct terms, a legal test could be effectively phrased based on the question: did the novelist *intend* to harm the plaintiff by such a depiction? Although other approaches abound, this appears to be the fairest. You cannot intend to harm a plaintiff you do not know, and evidence of artistic concealment of the fictional character's real-life model in the novel clearly militates against a finding of malice towards him. The suggested approach also has the advantage of being easily applicable to all types of fiction. As a matter of the rights of artists, it is indisputable that an artist should not be deprived of source material that fuels his legitimate vocation if it is clear that art rather than spite was his motivating force. However, again we find that, in the field of defamation in most jurisdictions, little, if anything, is said about an artist's genuine professional needs except occasionally in the many faceted and variously formulated, instances of defamation by fiction, as judicially construed in the American jurisdiction.[11] However, in this context, too, the radicalisation of fiction and its concomitant increased difficulty, has not improved the quality of judges' art discourse in the course of art's judicialisation. For that quality to be ameliorated, there must be a less inartistic judicial approach to the specialised area of art. Indeed, judicial experts on art would be especially welcome in this highly conceptually complicated field of libel.

[11] See generally, Frederick Schauer, 'Liars, Novelists, and the Law of Defamation' (1985) 51 *Brooklyn Law Review* 233 and Paul Kearns, *The Legal Concept of Art* (Oxford, Hart Publishing, 1998) Ch 4, 86–113.

B The European Convention on Human Rights

The rights of artists are sometimes specifically legally protected in national constitutional laws, such as, notably, in Austria and Germany, which establish the possibility for an artist, as a distinct entity, to found a legal action on the positive right constitutionally guaranteed.[12] This also in effect creates a preliminary positive 'presumption' in favour of artistic expression when that value competes with other societal interests such as the need to protect public morality. However, another important source of artistic rights in the human rights field is provided by international human rights instruments. Arguably the most significant of these is the European Convention on Human Rights (hereinafter sometimes referred to as ECHR). Article 10[13] of that treaty sets out the general right of freedom of expression in all Contracting States. Unfortunately for artists, the rubric of Article 10 does not make explicit provision for the protection of artistic freedom. Instead, political, artistic, and commercial freedoms of speech are informally distinguished by the judiciary of the European Court of Human Rights. It is arguable that a hierarchy of protection operates favouring political expression first, followed by artistic freedom, then finally, freedom of commercial expression.[14] However, it is submitted that this does not reflect the real judicial priorities indicated by the Strasbourg jurisprudence. Of key concern to us is the fact that artistic freedom has *never* been judicially preferred in practice to the need to protect morality. This is shocking. Another disturbing feature about judicial practice under the Convention is that the subtleties of the interaction of art and morality go unexplored. The established judicial habit is to simply rubber-stamp its previous decisions in this area without due attention being paid to the delicate problems raised by concepts such as art, pornography, obscenity and harm. There is no system of precedent in the Court's regimen and it is arguable that cases involving artistic freedom and public morality should be decided afresh in each new case, such is the conceptual complexity of the legal problematic in such

[12] On domestic constitutional legal provisions generally, including a comparative legal analysis, see Eric Barendt, *Freedom of Speech* (Oxford, Clarendon Press, 1985). Although the work is now in its second edition, the first edition is preferred by this author in terms of structure.

[13] Article 10 provides that: '1. Everyone has the right to freedom of expression. This right shall include freedom to hold opinions and to receive and impart information and ideas without interference by public authority and regardless of frontiers. This Article shall not prevent states from requiring the licensing of broadcasting, television or cinema enterprises. 2. The exercise of these freedoms, since it carries with it duties and responsibilities, may be subject to such formalities, conditions, restrictions or penalties as are prescribed by law and are necessary in a democratic society, in the interests of national security, territorial integrity or public safety, for the prevention of disorder or crime, for the protection of health or morals, for the protection of the reputation or rights of others, for the disclosure of information received in confidence, or for maintaining the authority and impartiality of the judiciary.'

[14] This is an informal arrangement that has been inferred from the case law by many commentators, its habitual reassertion proving to be in some respects misleading. See further, Colin Munro, 'The Value of Commercial Speech' (2003) 62 *Cambridge Law Journal* 134–58 and Ivan Hare, 'Is the Privileged Position of Political Expression Justified?' in Beatson and Cripps (eds), *Freedom of Expression and Freedom of Information* (Oxford, Oxford University Press, 2000) 105–21.

cases. More worryingly, it is the Court's primary job in this context to conscientiously uphold all freedoms relating0 to expression, and to accommodate restrictions on such freedoms comparatively reluctantly. At present what the Court does is to consistently enforce public-moral interests to the unequivocal sacrifice of artistic freedom. This is arguably a dereliction of duty given the Convention's foundational remit of fundamental rights protection. It is also a very surprising form of institutional laxness given that freedom of expression is often quoted as being the cardinal democratic right that the Convention is designed to protect.

The starting-point of relevant Convention case law is the seminal case of *Handyside v United Kingdom*.[15] The applicant published *The Little Red Schoolbook*, a book for children that, amongst other things, advised them on sexual matters. He was convicted for publishing an obscene libel under the Obscene Publications Act 1959 and the European Court of Human Rights judged that there was no breach of Article 10 of the Convention. It considered that a subsidiarity principle should operate that makes certain decisions the prerogative of the Contracting States alone, and this judicially-created latitude given to the individual states, notably for our purposes in moral areas, is termed the 'margin of appreciation'. This doctrine will be more closely analysed later in this essay. In *Handyside*,[16] the Court reasoned that because there was no uniform conception of morals in the Contracting States, they should be a matter of local concern only. It added that local authorities were in a superior position to itself in being able to gauge local moral feeling. Prima facie, such an approach by the Court is logical. However, a unifying standard of morality formulated by the Court would eradicate the injustices of the inconsistent local decisions on moral matters and encourage Contracting States to improve their standards by following an optimal one put forward by the Court. To avoid such an approach jeopardises artistic freedom because artists that produce morally controversial work may be at the mercy of narrow, parochial moral decisions at the local level. Art is famous for being at the cutting-edge of moral development and reflects critically on the moralities of the status quo. It has a moral function in this regard that the Court in *Handyside*[17] ignores. This function of art should not be made vulnerable at the hands of moral village politics. Artistic vision tends to transcend petty scruples and synthesises different concepts of morality in its own unique presentations. This generic artistic method of creating original moral directions is invaluable for society, not least in assisting it in challenging and undoing the evil of moral stagnation.

In the next case chronologically, *X and Y v United Kingdom*,[18] the European Commission of Human Rights reviewed the *Lemon* case[19] adumbrated above. It decided that the allegedly anti-Christian poem and illustration in *Gay News*

[15] *Handyside v United Kingdom* E Ct HRR A 24 (1976) 1 EHRR 737.
[16] ibid.
[17] ibid.
[18] *X and Y v United Kingdom* (1982) 28 DR 77.
[19] *Lemon* (n 5).

was a proper object of control by blasphemy law, and that consequently, there was no breach of Article 10. The Commission ignored the fact that there might be an artistic right to be unconstrained as to subject matter in the course of genuinely artistic endeavour and failed to appreciate that the likely audience of the offending items was small and specialised and unlikely to be corrupted or depraved by encountering the admittedly sensationalist artwork. In the subsequent case of *Muller v Switzerland*,[20] the European Court of Human Rights applied similar reasoning to the application of obscenity law by a Contracting State. It considered that the applicant's pictorial art might well offend the sensibilities of an averagely sensitive person, depicting as it did graphic sexual practices. However, it failed to find it relevant that the person who brought the offensiveness of the art to the relevant authorities was a teenage girl. It is clearly arguable that artists should not have to pander to the sensitivities of a minor when exhibiting their work in an adult environment that her father wrongly estimated would be innocuous for her. Moreover, the artist had exhibited the same work in other parts of Switzerland without official interference with it. Again we witness a provincial approach adopted by the Court as its own. The Court, in being supra-national, should make correspondingly elevated decisions.

In *Choudhury v United Kingdom*,[21] the European Commission of Human Rights held that Article 9 on freedom of religion was not breached by the United Kingdom. The United Kingdom was entitled to protect only Christians under its blasphemy law even though the state is religiously plural. This has relevance for freedom of artistic expression because if the Commission had found otherwise it may have then been obliged to examine whether or not Salman Rushdie's novel, *The Satanic Verses,* could in theory contravene the law even though the alleged blasphemy only appeared within imagined dream sequences in a work of art. It is still not clear whether characters in art are capable of having their allegedly blasphemous statements attributed to their creator, which is one step removed from literal blasphemy. Now that blasphemy law has been abolished in the United Kingdom, the answer will have to emerge from Convention cases involving an application from one of the other Contracting States that continue to operate a blasphemy law. It is to be hoped that the essential ingredients of artistic creativity that rest in the case of a novel on, inter alia, the autonomy of the opinions of characters within a novel, will not be undermined by a ruling that a novelist can blaspheme via those imagined protagonists. Otherwise, the very essence of one of creative writing's time-honoured mechanisms would be violated: the fictive would be treated as the factual.

In a later important case under the Convention, *Otto-Preminger Institute v Austria*,[22] the likely approach of the European Court of Human Rights to putative blasphemy expressed by characters in novels may be able to be predicted if

[20] *Muller v Switzerland* E Ct HRR A 113 (1991) 13 EHRR 212.
[21] *Choudhury v United Kingdom* (1991) 12 *Human Rights Law Journal* 172.
[22] *Otto-Preminger Institute v Austria* E Ct HRR A 295-A (1994) 19 EHRR 34, E Ct HR.

an analogy with the Court's approach here to putative blasphemy in films is appropriate. In the instant case, a religiously controversial film, caricaturing iconic Christian figures, was to be shown at the named Institute. Despite the fact that Article 17a of the Austrian Basic Law expressly protects artistic freedom, the relevant film, *Das Liebeskinzil,* was seized and forfeited by the local provincial authorities on the grounds that cherished religious doctrines had been disparaged. Considering Article 10's possible violation, the Court in Strasbourg supported the Contracting State's censorious stance: the offensiveness of the film outweighed any artistic virtue it had, and so Article 10 had not been breached, the imposed restriction on freedom of artistic expression being quite legitimate. This decision was made despite the fact that no-one who did not wish to see the film was in any way obliged to see it. In addition, the film was to be shown in what was described as an 'art cinema' so only the art-interested would have been attracted to seeing it in its natural setting as an 'art film'. The clear principal focus of the film was artistic stimulus not religious irreverence. Yet again we find artistic freedom swept aside by the overwhelming force of local moral indignation at its practice. The artist Karel Appel[23] said that 'art must shock'. Ignoring the imperative, the legal acceptance that it merely has the right to would be welcome.

The final case relating to the art versus morality debate is *Wingrove v United Kingdom*.[24] This case was heard over a decade before the law of blasphemy was repealed in the United Kingdom. The applicant, Nigel Wingrove, was denied a certificate for his video-film to be shown, first by the British Board of Film Classification, and then the Video Appeals Panel, on the grounds that it potentially contravened United Kingdom blasphemy law. The film, *Visions of Ecstasy,* was an erotic interpretation of the story that Saint Teresa of Avila had had ecstatic visions of Christ. It is not feasible that this video was as offensive as that which is legally available in the pornographic field on the Internet. No-one suggested that the film was in anyway comparable in severity to routine hard-core pornography. Despite this, the European Court of Human Rights held that Article 10 had been violated. The Court used its habitual, non-reflective argument that a standard of morality was best adjudged in the region where it was allegedly upheld. It also approved again the national operation of a blasphemy law as a legitimate restriction on artistic freedom. Again it was unwilling to formulate a supra-national meta-standard of morality of its own; it was content to remain consistent with its policy of abandoning artistic freedom when confronted by the very limited tolerance towards it, as demonstrated, for example, at varying levels of regulation by the Contracting State in relation to the

[23] Karel Appel was born in 1921 and became a member of the Cobra movement which was constituted in 1948 by a group of artists from Copenhagen, Brussels and Amsterdam who were united in rejecting passive and lifeless art in favour of more violent subjects. Highly expressionistic, Appel painted in thick, naive strokes using very lurid colours, paying attention to astonishing brutal effects above formal perfection of technique.

[24] *Wingrove v United Kingdom* [1997] 24 EHRR1 .

blasphemy issue at hand. In short, and with respect to the artistic freedom and morality cases in general, the Court is revealing priorities which are inimical to its rights-advancing role. It is bewildering that its constant omission to protect artistic freedom in favour of moral censorship has not been challenged and rectified.

The protection of artistic freedom when threatened by countervailing moral concerns is jeopardised in particular by the Court's subsidiarity tool, the margin of appreciation. Basically, the Court upholds a certain amount of discretion on the part of the Contracting State when it comes to controversial or delicate matters of specifically local concern. The idea behind this mechanism, as propounded by the Court, notably seminally in *Handyside*,[25] is that local authorities are in a better position to evaluate the moral climate, inter alia, in the local environment than the comparatively distant Strasbourg Court is. The argument is prima facie appealing. But what it in effect involves is the Court relinquishing its supervisory role in deference to local moral opinion as determined by local bodies. What is the point of someone making an application to the Court if the Court does not pronounce its own ethical judgment that is substantively separate from the local ruling against which such an application is made? In the area of morality, the margin of appreciation is said by the Court to be 'wide', a concession to the varying local-moral standards that exist in the allegedly morally disparate Contracting States. However, the Court gives no scientific evidence for such a disparity, and engages in no comparative law analysis, for example, to support its view that where morals are concerned there is no moral 'objective character' discernible across the Contracting States. Moreover, as so many Contracting States now have very morally plural societies, a decision on what is a state's moral position as a singular corpus may be even empirically impossible to ascertain. In addition, if in the art versus morality cases the Strasbourg Court observes only local mores rather than an international moral meta-standard, morally controversial art is judged by more conservative parochial values than the cosmopolitan ones habitually found in a large metropolis where morally cutting-edge artists enjoy greater moral freedom. Finally, the European Convention on Human Rights is meant to be used as a 'living instrument' and interpreted 'dynamically'. This entails provision for the morality of art to be assessed by the most contemporary value judgments. With due respect, such judgments are seldom found to be initiated and sustained in a regional village atmosphere that the margin of appreciation permits to dictate moral imperatives.

Yet, in another sphere of rights protection, the European Court of Human Rights has commendably demonstrated a greater awareness of art-relevant issues. This is the area of sedition. Whereas the Court has been markedly disinclined to defend artists against the charge of immorality, it has seen fit to protect artists from condemnation for more serious crimes akin to seditious libel. This

[25] *Handyside* (n 15).

stance is somewhat paradoxical, and the cases concerning art and sedition have received little attention in comparison to the cases concerning art and immorality. One unreported case of 1999 on art and sedition is *Karata v Turkey*.[26] The applicant in this case was a Turk of Kurdish origin. He published a collection of poetry called *The Song of a Rebellion*. At the national level, he was convicted of disseminating separatist propaganda and imprisoned. His poetry was confiscated. The applicant made an application against Turkey to the European Court of Human Rights. Had there been a legitimate restriction of the artist's freedom of artistic expression under Article 10? The Court emphasised that the material concerned comprised poetry, which, it said, reached a very small readership, and that the poet's punishment by the Turkish authorities was disproportionate. It focused its judgment on the limited potential impact of the verse in issue on national security, territorial integrity and public order. The poet explicitly stated that the poetry was not a reflection of his own political opinions; but no argument was put forward based on the autonomy of art. Such an argument might have immunised the poetry from inartistic interference from the outset, but at least the Court in this case acknowledged in the course of its deliberations that the poetry collection was primarily a literary, as opposed to a political, work. Strangely, the European Commission of Human Rights, prior to the Court's decision-making, had sided with the Turkish authorities. This is surprising because in the art and immorality cases the Commission had steadfastly defended artists against censorship, whereas the Court had, in that context, opposed such arguments. It is surprising that the Commission and the Court failed to cross-reference the immorality and sedition cases to make their different overall stances on artistic freedom consistent in both contexts. This omission reveals an unholistic institutional approach to artistic freedom. This is antithetical to a consistent juridical awareness, and associated doctrinal development, of the legal distinctiveness of artistic freedom under Article 10. However, in *Karata*,[27] the Court is to be commended for its specialistic recognition of the uniquely artistic context of any apparent aggression towards the integrity of Turkey as a sovereign state that the applicant's poetry could have been interpreted as exhibiting.

In this respect, the Court has been reassuringly consistent. In *Alinak v Turkey*,[28] a 2005 case, the applicant had written a novel, using fictional characters, that criticised hostility generated by Turkish security forces against the residents of an actual village. The Turkish Security Court seized the book. The European Court of Human Rights noted that the medium of the criticism was artistic and that a novel reached a smaller readership than the mass media. It duly held that the seizure of the work of fiction was not a proportionate reaction to the alleged political abuse of the right to freedom of expression by

[26] *Karata v Turkey* [1999] ECHR 23168/94.
[27] ibid.
[28] *Alinak v Turkey*, judgment of 29 March 2005 (officially unreported).

its author. It is perhaps significant that whereas in the art versus morality cases the facts involve visual art, in the art versus sedition cases the facts involve creative writing. Given the reasoning in its sedition judgments in favour of artistic freedom, and against it in the immorality cases, it could be that the Court is of the opinion that visual art tends to reach a wider audience than creative writing, and is therefore more extensively harmful than the written word could be. The demographic validity of any such assumption is a matter of conjecture.

C International Human Rights Instruments, Universal and Regional, Excluding the ECHR

There is, of course, international concern for the human rights of artists beyond the European Convention. A fundamental question of global interest is whether, theoretically, legal constraints can be imposed on artistic freedom given that the nature of artistic enterprise necessarily implies in theory, and reinforces in practice, the notion of the transgression of limits, as part of the very essence of art, in terms of such ideas as creative inventiveness, novelty, inspiration, and adventure. Historically, the Universal Declaration of Human Rights first recognised the need to internationalise the relationship between art and liberty.[29] In its Article 19, the Declaration protects freedom of expression in general, then paragraphs 1 and 2 of its Article 27 preserve, respectively, the right of everyone to participate in the cultural life of the community, and the right of every author to secure protection of his/her moral and material interests resulting from literary and artistic production. Artistic liberty per se is not explicitly referred to but is implicitly protected under both paragraphs. The Declaration, however, is not a binding international human rights instrument, which restricts its practical if not iconic value: even though merely rhetorical, it has been a catalyst for two binding international covenants on artistically related matters. The first of these, the International Covenant on Civil and Political Rights, in its Article 19, paragraph 2, reiterates the commitment to the international protection of freedom of expression in general, and, though not recognising that some art is non-cognitive but simply affective, it proceeds to specifically protect, inter alia, the imparting of information and ideas in the form of art. Though this binding provision is helpful to artists, the paragraph emphasises only the furtherance of art's incidental function, sometimes of ideation rather than the promotion and

[29] The initial enthusiasm for freedom of expression of all types was exhibited in such eighteenth century documents as the First Amendment of the US Constitution and the French Declaration of 1789. It is instructive that whereas the Americans favoured an absolute conception of expressive freedom, the French preferred a relative concept of liberty based on the writings of Rousseau. The international human rights instruments which evolved much later than these seminal national approaches, still reflect subtle aspects of this dichotomical thinking, but in a much more complex way. This variation results from the need for significantly more philosophical and practical compromise at the international legal level, where a relative conception of freedom of speech is more generally favoured, to accommodate, as diplomatically as possible, international political and moral diversity.

protection of art in all its ontological complexity. Moreover, there is no detail given in the broad and open-textured language of the provision that assists the recognition of art for protective purposes. An important feature of paragraph 3 of the law here is the prescriptive accommodation of others' competing interests with those of the artist, which must be strictly observed under Article 19 as a contrasting priority in the form of a list of legitimate restrictions on artistic freedom. This countervailing set of interests, which includes the rights and reputations of others, and the need for the more communal protection of national security, public order, public health or public morals, places a significant, and arguably draconian, practical limitation on artistic liberty that also appears in the European Convention on Human Rights. However, these conflicting restrictions must not undermine the essence of the right to artistic freedom within the range of the cardinal basic human right of freedom of speech, including symbolic speech. In the International Covenant on Civil and Political Rights, there is no reference made to democratic society, which is a central feature of the European Convention, because of the Covenant's hybrid political global context. This begs the question whether the true observance of human rights can only work successfully in a democratic framework, as some commentators on rights insist. In ignoring the arguably necessary democratic medium for rights, the Covenant expediently avoids antagonising non-democratic states. To do the contrary would be to impose on them, in the universal Covenant's terms and interpretation, a key plank in the traditional Western theoretical structure and political value-system of rights protection.

The sister instrument of the International Covenant on Civil and Political Rights is the International Covenant on Economic, Social and Cultural Rights. This human rights covenant, in its Article 15, paragraph 1, does not stress artistic freedom as a primary issue. Instead, it points to the importance of participation in cultural life, the benefits of scientific progress, and the intellectual property rights resultant from authorship in the scientific, literary and artistic fields. It is only belatedly, in its Article 19, paragraph 3, that freedom of artistic expression is implied by the nebulous, if imperative nomenclature, involving the 'indispensable' freedom of 'creative activity'. As in its partner covenant, the instrument on economic, social and cultural rights attempts to synthesise the freedom and solitude of the artist and the values involved in his/her public usefulness and participation. It is submitted that this exaggerates the importance of state control over the necessary privacy of creative endeavour and its personal rewards; and, in general, the International Covenant on Economic, Social and Cultural Rights mistakenly sees the role of the artist as one of public service rather than individual fulfilment. This underestimates the tension between the right of artists to shock and the accepted moral standards of a given, basically inartistic, community setting.[30]

[30] The dynamic created by the reception of art in society often involves an uncomfortable interaction of opposing moral positions. In HLA Hart's terms, this can be accurately expressed as a reaction of society's 'accepted' morality to art's 'critical' morality. The difficulty for art here is that 'society' is

As well as universal arrangements for the protection of human rights, regional arrangements comparable to the European Convention system also exist in America and Africa. The 1969 American Convention on Human Rights reflects the terms of the International Covenant on Civil and Political Rights. Its Article 13, paragraph 1, protects freedom of expression in general, including in the form of art. The Article's paragraph 2 bans prior censorship as a leading principle, but recognises that artistic freedom can be compromised by others' interests, much as conveyed in the legitimate restrictions placed on freedom of expression in general in the European Convention on Human Rights. These include concessions to such interests related to defamation, national security, public order, public health, public morals and unspecified 'rights of others'. This last residual category is potentially threatening to artistic freedom because of its vagueness, which could conceal various justifiable counter-claims to the exercise of artistic liberty that an artist cannot foresee. Article 13, paragraph 4, stipulates that another restriction on artistic freedom, inter alia, pertains to the moral protection of childhood and adolescence. It is submitted that this stance is uncontroversial except that the rule here could have provided for the use of warning signs at art exhibitions as a paternalistic solution to the situation of minors, instead of possible legal action on their behalf by their parents or guardians. Another international regional arrangement for the protection of human rights is the 1981 African Charter on Human and Peoples' Rights, which has idiosyncratic provisions on freedom of expression. This charter begins conventionally by protecting the right to express and disseminate opinions in its Article 9, paragraph 2, and by providing for free participation in the cultural life of the community in its Article 17. However, it also affirms the duty of the state to protect the morals and traditional values recognised by the community, a duty the performance of which may restrict free speech. Individuals are also oppressed in Article 27, paragraph 2, by a host of onerous duties to respect the rights of others (the rights being unspecified), and to have due regard for collective security, morality and the common interest. There is no recognition of the autonomy of artists as, under Article 29, paragraph 7, they and their fellow citizens must preserve and strengthen 'positive African cultural values' and promote the moral well-being of society.[31] This is virtually a prescription for an official literature even though the measures may have been well-intentioned in being designed to cultivate a post-colonial communal spirit of solidarity. There is the strong intimation that any art which could be judged negative or amoral,

usually unaware that art has a moral purpose at all, let alone one that impacts on accepted morality as a catalyst for that morality to evolve according to change in societal attitudes. This lacuna in societal awareness makes art vulnerable to maltreatment by establishment norms that are misconceived to be superior and static.

[31] This political stance misconceives art as being comprised of moral opinions. Art is a specialised form of cultural value not a vehicle of opinion, and any morality involved in it is not political engineering, nor is it designed to wield political influence. Sometimes, as an incidental and often unintended reflection of its aesthetic function, a political message of sorts can be inferred, but art is not involved in literal argument, being an autonomous symbolic medium.

or any other type of offending unofficial 'message', could be censored in a typically totalitarian fashion. This possibility is obviously inimical to the true spirit of freedom of expression, and its products' sometimes critical approach to the status quo, quite properly within the poetic canons of artistry. Any alleged offensiveness by an artist is misunderstood if taken as literally, rather than symbolically, real, and the African Charter's restrictive elements militate against the very essence of art's ontological and culturally recognised, oblique and independent, and thus syncretically conceptually-insulated, relationship with the real-life, extrinsic brouhaha of ordinary and inter-personally consequential human affairs. Instead of accusing artists of being in some way conventionally immoral or simply unacceptable non-conformists, there should be a general legal recognition of art's moral autonomy in accordance with its own internal specialist criteria of reference. Having proceeded to acknowledge and respect artistic autonomy, legal systems involving human rights can attribute a particularly elevated type of esteemed *virtue* to art, which can be legally and morally identifiable as indelibly associated with creative virtuosity, a word with the same semantic root.[32]

Artistic freedom should be secured based on two arguments, one from the standpoint of individual self-fulfilment which is self-evident, and (in the case of cognitive art, in particular, which communicates ideas) another that maintains that artistic expression can comprise or generate information that can lead to the ascertainment of truth. Moreover, an argument exists that art should be insulated from legal purview entirely, in accordance with the fact that art is a *sui generis*, culturally acknowledged, unique form. In addition, as well as art being independent based on its own ontology as an autonomous product, aesthetic perceiving or dwelling upon an art form gives autonomy to the self-activating interplay that can be termed 'the art experience'.

It is to the benefit of society in general for art to be produced: creativity is a noble and commendable exercise at all levels, and the most highly prized examples of art lift humanity to heights of awe and pleasure, and contribute to what is worthwhile and creditable about human civilisation. This fact should find reflection in the recognition of artists as rights-holders in all spheres of their artistic activity, including their role as critical-moral agents. This critical-moral capacity involves the presentation of new moral stimulus or insights that challenge the societal-moral status quo, albeit with the subtlety sometimes of an inherently ambiguous medium. The exclusive focus of the law should be extreme, 'worthless' pornography, such as that associated with the exploitation of children and with the portrayal of serious violence, examples of which occur on the Internet. This argument is supported by theoretical reasons why individuals should not be limited in their artwork on account of an allegation that

[32] We can return to Van Gogh. In his case, there is a particularly potent argument that his Christian life and inspirational art had an essentially sacred dimension. This takes us back to the mystical element to art that art history, as a genus, has frequently acknowledged as inexplicable in purely rational terms.

a given product's showing is detrimental to public-moral standards. One such reason is that obscenity as a phenomenon can only emanate from a non-artistic medium. Only when art is viewed out of context can obscenity result, because, if the viewer adopts the appropriate art-appreciative attitude, that specialised psychic approach denudes the art of any potentially offensive literal impact. Moreover, if something is displayed as art in an art gallery, there is a natural and necessary presumption that the object is art. The oblique communication of art militates against it having detrimental literal effects; it is symbolic, not quotidian fact; its physical position in an art gallery affirms its artistic status unqualifiedly. In addition, if one espouses the theory that the viewer co-creates an artwork in the course of that object's mental reception, obscenity is necessarily excluded from the viewer-to-object interaction since the creative liaison between viewer and object does not allow for anything extrinsic to interfere with the culturally specialised purity of that relationship, which can be broadly described as aesthetic.

Unlike the ontology of pornography, the ontology of art presupposes the culturally valued autonomy of a privileged class of imagery. This is an ineluctable and inevitable insularity that the law, virtually uniquely, frequently disrespects, usually because of law's a priori schemas and a habitual element of prejudication based on a conservative adverse reaction to charges of immorality in general. Moreover, the judicialisation of art sometimes conjures up institutional prejudices about 'ivory tower' approaches and their juridical insignificance. The appreciation of art is not a rarefied pursuit and it is in the interests of civilisation in general that artists have rights to engage in critical-moral activity that shifts understanding on accepted, complacent or demoded moral practice. To misunderstand art's intrinsic moral role leads to injustice for artists, and this is indefensible as a common legal phenomenon.

For law to maintain its image of being a neutral, fair and refined culture, it must desist from revealing itself as unsophisticated in its dealings with controversial but ultimately edifying art. To demand that art has a uniform moral pallor in conformity with the comparatively dull complexion of allegedly accepted moral mores, is to force artists to restrict themselves in creating works that merely replicate the attitudes that congregate to form what could be a *fictive* censorious consensus (because there is little empirical evidence to suggest that 'accepted morality' is other than a mistaken legal presupposition in the first place). Some, but too few, written national constitutions offer as a counter-proposition that art should be free as a primary presumption when art is confronted by what is often its public-moral nemesis. To prosecute artists and to deny them their rights qua artists leads not only to injustice but also to auto-censorship; more worryingly, it is the prelude to the prescription of an official art and that art's close association with totalitarianism.

III THE INTELLECTUAL PROPERTY RIGHTS OF ARTISTS

A Copyright Law in England, France and the USA

Copyright comprises the exclusive right to produce copies of, and to control, an original work, which is granted by law for a specified number of years.[33] The copyright law of the United Kingdom is to be found in the Copyright, Designs and Patents Act 1988, as amended.[34] This Act came into force largely on 1 August 1989; some minor provisions came into force later, in 1990 and 1991. Various amendments have been made to the original statute, the majority as a result of European Union directives.[35] Artistic works are amongst the works eligible for copyright protection and such protection is automatic, but, significantly, only when the relevant artistic ideas are put in material form. Before 1 January 1996, the relevant copyright term in the United Kingdom was the life of the author and 50 years. An extension to 70 years was introduced by the Copyright and Rights in Performances Regulations of 1995. These new Regulations implemented a European Council Directive,[36] the objective of which was to make the copyright duration uniform throughout the European Union.[37] In the United Kingdom, it is assumed that the author of the work is the first owner of its copyright. However, if the created work is made by an author in the course of his/her employment, then the author's employer is the first to possess the contingent copyright. The copyright period does not alter according to who owns the copyright, unlike in the USA.

In the USA, copyright protection was once granted under both federal and state laws. In 1979, Congress abolished most state copyrights in favour of an overarching federal copyright statute. One aim of copyright in the USA is to promote the advancement of the 'useful arts', but, ironically, if an artwork is a 'useful article', it is only copyrightable if its aesthetic features are separable from its utilitarian characteristics. A balance is sought that encourages creativity and yet gives the public free access to created works. Although one should attempt to avoid generalisations in this field, probably in contrast to the situation in the United Kingdom, and definitely to that in France, the USA law does not recognise any inherent or natural right of an artist to prevent others from copying his/her work. Put more boldly, the artist's interest in the USA is secondary to that of that state's public, so copyright law there gives artists rather more

[33] See generally, W Cornish, *Intellectual Property: Patents, Copyrights, Trademarks and Allied Rights*, 7th edn (London, Sweet & Maxwell, 2010).

[34] For a straightforward account of copyright in UK law, see further, P Pedley, *Copyright Compliance: Practical Steps to Stay within the Law* (London, Facet Publishing, 2008).

[35] See further, C Colston and J Galloway, *Modern Intellectual Property Law*, 3rd edn (London, Routledge, 2010).

[36] Directive 2001/84/EC.

[37] See, more generally, T Cook, *EU Intellectual Property Law* (Oxford, Oxford University Press, 2010).

limited property rights in their works than the equivalent law in the other two jurisdictions analysed here does. The public's ultimate benefit from creativity is the overriding priority of US law but, crucially, as in the United Kingdom and France, in US copyright law what is protected is not an original idea itself but the expression of that idea in a tangible medium.[38] Again, similar to the situation in the United Kingdom and France, under US law copyright attaches automatically when an original work is created, but in the USA registration with the Copyright Office puts a copyright-holder in a better position if litigation occurs in relation to the copyright. As in the United Kingdom, copyright law in France (the *droit d'auteur*) developed in the eighteenth century. However, French copyright law is based on a different philosophy from that of copyright law in common law systems, and has been widely influential in other civil law jurisdictions. It was also seminal in the development of the Berne Convention.[39]

In France, copyright protection is afforded to 'works of the spirit/mind'[40] so clearly, there is the expectation that the work is a product of the human intellect. Because, in France, there is a strong emphasis on the 'author' of the work, a protected work is seen as an extension of the personality. This means that 'moral rights' are very prominent in French copyright law but, despite this, it is apparent that in recent times several of these rights, such as the right to respect for the work's integrity, have been weakened when the moral rights of an artist, for example, have conflicted with the property rights of the owner of the artwork. The current law relating to copyright in France is the Intellectual Property Code and, within this document, there are two distinct sets of rights: moral rights and proprietary rights. In addition, on 7 March 2006, the French National Assembly passed what is known as the DADVSI Act, which implemented, with some modifications, the 2001 European Union Copyright Directive. This was a controversial development, which followed considerable debate. As a result, the DADVSI Act makes sharing copyrighted works peer-to-peer an offence but legitimates the sharing of private copies of certain tape recordings and other media.

In the United Kingdom, the USA and France, the dominant concept in copyright law is originality. In US law it is coterminous with a creativity requirement, and in French law, there must be evidence of the impact of a personality in the work produced.[41] Although in UK law originality is formally independent of any requirement of a specifically creative dimension to the work, such creativity

[38] Trying to separate, conceptually, ideas from expressions, has generated much legal scholarship in the copyright field, but there is inadequate space here to critique this debate profitably. If ideas without any concrete expression were protectable, evidential matters would be difficult to resolve, and would inevitably undermine copyright law's practicality.

[39] The Convention's method of working is examined briefly later on in this essay. See further, AL Sterling, *World Copyright Law,* 3rd edn (London, Sweet & Maxwell, 2008).

[40] In French, they are termed 'oeuvres d'esprit'. The physiological implications of this term were obviously intentional.

[41] See further, Caroline Carreau, 'Merite et droit d'auteur' (1981) 109 *Revue Internationale du Droit d'Auteur* 8. Hers is an informative, if rather idealised, account of law and artistic quality.

is arguably always present in an original work, implicitly if not explicitly.[42] Broadly speaking, notions of creativity are semantically allied to notions connected with the artistic, so in the USA and France, where creativity is important in an original work, artistic considerations might be expected to be more prevalent in the general copyright context than in the UK. When specifically 'artistic works' are legally examined, as we shall see a little later in this essay, courts inevitably have to address the difficult question of the precise meaning of the epithet 'artistic'.[43] In UK law, the artistic 'character' of a work is to be judicially discerned independent of artistic 'quality' or 'merit', except in the exceptional case of 'works of artistic craftsmanship'.[44] Different judges will have different ideas about what artistic character is.[45] The pressing problem of needing a concrete and finalised judicial definition of art in the copyright context may be insoluble as well as intractable. In all three jurisdictions studied here, law court judges do not have the luxury of art philosophers in being able to leave such a definition open-ended. Neither is it obvious, more fundamentally, that art assessment should be part of the legal adjudicator's role, since they are rarely experts in this very subjective area. As one prominent Justice of the US Supreme Court, Oliver Wendell Holmes, famously opined:

> It would be a dangerous undertaking for persons trained only to the law to constitute themselves final judges of the worth of pictorial illustrations, outside of the narrowest and most obvious limits. At one extreme some works of genius would be sure to miss appreciation. Their very novelty would make them repulsive until the public had learned the new language in which their author spoke. It may be more than doubted, for instance, whether the etchings of Goya or the paintings of Manet would have been sure of protection when seen for the first time.[46]

[42] See further, Paul Kearns, *The Legal Concept of Art* (n 11) Ch 3, 61–85.

[43] See further, J Pila, 'Copyright and its Categories of Original Works' (2010) *Oxford Journal of Legal Studies* 30(2), 229–54.

[44] Artistic works are defined in s 4 of the Copyright, Designs and Patents Act 1998. Section 4 reads as follows: '(1) In this Part "artistic work" means – (a) a graphic work, photograph, sculpture or collage, irrespective of artistic quality, (b) a work of architecture being a building or a model for a building, or (c) a work of artistic craftsmanship. (2) In this Part – "building" includes any fixed structure, a part of a building or fixed structure; "graphic work" includes – (a) any painting, drawing, diagram, map, chart or plan, and (b) any engraving, etching, lithograph, woodcut or similar work; "photograph" means a recording of light or other radiation on any medium on which an image is produced or from which an image may by any means be produced, and which is not part of a film; "sculpture" includes a cast or model made for purposes of sculpture.'

It is beyond the ambit of this essay to critique all elements of this section but it is important to note that only photographs are precisely defined here, and that works of artistic craftsmanship are unique in being copyrightable based on a judicial assessment of their quality. On works of artistic craftsmanship in particular, see David Booton, 'Legal Determinations of Artistic Merit under United Kingdom Copyright Law' in (1996) 1 *Art, Antiquity and Law* 2, especially at 138, where he says that '[t]he legislation requires that it is the craftsmanship which must be artistic and not the work itself. It follows that whether or not the work itself is artistic will not be determinative of whether it is a "work of artistic craftsmanship". It is submitted therefore that any test which has as its basis the examination of the finished work itself is wrong in law.'

[45] See especially, *George Hensher Ltd v Restawhile Upholstery (Lancs) Ltd* [1975] RPC 31.

[46] 188 US 239 (1903) 251.

The list of protected artistic works in UK law is both very specific and exhaustive, and some contemporary art may be jeopardised by not being legislatively included here.[47] It is clear, moreover, that seemingly meaningless or trivial art may be denied copyright protection following the general principle that only material which is worth copying is copyrightable.[48] It appears counter-intuitive that a quality criterion is excluded here but the law assumes that objective judgment is used in such appraisals, in much the same way as it assumes objectivity in the judicial discernment of artistic character in a given work (not least because law court judges are not permitted to be 'arbiters of taste', at least in common law jurisdictions).

In UK law, photographs are copyrightable even though the method of their production involves a mechanical tool for their execution, necessarily distancing the role of the 'creator'. During the evolution of legal practice, it has been established that photographs[49] are clearly classifiable as 'writings' within the meaning of the relevant copyright clause of the US Constitution (even though that involves a degree of imaginative linguistic interpretation). More controversially, it has been assumed that some expression of personality can be inherent in a photograph, especially in the USA and France. In the latter-mentioned jurisdiction, the personality required in a work for copyrightability is provided by the photographer's use of his/her aesthetic judgement even though, for example, many good photographs have in fact been taken accidentally, a circumstance that militates against any presumption that some personal skill is inevitably involved in producing a copyrightable photograph. Conceptually, this area of copyright law is very unsatisfactory.[50] The Internet has created problems for copyright law. In principle, digitalised images[51] differ little from ordinary photographic images except in terms of technological reproduction. The central

[47] One problem the law faces is that some art is only defined as art retrospectively, and the law is reluctant to be visionary when establishing copyright classifications. Consequently, it usually only legislates for traditional, acknowledged art forms, which some argue is all that can reasonably required of it. However, it can be justifiably contended that copyright legislation is not revised often enough to cover contemporary artworks as and when they arise.

[48] When an artist's work appears to comprise merely scribbles, it could, in theory, be denied copyright protection, but this has not been the case for the work of Cy Twombly, or more recently, David Shrigley, both of whom appear to have been accepted by the law as producing copyrightable art because they are unqualifiedly embraced by the contemporary art world. This is encouraging for artists. However, later in the main text of this essay, the law's apparent reticence to move with the times in the context of art's advancement is duly considered. (The principal complaint again here, as indicated in n 47, is that legislation is not enacted quickly or frequently enough to accommodate artworks of an avant-garde nature).

[49] On the reasons why it is economically important to grant photographs copyright protection, see Bernard Edelman, *Ownership of the Image*, translated by E Kingdom (London, Routledge & Kegan Paul, 1976).

[50] There is considerable academic literature on this topic, which has accrued historically from the time of the most basic camera's invention.

[51] See S Stokes, 'Art, Digitisation and Copyright: Some Current Issues' (1998) *Art & the Law* 361. For an interesting and novel perspective, see also, S Gordon, *The Future of the Music Business. How to Succeed with the New Digital Technologies. A Guide for Artists and Entrepreneurs*, 2nd edn (San Francisco, California, USA, Backbeat Books, Hal Leonard Corporation, 2008).

question in this area is whether such images are simply automated, computer-generated phenomena like simple Xerox copies, without further enhancement, and without a discernibly distinct author, or whether they have sufficient originality to qualify for copyright protection. This opens up a huge new challenge for copyright law regarding criteria for copyrightability, comparable to the historical realisation that a normal camera could produce images worthy of copyright protection. In addition, as mentioned earlier, copyright law has been slow to accommodate new art forms. In UK law, for example, collage is arguably the newest art form to achieve copyright protection under the 1988 Act, even though it has been a known art form for many decades. The law has rarely kept up with the advent of highly contemporary art forms, and has not addressed itself to protecting art that is very complex, or hybrid in terms of art classification, and, consequently, difficult to regulate by standard legal tests and formulae. A glance at the example of artworks known as 'ready-mades', alluded to earlier in this essay, clearly reveals the nature of some conceptual difficulties which the law is faced with in the copyright realm. 'Ready-mades' are basically everyday objects presented as art. They probably fall into the traditional art category of sculpture. But even if they could be prima facie copyrighted as sculpture as a matter of art classification, would their 'ordinary' nature deny them the quality of originality, which is vital for copyright protection? A related question that may arise could be the appropriateness of examining whether, if the work is perceived by its author as an artwork, that would indicate its originality. Another possible legal criterion for copyrightability here could be whether the work was created by a recognised artist, which might again suggest originality. Other relevant considerations might be whether the work is permanent or merely temporary, or whether the work is a collection of found articles that are artistically arranged in what is known as an *assemblage*. In another context, it may be enquired whether copyright is infringed by 'appropriation art' (such as a parody of an original work), where a different artist's (or artists') efforts may be drawn upon to form a 'new' artwork (for satirical purposes, for example). Other artistic paradigms that could involve problems for copyright lawyers include art such as that of North American Indians, or Australian Aboriginal art, in which the artistic efforts involved might be collective or without evidence of a specific author's artistry. It is arguable that a new development is necessary in copyright legislation that accommodates the particular problems presented by such folklore-based art. This could involve the modification of the originality principle in certain artistic areas, which would potentially revolutionise the status quo relating to copyright's universal predominant criterion.[52]

[52] See further, R Deazley, *Rethinkng Copyright: History, Theory, Language* (Northampton, Massachusetts, Edgar Elgar Publishing Ltd, 2009). In addition and also of relevance, is W Cornish, 'Conserving Culture and Copyright: A Partial History' (2009) *Edinburgh Law Review* 13(1), 8–26.

B Moral Rights

i Introduction

The concept of a 'moral right' derives from the French term *droit moral* which relates not to ethics in a general sense but to the right authors have to benefit from and protect their creations,[53] and their on-going coherence or even survival. One central idea behind the protection of an artist's moral rights is that in his/her creations the artist has imprinted and revealed his/her distinctive creative personality, and that this is the primary reason for the artist to have a continuing proprietary and protective right over his/her creative works.[54] This gives the artist authority over his/her creations so that the work itself, as well as his/her concomitant reputation, are appropriately safeguarded. Moral rights also ensure that the artwork's consumers have the benefit of the authentic product. In addition, the financial worth of a piece of art may, obviously, increase if the artist is conclusively identified. This is a crucial facet of the workings of the art market.[55]

In an artistic work, the artist suffuses his art with elements, or the entirety, of his/her own personality. However, in certain instances this is far from obvious especially in the realm of minimalist art and in specific works, initiated by Duchamp, called 'ready-mades'. These are often seemingly ordinary objects that have been enhanced by the artistic label they are given by the artist or by the artistic context of their display. Artists' moral rights in French law are perpetual; in the United Kingdom they cannot be assigned but can be waived, which raises the question of whether they are truly inalienable.[56] Moreover, in the UK the moral right of paternity has to be asserted by the author, which again clearly compromises the purity of the right in terms of absolute protection. It is submitted that this requirement imposes too much responsibility on the artist when many other personal rights are, contrastingly, more passively and easily protectable. The whole basis of moral rights is immersed in the notion of inherent rights. In addition, there is no 'exhibition right' in the UK (ie the right to control the public display of an artistic work) but that right does exist in the USA,

[53] Their artistic works are not required to possess a certain quality for moral rights to apply to them, which is consonant with more general copyright law. Very minimalist or trivial art arguably fails to attract copyright protection on the basis of a perceived lack of skill or effort on the part of its author.

[54] See further, LA Beyer, 'Intentionalism, Art and the Suppression of Innovation: Film Colorization and the Philosophy of Moral Rights' (1988) 82 *Northwestern University Law Review* 1011.

[55] See further, H Hansmann and M Santilli, 'Authors' and Artists' Moral Rights: A Comparative Legal and Economic Analysis' (1997) 26 *Journal of Legal Studies* 95.

[56] Moral rights, as peculiarly personal rights, are sometimes thought to be inherent rights, embracing and protecting as they do matters such as emotion, intellect, pride and privacy. In all three legal jurisdictions examined in this essay, moral rights almost always operate outside the conventional practices of commercial law because of the unique subjectivity of what they protect. This accentuates their historical lack of popularity in the UK and the USA, where copyright law's economic implications tend to be paramount.

whose legal stance is preferable and in consonance with the position in most civil law systems. However, until the early 1990s, US federal law contained no law expressly providing for moral rights, so the USA is behind the UK and France concerning the development of this important species of intellectual property right. A fortiori, when the Visual Artists Rights Act (VARA) 1990 was eventually enacted in America, it did not even satisfy the minimal protection achieved by other states, notably as required under the Berne Convention. This is despite the fact that some individual state laws in the USA, notably New York and California, possess laws protecting, inter alia, the moral right known as that of 'integrity'.

ii The Legal Positions in the UK, France and the USA[57]

To recap, in the United Kingdom, the Copyright, Designs and Patents Act 1988 largely came into force on 1 August 1989, which has proven to be crucial for the protection of moral rights in that jurisdiction. Prior to the Act, moral rights were not explicitly a part of UK copyright law. Instead, discrete areas of UK law afforded related protection, namely in the forms of contract, passing-off and defamation. Section 43 of the Copyright Act 1956 also expressly provided protection against false attribution of authorship but this was not at the time distinguished as a moral right per se. This picture changed completely under the subsequent 1988 legislation, sections 77 to 89 of which identify four types of moral right that afford protection to artists (and other authors but our focus here is squarely on artists). In no particular order, there is a right to protect an artist against false attribution of a work to him/her; a privacy right relating to certain photographs and films; an integrity right which gives artists a right to object to any derogatory treatment of his/her work; and, finally, the right to be identified as a work's maker, known as a paternity right.

The right regarding false attribution applies, inter alia, to artistic works. An occasion for an artist, in particular, to object to the false attribution of a work is provided for in the following two circumstances, the latter being the more important:

1. When the public is issued with copies of the artistic work (when appropriate) containing a false attribution.
2. When an artistic work, or a copy of it, is exhibited in public with a false attribution.

The false attribution right embraces adaptations. In the case of artistic works, this involves a copy of an artwork being falsely presented as a copy made by the author of the art. In addition, as a matter of practice, the right to object to a false attribution is often invoked in relation to parodies or satires: these tend to resemble the original artwork very closely.

[57] The content of moral rights is not identical in each system analysed here, which creates inconsistency which is undesirable given, for example, the unifying legal objectives of the Berne Convention.

Unfortunately, the artist's privacy right is quite complex, arguably unnecessarily so. It relates mainly to photographs. If a photograph is commissioned, for example, the copyright's ownership vests in the photographer not the commissioner. The direct consequence of this is that the photographer can use the negatives for whatever purpose without having to seek out the consent of the commissioner. There are problems that arise from this, especially regarding photographs for domestic and various other private purposes. The moral right of privacy grants the commissioner some justifiable privacy in these circumstances. Until the Human Rights Act 1998 (which came into force on 2 October 2000) facilitated the opportunity for judges in the UK to develop a general right to privacy, this moral rights-based privacy compensated in part for the more general lacuna. The commissioner of a private photograph always has to pay attention to the precise requirements that (a) the photograph has to be commissioned for domestic and private purposes and (b) that such a photograph must attract copyright. The *incidental* inclusion of such material in an artistic work is exempted from the ambit of the right (as one of the minor exceptions to it).

The integrity right is a right to object to derogatory treatment of an artwork.[58] Such treatment is very varied. It can comprise the addition, deletion, alteration or adaptation of an artwork that involves its distortion or mutilation. But the integrity right also covers acts that are otherwise prejudicial to the honour or reputation of the artist. There must be proof that the artist's lawful personal or intellectual interests in the artwork have *really* been prejudiced by its distortion or mutilation. All pertinent interests must be assessed including the nature and purpose of the art and the scale of its alteration. The following factors may also be relevant:

- whether the art is more utilitarian than truly artistic in character;
- whether any alteration of it is irreversible;
- the size of the audience to which the changed art is exposed;
- whether the artist created the art in the course of his/her employment or self-employment; and
- the practical impact the distortion or mutilation of the artwork has had on the artist's professional interests.

These considerations must be weighed objectively to bring about a pragmatic balance of interests between the artist and the user (or abuser) of the artwork (who has allegedly so exploited it).

The paternity right, as its name implies, is a moral right that favours the principle that the true creator of the artwork has the right to be identified as its author.[59] This identity must be clearly displayed, in a prominent manner, in

[58] See further, Jonathan Griffiths and Uma Suthersanen (eds), *Copyright and Free Speech: Comparative and International Analyses* (Oxford, Oxford University Press, 2005) Ch 9, 213.

[59] See, on moral rights, the right of paternity in particular, Ursula Smartt, *Media and Entertainment Law* (Abington, Routledge, 2011) 318–21.

order to attract the attention of any person who somehow acquires a copy of the work. The work must be one that attracts copyright protection, and, unusually in this area of law, the right does not automatically arise in the UK, as indicated above. It therefore has to be asserted appropriately by the artist who wishes to benefit from it. In addition, there are circumstances that are expressly excluded from the operation of the right. The paternity right applies neither to publications in dictionaries, encyclopaedias, newspapers and periodicals, nor to computer programmes, computer-generated works and typefaces. The *incidental* inclusion of the work will in certain circumstances preclude the right's infringement. The central objective of the paternity right is to protect the artist's work from immoral (and, therefore, illegitimate) commercial exploitation.

It is important to reiterate that moral rights have not until recently been protected anywhere in the USA, in contrast to their strict enforcement history in continental European legal systems, for example. This is at least partly because the emphasis in US copyright law is on pecuniary reward rather than the protection of creative attribution. Indeed, until 1990, at federal level, no explicitly moral rights provisions had been enacted. Instead, 'moral rights' had received protection only through judicial interpretation of miscellaneous copyright, trademark, privacy, and defamation statutes. However, VARA gave legislative force to the contention that an artist's professional and personal identity is inherent in each of his/her created works, which, in turn, embody his or her reputation. US copyright law was thereby changed in order to give artists who created appropriate artworks such moral rights as those of integrity and attribution. However, VARA only applies to visual art. Moreover, less than a dozen US states have individually recognised moral rights. Nevertheless, VARA gives qualifying authors the right to prevent the destruction of a work of art if it is of 'recognised stature', the right to claim authorship, the right of false attribution, a right against adverse distortion, mutilation or modification of an artwork, and the related right to prevent use of one's name on any such work. As alluded to earlier, artists may obtain moral rights protection under state laws in New York and California that resemble those found in VARA.

Under VARA, moral rights vest in the author of a 'work of visual art' automatically. Visual art, for the purposes of that 1990 Act, includes paintings, drawings, prints, sculptures, and photographs, existing in (i) a single copy or (ii) a limited edition of 200 signed and numbered copies or fewer. For photographs to be protected, they must have been taken for exhibition purposes only. All these works, but no others, are protected as works of 'recognised stature'. Surprisingly, applied art, inter alia, is explicitly excluded from the Act's ambit of protection. Unlike in France, for example, moral rights in the USA end with the life of the author. Unlike in the UK, for example, moral rights in the USA are not coterminous with copyright.[60]

[60] See further, on the interaction of copyright laws, P Rogerson, 'Conflict of Laws: Foreign Copyright Jurisdiction' (2010) *Cambridge Law Journal* 69(2) 245.

France was the first nation to substantively provide for moral rights as part of its national law, even though the precise term 'moral rights' did not enter its legal vocabulary until later. In France, moral rights never expire, which is not the case in most other jurisdictions. They are vigilantly protected in France as powerfully as economic rights, and the regime of moral rights in France has been gradually expanded as the law has progressed from the nineteenth-century into the twenty-first. This is in contrast to the situation in common law systems, which until quite recently tended to view moral rights as extrinsic to their traditional legal remits and philosophies. Amongst the rights available under French law is the right to decide on a work's first publication or other release, the right to correct or withdraw works that the author wishes to disown, the controversial right of the artist to insist on completion of the original where that is contingent on its execution by another or others, and the right to formally denounce the destruction or displacement of the original work. These rights are most recently derived from the law of 11 March 1957, and are now to be found in Article 121 of the current French Intellectual Property Code.[61]

In France, artists who are no longer content with their creations may withdraw or alter them, but such authors must indemnify the copyright-holder regarding any financial loss that is attributable to this. The paternity right in French law, unlike in most jurisdictions, allows artists to remain anonymous and to renounce any artworks that he/she (allegedly) did not make. The integrity law in France dictates that if an author's work is destroyed, there is a legal remedy of compensation, quite logically, because there has been a violation of his/her right to respect for his/her creation. Another moral right protected in France is the exclusive right of the artist to disclose his/her work, and a peculiarity of French law is that the right for a person not to have an artwork falsely attributed to him/her is not a separate provision in intellectual property law but part of the right of paternity.

On an international level, the Berne Convention was adopted in 1886, and has been often revised. The Convention provided for a union of member countries which is accessible to all states that comply with its conditions. It established a system of equal treatment that internationalised copyright for those who ratified it. It also founded strong minimum standards for copyright law, to which the Member States were obligated to adhere. Published and unpublished works are given protection when the authors are nationals of Berne Union states. Amongst other things, such states must ensure the provision to relevant authors of moral rights. Specifically, since moral rights are in essence to protect an author's reputation, they continue to be possessed by an author of a work even if that author has transferred the physical work and its copyright to another party. The Berne Convention also provides qualifying authors with

[61] See further, Ruth Redmond-Cooper's chapter on moral rights in D McClean and K Schubert (eds), *Dear Images: Art, Copyright and Culture* (London, Ridinghouse, 2002) 69–79. Redmond-Cooper's scholarship is favoured here because she is very highly qualified in French as well as English law.

resale rights so that they are entitled to 'royalties' each time the relevant work is sold. We shall now investigate the notion of a resale right or *droit de suite* as it was originally known more comprehensively.

iii The Droit de Suite (The Artist's Resale Right)

The *droit de suite* or artist's resale right is a concept independent of moral rights and its fundamental purpose is to provide visual artists with a usually modest share of the revenue from sales that occur *after* the initial sale of their artwork. It has been praised as being a measure of justice for them based on due respect for their creativity. However, conversely, it has also been criticised for being an inappropriate tax that is essentially ineffective. It is difficult to generalise about the *droit de suite* because it mutates depending on the legal jurisdiction where it is afforded. Nevertheless, some broad statements can be safely made about its workings as a genus. The resale right relates to public rather than private sales – by dealers and auction houses, for example, rather than between private individuals directly; and it covers work above a specified value. It enables an artist to share in the increased value of his/her work, at the same time providing him/her with the incentive to engage in further creativity. The *droit de suite* is also exclusively concerned with the resale of physical entities, not reproduction rights the artist may accrue. It has been strongly objected to on economic grounds, by some dealers, as a misplaced social welfare measure that is conceptually unrelated to copyright and difficult to administer. The right was established in France in the 1920s, and the previously-cited EU Resale Royalty Directive harmonises relevant legislation on the right in the various EU states, including the UK.[62] This will be examined in due course. Unsurprisingly, given its record regarding moral rights, the artist's resale right has not been popular in the USA, although a form of the *droit* is in place in California.

Supporters of the philosophical basis for a resale right argue that some great works are rarely recognised at first sale, so the artist is inadequately rewarded. Accordingly, resellers and buyers should compensate for this injustice. This is connected with the argument that the resale of artworks involves exploitation of the artist, who is unable to share the profits gained by undeserving others. Essentially, the right can be defended on the logical ground that, because of it, the artist can share in the realisation of his work's latent value at first sale through its subsequent resale. However, critics of the right claim that existing welfare initiatives exist for impecunious artists, and that artists can always use contract law to secure a share in future resales. They therefore deny the necessity for legal paternalism of this kind, that they allege is founded on nothing but an anachronistic, romantic caricature of the 'struggling artist'. They also allege that the overall demand for art is fixed so benefits for celebrity artists will be at

[62] For further information see J Phillips, *Copyright in the UK and the European Community* (London, Butterworths, 2009).

the expense of emerging creators. They note that in France approximately three quarters of resale payments seem to go to the families of a small cohort of famous artists such as the Cubists. In addition, opponents of the *droit de suite* point out that it clearly benefits the wrong artists (ie already prominent artists rather than those that really require financial assistance) or at the wrong time of their career. They also put forward the economically-based suggestions that demand for contemporary works is reduced by what they contemptuously term 'this philanthropy tax', and that the right is virtually redundant because major works are sold or donated to cultural institutions and so, in practice, are not resold. They also assert that the right is easily evaded by resellers who ignore the law and rely on the lack of initiative by artists in taking them to court. However, this observation also reinforces the justification for the right as being a necessary paternalistic gesture on the part of the law towards artists who are often impractical and not financially minded, based on the principle of 'material reciprocity', that has been firmly advocated by institutions such as UNESCO, which contend that the right must be recognised as inalienable and non-waivable.

As alluded to earlier, on 24 April 1996, it was proposed that national laws relating to the artist's resale right should be harmonised across all EU Member States by the creation of a controversial European Parliament and Council Directive on the matter. The UK at this time was one of the only Member States which was reluctant to recognise the *droit*. The Directive was designed to come into force within five years from the beginning of the year following that in which the Directive was intended to be activated, with the caveat that a derogation be respected in the case of a Member State which did not yet utilise the *droit*. Initial opposition to the measure by the UK alone was unsuccessful in barring the adoption of the Directive which we infer was thought to be a welcome development by other Member States. However, the UK gradually revised its position on the ethics of the *droit*, and on 14 February 2006 an artist's resale right was created from regulations made under the European Communities Act 1972.[63] In the UK, the right exists for as long as copyright remains in an artwork and provides for the artist to gain a 'royalty' when there is a qualifying sale of his/her work. The right only covers original works or those of which a limited number of copies have been made under the direction of the artist. A sale is only deemed to be a qualifying resale when the price of the artwork being sold is greater than a thousand, and either the seller or buyer is acting in the capacity of a professional art dealer. However, consonant with the belated introduction of the artist's resale right in UK law, the UK has also been tardy in creating a related right that has been enjoyed by many EU states since 2006. On 1 January 2012, UK artists' estates eventually became entitled to receive a percentage of the resale purchase price of any of their artworks whenever such a resale involves an EU 'art market' professional. The law on this comprises the

[63] See further, JN Adams, 'The United Kingdom's Droit de Suite' in Stamatoudi and Torremans (eds), *Copyright in the New Digital Environment* (London, Sweet & Maxwell, 2000).

Artist's Resale Right (Amendment) Regulations 2011, the fine details of which are beyond the ambit of this essay (but it is practically important to note that these new rights do not apply to resales before 1 January 2012). The artist's resale right is therefore rightly now extended in UK law to heirs and beneficiaries of artists whose art qualifies for the making of such provision.[64]

IV SOME GENERAL CONCLUSIONS

This essay has critiqued, for the first time holistically, the human and intellectual property rights of artists. Regarding human rights, we have primarily explored the difficulties that affect art when it is confronted with legal measures that aim to preserve public morality. In obscenity law and related laws, the lack of juridical attention to the specialisation of art matters (that form a socially recognised distinct culture) has been highlighted. In particular, the laws seldom respect the fact that art has a unique ontology that does not easily fit the workings of general legal mechanisms designed and utilised for censorship purposes. The critical-moral role of art tends to be ignored by the judiciary, who are insufficiently activist regarding society's necessary moral evolution. Art's role in stimulating debate in the moral realm is crucial for this development but judges prefer to adhere to the moral status quo in a demonstrably conservative way. It is arguable that, instead, they should be vigilant guardians of the law as a 'living instrument', like the judges of the European Court of Human Rights, and shape the law to move with the prevailing moral, social and political consciousness on matters of common cultural concern.[65] Regarding art, their outlook should be more futuristic. They should acknowledge that morally controversial art forms one of the vital tools for the stimulus of society and its subsequent maturing, notably in its tolerance of sexual-moral diversity as frequently demonstrated in the arts. In the case of blasphemy law, now abrogated in the UK,[66] some sort of common sense could arguably enable comparable legal regimes which retain a blasphemy law to accept that God's wisdom may well extend beyond human assumptions or misassumptions about His own reputation and how He wishes

[64] For a detailed critique, see Henry Lydiate, 'Artist's Resale Right' (2012) *Art Monthly* 353, 41.

[65] Because of the living instrument doctrine of the Strasbourg Court, its judges must give the European Convention on Human Rights a dynamic interpretation when adjudicating, so as to be in tune with the most up-to-date trends of postmodern society in the Contracting States they serve. However, as we discovered in the first part of this essay, those judges are not sympathetic to the latest exponents of artistic freedom when they create works that are considered to be too morally challenging and thereby contravene local public morality laws.

[66] The abolition of blasphemy law came into force there in 2008. The Racial and Religious Hatred Act 2006, as its name suggests, has the underlying objective of curtailing the stirring up of hatred of a racial or religious character in that state, putting a new social priority regarding *religious* harmony in place legislatively to complement the pre-existing and well-established proscription of incitement to *racial* hatred. The 2006 legislation was specifically needed to protect Muslims, who are classified as a religion rather than a race.

to protect it.[67] In defamation law, the phenomenon of defamation by fiction, palpably in the USA, could be developed to set fiction apart from ordinary factual documents in a much more exclusive way, thereby protecting novelists from anxiety about what they portray in the imaginative realm, a facility often drawn from the example and lessons of life itself, which tend to be the pillars on which the best art revolves.

Copyright law is tailor-made to regulate, inter alia, artistic works, whereas obscenity laws (and other libels) have much more general application. The importance of originality for copyright protection is relatively easy to satisfy whereas a defence of artistic merit, for example, in an obscenity context, is merely a residual means of exonerating art of a particular quality from condemnation as obscene, the effects of which are sometimes as draconian as the destruction of the relevant artwork. For copyright protection, quality is not a factor, and it is exceptional for an artwork to go unprotected. Copyright law is much more sympathetically attuned to art's promotion than public-moral laws, whose objective is to repress.[68]

The law that affords moral rights to artists is a recent development in common law systems, whereas in France those rights are relatively well-developed. This is for cultural reasons but the mere adoption of moral rights in the UK and USA suggests that the French example was a very positive one. The long-standing moral rights specified in French law reflect a degree of empathy between French legal culture and artists. The same cannot be said regarding the UK and the USA. In their legal systems, the schema of moral rights is more economics-based than person-centred. This may be because whereas the objective of French copyright law is focused directly on the creator (*l'auteur*), UK and US copyright regimes are financially-oriented rather than reputation-based. The French ideological scheme of requiring the impact of a personality in a work of the spirit/mind for copyright purposes signifies an appropriate humanity within French law's governance, where there is a clear nexus made between the artistic vocation and the created artwork. This reveals apt specialised artistic awareness on the part of the French copyright system in general, in contrast to that of the comparable UK and US regimes, where the relevant law is more mechanical. However, the introduction of moral rights into mainstream UK and US copyright law is reassuring for artists and the art-interested, and may well result in an expansion of sympathy for artists, whose moral interests as a specific group

[67] It is beyond the ambit of this essay to consider the social and theological rationales behind the need for current blasphemy laws. However, it must be emphasised that this is a sensitive and controversial area. It is widely acknowledged, and respected, that many people still possess devout faith of a Christian nature, for example, which some communities (especially Catholic ones, such as provincial ones in Austria) seek to insulate from unnecessarily uncouth abuse, invective or vilification.

[68] Art is unlikely to be so obscene as to contravene any laws against 'extreme' pornography, which typically portrays, amongst other things, serious sexual violence, bestiality and necrophilia. In particular, therefore, art is unlikely to be caught by the English Criminal Justice and Immigration Act 2008, which came into force in 2009, and which proscribes the possession of several kinds of morally heinous and very disturbing pornography.

were for a long time neglected in those states' rather less artistically insightful copyright laws.

The concept of an artist's resale right is controversial, and there are good arguments for and against it, that have been adumbrated above. On the practical front, it is arguable that this *droit de suite* is ultimately of negligible economic use because the art market may simply move from London and Paris to states such as the USA where the notion of an artist's resale right is comparatively under-explored. A personal submission is that this event is unlikely. It must also be borne in mind that resale rights usually render only modest rewards for artists, that the existing art market already easily accommodates. Moreover, the establishment of such a right is in principle very equitable, especially bearing in mind the treasures which some artists produce, that also become of immense financial importance (in uncomfortable juxtaposition, in many cases, with the financially penurious incomes of the artists' younger years). Moral rights and the *droit de suite* represent the gratitude of society for the fruits of creativity: as well as achieving a degree of economic justice, they aim to ensure that the artistic vocation as a genus is encouraged rather than defeated, which is, sadly, a situation that legal agents that promote the censorship of art simply fail to consider, let alone replicate.

10

*Artistic Liberty and the European Court of Human Rights**

I INTRODUCTION

ARTISTIC FREEDOM IS the Cinderella of liberties, seldom in the spotlight, and never in the limelight. The neglected theme of this essay is, accordingly, the judicial protection of artistic expression under the European Convention on Human Rights (referred to hereinafter as the Convention or ECHR). The essay's central contention is that such protection is starkly and surprisingly penurious, especially when juxtaposed against the strenuous protection of political speech; and a concomitant argument that there is preferential protection for political speech by the European Court of Human Rights (referred to hereinafter as the Court) inevitably raises the issue of whether a hierarchy of speech protection is discernible. This is, sadly, an unnecessarily opaque initial issue to resolve since it centres on only an inference of such a hierarchy of protection for different species of free speech by the Strasbourg Court; and the position is obfuscated by the fact that the Court sometimes seems to deny that it has established such a system. In *Thorgeison v Iceland*,[1] for example, that Court said that there was 'no warrant' in its jurisprudence for differentiating between apparently political speech and other forms of expression of public concern. However, despite this apparently emphatic declaration, that decision must be put in the context of the facts with which the Court was dealing, namely journalistic material pertaining to the grave abuse of state power through police brutality. In this context, the Court was emphasising the importance of non-political speech in respect of a particularly draconian misuse of state coercion. It probably did not mean to be stating a firm policy about the equality before it of all types of expression. Indeed, such a statement would clearly undermine a plethora of commentators' views about the clearly-established hierarchy of speech priorities adopted by the Court, by which it is now commonly understood that political speech is more keenly protected than

* I would like to thank Professor Rodney Brazier for reading and commenting on this essay. Any errors are my own. A precursor of this essay was first published in the first (inaugural) volume of the *Irish Law Journal* (2012) as 'The Judicial Nemesis: Artistic Expression and the European Court of Human Rights'. The precise page numbers of that article are unknown at the time of writing.

[1] *Thorgeison v Iceland* (1992) 14 EHRR 843.

artistic speech and commercial speech.[2] Moreover, it is usually academically inferred[3] that artistic speech has priority of judicial protection over commercial speech, an assumption that is clearly not borne out by the case law, as this essay will gradually reveal.

The formally disavowed taxonomy of expression by the Strasbourg Court has in fact been firmly established for many years, but for some commentators, it is far from self-evident that such a classification system is a constructive policy, as the Court's own reluctance to acknowledge its role in the phenomenon may be testament to. It will become apparent in this essay that I am in favour of the judicial acknowledgment of the autonomy of art, so the author is disposed to seeing advantages in a certain type of prior recognition of art as a specific category, in need of defending against the countervailing pressures of public-moral concerns. I am, however, totally against a freedom of speech ranking system, especially one that in practice puts artistic freedom last. In addition, although I strongly support the notion of artistic freedom specifically, I acknowledge that there may be in fact several dangers in trying to decide free speech cases by the use of predetermined categorisations of it. For example, free speech legal analysis requires very close attention being paid to the precise context in which the speech appears, and the judicial appreciation of a diverse range of relevant factors in an individual case may be precluded or abbreviated if undue significance is attached to a priori categories, into one of which the speech is dictated to fall. The identity of the subject matter of the speech, and the medium of the communication, for example, may be crucial, and defy the scheme of prior categorisation by their singularity or complexity. Such circumstances might suggest ameliorating judicial approaches to involve only an ad hoc balancing of contrasting interests in preference to a prior labelling of the particular speech as political, artistic, or commercial. This would result in an approach that is unaffected by any preliminary 'weighting' of the speech concerned, which weighting could be viewed as not only too general, imprecise and artificial but also an impediment to the rendering of true justice. Moreover, always giving primacy to political speech, in a table of speech priorities, could, of course, have the damaging effect of undermining the level of protection that should justly be afforded to all other legitimate species of speech.[4] Judicial preference for such primacy will be shown in this essay to involve the practice of an implicit unfairness under the European Convention on Human Rights, which occurs co-extensively with

[2] See further, Colin R Munro, 'The Value of Commercial Speech' (2003) *CLJ* 62, 134–58. The Court itself has become increasingly less reserved about expressing its strong protection of political speech.

[3] See further, Ivan Hare, 'Is the Privileged Position of Political Expression Justified?' in J Beatson and Y Cripps (eds), *Freedom of Expression and Freedom of Information* (Oxford, Oxford University Press, 2000) 105–21. In my introduction, I am indebted to Ivan Hare for elucidating the dangers of the a priori segmentation of different types of expression.

[4] It is possible to envisage categorisations of speech beyond the tripartite hierarchy of political, artistic, and commercial speech. A category known as 'symbolic speech', for example, goes beyond artistic expression to include gestures and inartistic insignia.

the unexplained, and therefore unreasoned, relegation of artistic expression in a protection hierarchy. Not only is artistic freedom as legitimate a public freedom as political liberty, but deprioritising it has had the practical effect of virtually negating it in its entirety as a bona fide protectable right, as the Strasbourg jurisprudence worryingly and transparently reveals.[5]

Consequently, in this essay,[6] the real efficacy of the current legal protection of artistic expression under the European Convention on Human Rights is scrutinised very closely. Excluding the introduction and general conclusions (Part I and Part VI, respectively), the essay comprises four main parts. In Part II, theoretical ideas on art, obscenity, pornography and harm, as conceptualised in the legal process, are presented. This detailed analysis highlights the subjectivity and complexity of this socio-moral area, an important circumstance which, crucially, goes mainly unrecognised in the judgments of the Contracting States of the Convention and the European Court of Human Rights, hence its instructive juxtaposition here.[7] This lack of demonstrable, necessary and sophisticated knowledge on the part of the relevant courts leads, ultimately, to injustice being done to art and its associated processes through a surprising degree of apparent judicial ignorance of art's unique ontology and method of operating, and its key valued role as a critical-moral counterbalance to established morality. This part of the essay ends with an original suggestion of the proposed reform of the national and supra-national legal approach when art and public morality are in issue, based on a legal presumption of artistic character in allegedly offensive sexually-explicit material.[8] Then, in Part III of the essay, the author analyses the generally antipathetic approach of the Strasbourg Court towards art under Article 10[9] of the Convention,

[5] See further, Part III.

[6] A shorter precursor of this essay appeared in P Kearns, 'Antipathy to Art in a Recalcitrant Court', (2006) *Amicus Curiae: The Journal of the Society for Advanced Legal Studies* 67, 25. A more comprehensive article, on a broadly similar theme, can be found in P Kearns, 'Art's Demise in the European Court of Human Rights' (2007) XII *Art, Antiquity and Law* 2, 137–69.

[7] It is difficult to imagine why courts of law dealing with art-related issues are so reluctant to inform themselves about, for example, ethically contentious art's relationship with established morality. In the case of the European Court of Human Rights, the acquisition of such knowledge should be mandatory in accordance with the Convention's principle of effectiveness.

[8] In copyright law, such as s 4 of the UK's Copyright Act 1988 on artistic works, the ascertainment of artistic character in a given object is necessary for its copyrightability. It is my suggestion that this minimalist criterion should apply in obscenity and related laws, instead of artistic merit, in order to protect all art, not just meritorious art, from charges of illegal immorality.

[9] For my purposes, the particularly relevant characteristics of Art 10 are referred to in the main text of this essay, at the beginning of Part III. Reference to Art10 will occur frequently throughout the essay. Article 10 provides that: '1. Everyone has the right to freedom of expression. This right shall include freedom to hold opinions and to receive and impart information and ideas without interference by public authority and regardless of frontiers. This Article shall not prevent states from requiring the licensing of broadcasting, television or cinema enterprises. 2. The exercise of these freedoms, since it carries with it duties and responsibilities, may be subject to such formalities, conditions, restrictions or penalties as are prescribed by law and are necessary in a democratic society, in the interests of national security, territorial integrity or public safety, for the prevention of disorder or crime, for the protection of health or morals, for the protection of the reputation or rights of others, for the disclosure of information received in confidence, or for maintaining the authority and impartiality of the judiciary.'

on freedom of expression, and its dubious and unqualified preference for the preservation of accepted morality over the necessity for artistic freedom when those interests appear to conflict. Next, Part IV of the essay presents the first comprehensive critique of the somewhat neglected case of *Karata v Turkey*,[10] and affirms its importance for artistic freedom in itself, as well as beyond its own particular context of political controversy, which is sedition. Part V adumbrates a comparison between the American and Strasbourg approaches to the protection of artistic freedom. My general conclusions complete the essay.

II THE COMPLEXITY OF THE CENTRAL ISSUES: ART, OBSCENITY, PORNOGRAPHY AND HARM

Within the ambit of Article 10[11] of the European Convention on Human Rights, on freedom of expression, Article 10(1) guarantees the right to such freedom but then, in Article 10(2), there is express provision made for legal limits to be placed on that right by the Contracting States of the Convention in certain prescribed circumstances. One such circumstance is when Contracting States impose restrictions on, inter alia, artistic freedom, for the countervailing protection of morals. It is this legal area with which this essay is primarily concerned. The main responsibility to protect rights lies with the Contracting States but the European Court of Human Rights exercises, at least in theory, a substantive monitoring function. Definitional and other problems can arise when very difficult, contentious concepts such as art and morality are counterpoised in the legal process, and this occurs first at a national level prior to any relevant case subsequently proceeding to Strasbourg. In Strasbourg, in essence, the issues adjudicated upon by the national courts of the Contracting States are intended to be freshly reviewed in accordance with the Convention's foundational purposes.

Unsurprisingly, the Contracting States of the European Convention on Human Rights all have individual approaches to the sensitive issue of the protection of morals. The primary focus, in this part of the present essay, on the Contracting States, and their lack of attention to the important complexity of the conceptual issues relating to the art-morality dynamic, is because the European Court of Human Rights extends to those states a discretion as to how to formulate legal rules on morality according to local-moral values. This is called the margin of appreciation doctrine, and when morality is in issue that margin is 'wide', ie the

[10] This is the officially unreported case of *Karata v Turkey* [1999] ECHR 23168/94. In some sources, confusingly, the name Karata becomes Karatas. This case is seminal because it shows the European Court of Human Rights for the first time amending its generally restrictive attitude to freedom of artistic expression. For reasons of space, primarily, the analysis in this essay is restricted to public morality cases, and sedition cases when they have relevance for public morality. It is beyond the ambit of this essay to consider Strasbourg cases that are concerned with defamation or terrorism in relation to artistic freedom, interesting though such cases may be.

[11] For more information on Art 10, see n 9.

Court confers a broad discretion on the authorities of the Contracting State.[12] Although in theory the Court then retains a supervisory function, a personal view is that the margin of appreciation, at least in the area of artistic freedom, in effect allows the given Contracting State virtual carte blanche to assess the prevailing moral community feeling within its jurisdiction and to accommodate that sentiment in appropriate paternalistic laws.[13] This arrangement is arguably an abdication of responsibility by the Court in favour of a subsidiarity principle that undermines its important prerogative to decide through its own reasoning its own interpretation of moral justice. When, arguably, 'immoral' art enters the arena as the target of national public-moral laws, the Strasbourg Court, in hearing the case under its own jurisdiction, is in theory faced with the unenviable prospect of juggling various important concerns involving art and immorality. However, through the use of the margin of appreciation, the Court in practice simply reserves decision-making involving this seemingly intractable, delicate problem for the national courts, in all cases involving artistic freedom in the context of morality, despite those courts' narrower focus of moral vision and lower level of judicial expertise. To set in relief the indisputable lack of close analysis of relevant issues at a national level, which is revealed in the judgments relevant to the artistic freedom of the Strasbourg Court, and adumbrated in Part III, a preliminary critique of the often legally inter-linked subjective factors of art, obscenity, pornography and harm, is vital. This is not least because, firstly, it reveals the inadequacy of courts' habitual dealings with the difficult nature, but absolute necessity, of such information in art-related cases, and because, secondly, the elucidation of the precarious and sensitive interaction of these factors in a court of law will assist, if heeded conceptually and practically, the smooth operating of objective legal adjudication, certainty and consistency.

It is widely opined that pornography, as opposed to art, is not philosophically or socially regarded as a precious commodity, but rather as a gratuitously venal, ignoble, expedient, and self-indulgent device. It is therefore fundamentally problematic to apply classical scholastic arguments for the protection of freedom of expression to pornography because of the lack of intrinsic value that is habitually found in it. As Dworkin observes, although a right to freedom of expression can, of course, be justified in the interests of individuals and society in general, including regarding even morally shocking entities, pornography is difficult to defend using free speech justifications, not least because it cannot be realistically argued that increasing society's pornography resources is really an

[12] A 'wide' margin of appreciation is given in the context of moral issues because those concerns do not have what the Strasbourg Court calls an 'objective' character. In other words, what is considered moral will differ from state to state and, accordingly, the Court considers that states should be given a broad discretion when resolving morality-related legal conflicts within their own jurisdictions.

[13] The role of the Strasbourg Court should be to impose supra-national moral solutions, from its judiciary's international perspective, when reviewing morality-based legal decisions in Contracting States.

epistemic benefit.[14] Although this dismissive approach appears morally sound in terms of decency and propriety, it is arguable that the circulation of morally dubious, explicit, usually sexually-related material can nevertheless find a justification on the basis of a variant of the liberal argument related to the ascertainment of truth. What is advocated in that argument is the proposition that the prohibition of any explicit, implicit or associated free flow of ideas in pornography could prevent the acquisition of (possibly incidental) ideas that possess true value. In addition, 'harm' to society allegedly caused by pornography is still not conclusively proven, at least in relation to adults, and the legal eradication of pornography could conceivably lead to the enforcement of a particular, unduly dull, sanitised conception of morality, to the detriment of, for example, priapically innovative, non-anodyne, daring artistic expression. Conversely, a reason to rid society of pornography might be the qualitative consideration, from an art-critical perspective, that almost all of it is aesthetically and conceptually meritless. This common observation is galvanised by the assertion that pornography is conative[15] rather than cognitive, ie that it is a stimulus to physical, base and unreflective action rather than an inspiration for creditable thought. Nevertheless, especially in the present era known as postmodernism, many artists challenge accepted morality in their works in what could be termed a critical-moral way, and might use pornographic approaches to this end;[16] so, it is clearly feasible that even allegedly offensive or obscene works may possess real merit from a sociological and art-interested viewpoint. In addition, notions of obscenity, indecency, and pornography are defined, impractically and inconclusively, by reference to what have been termed vague and elastic formulae that invite protracted discussions about morality that do not fit comfortably within the workings of a criminal trial.[17] There is therefore the associated legal-institutional problem of the precise identification of undesirable facets of creativity. Moreover, there is a conceptually based persuasive argument that obscenity simply cannot inhere in art because art's ontology and cultural distinctiveness require a contemplative engagement with it that negates, in its concomitant exclusively aesthetic mental processing, even the remotest possibility of literal harm: a harm that could arguably only occur in an art-absent context, oxymoronically, or through audience art-ignorance.[18]

The legal regulation of art for moral reasons is, of course, complicated by the renowned philosophical difficulty in defining art, at least with the precision legal certainty requires. It may be easier to try to define art by its purpose rather than its content. A personal suggestion is that art is differentiated from ordinary facts

[14] See further, R Dworkin, 'Is there a Right to Pornography?' (1981) 1 *Oxford Journal of Legal Studies* 177, especially 193.

[15] Conation involves the wilful endeavour to prompt physical action.

[16] See further, D Harvey, *The Condition of Postmodernity: An Enquiry into the Origins of Cultural Change* (Oxford, Blackwell, 1990) and F Jameson, *Postmodernism*, or, *The Cultural Logic of Late Capitalism* (London, Verso, 1991).

[17] G Robertson and A Nicol, *Media Law* (Penguin Books, 2000) 153.

[18] Art's fictive essence insulates it from projecting literal harm into the factual world.

by its capacity to stimulate (only) intellectual reflection in its audience. It can thereby be defined according to its quasi-teleological function of prompting (only) contemplation, and never anything but the most insignificant action. Alternatively, art can be defined in very broad terms, and no more precisely, as 'the application of human skill';[19] but then the notion of 'skill' therefore remains to be elaborated upon.[20] What is clear, though, is that art is a very subjective entity and invites individual, heuristic and informal endeavour on the part of its viewers or readers.[21] This, in part, may explain why law is often presumed to be antithetical to it. It is also one view that while art is associated with imagination, creativity and even playfulness, law is hallmarked by control, sobriety and discipline.[22]

These are strictly dichotomised characterisations of art and law, and the impact of the latter on the former exaggerates the distinction further. The consideration of any pornographic properties or connotations of art by law in a legal arena exacerbates the already oppositional nature of the art-law dialectic by introducing additional subjective factors that further complicate the problematic. Moreover, the very term 'pornography' unhelpfully semantically reinforces its association with art since pornography always infiltrates a book, poem, painting or photograph, for example, and so is ineluctably conceptually entwined with something at least artistic in the broadest and loosest sense. Nevertheless, conceptual distinctions between pornography and art can and have been made, especially in the realm of psychology. According to some psychologists, one psychological fact is that pornography appeals to, and provokes, a type of sexual regression, a notoriously complex process that is not susceptible to legal examination in a definitive way.[23] However, it can be stated here, in a readily comprehensible way, that such regression is characterised by the reducing of life to varieties of sexual preoccupations that perpetuate pre-adolescent fantasies, which, in turn, reject reality.[24] Regression, then, in the typical pornography consumer, inhibits the normal courses of the human maturing processes, and incites the consumer to devolve psychologically to a more irresponsible condition, based on unrealistic sexual expectations, devoid of the wholesome quality of love. Since Aristotle, amongst others, wisely predicates that the purpose of art is to reveal internal value rather than to laud purely cosmetic appearance,[25] it is evident that pornography-induced regression is inimical not just to normal human development, but also to art's unsuperficial, 'interior', intellectually-edifying purpose (in contrast to pornography's surface,[26] degenerate, repressive,

[19] See further, *The Concise Oxford Dictionary* (Oxford, Oxford University Press, 1964) 64.

[20] 'Skill' can be defined as expertness or practised ability or dexterity, all of which are rather too general to assist us in our enquiry here.

[21] An artwork invites creative exploration on the part of its audience to the degree that some postmodernist scholars have argued that the readership in effect co-creates the work.

[22] C Douzinas and L Nead, *Law and the Image* (Chicago, University of Chicago Press, 1999) 3.

[23] I Kristol, 'Pornography, Obscenity and the Case for Censorship' *New York Times Magazine* (1971) 115.

[24] E Van den Hagg, *Censorship: For and Against* (Oxford, Hart Publishing, 1971) 147.

[25] This aphorism of Aristotle is available at http://creatingminds.org/quotes/art.htm.

[26] It is a particular tendency of postmodernism to promote superficiality.

retarding influence). On this basis, a philosophical distinction can be made between the two phenomena traditionally called art and pornography which has an empirical basis. In direct contrast to pornography's *regressive* and *negative* influence, artistic antennae are forever sensing the way *forward* in the true *positive* spirit of creativity.[27]

With regard to the interactive realm of the actual viewing of pornography, it is obvious that pornography stimulates the audience at a unedifying if elemental level, in contrast to the relatively deep and demanding level of audience participation and reception that art requires. In addition, it can be advanced that whereas literature embodies a multitude of intentions, pornography possesses only one aim, which is a sexual reaction to it on the part of its consumers.[28] This highlights the transient goal of (mere) sexual pleasure as pornography's key objective in contrast to literature's holistic appeal of a durable nature. Thus viewed, pornography becomes legitimately stigmatised as a crude, unenlightening, ignoble and practical device, whereas art is comparatively refined, psychologically enriching, and commendably complex in its psychic effects. A distinction may then be drawn again between the visceral reaction to pornography and the prompting to reflection of art. It therefore becomes unduly defeatist to proffer that any attempt to circumscribe what is objectively pornographic or obscene is doomed to failure.[29] Moreover, it is important to retain conceptual clarity in this area, especially when such terminology is imported into the law. In this light, the Preamble to the English Obscene Publications Act 1959, for example, appears prophetically over-simplistic, and potentially confusing, because in relation to obscenity and pornography it appears to draw a distinction between them which is semantically contradictory by stating that '[l]iterature is to be spared the rigours of the law, even if obscene, but pornography – material of no intrinsic merit of any kind – remains subject to suppression.'[30] This highlights another problem. Artists habitually violate boundaries, and one argument is that either the law protects art as a whole *or* protects society from pornography: it cannot do both.[31] It will be sobering for us to consider the Strasbourg solutions to the alleged immorality of art in the light of this approach, because we will discover there a distinct preference for purported moral rectitude over virtually any artistic freedom.[32]

[27] In John Finnis, *Natural Law and Natural Rights* (Oxford, Oxford University Press, 1980), Finnis claims that aesthetic experience is an objective good, the value of which is self-evident.

[28] S Marcus, *Pornutopia* (Encounter, 1966) as cited in B Williams, *Report of the Committee on Obscenity and Film Censorship* (Cmnd 7772, 1979) para 8.10, 106.

[29] *Pace* D Lacombe, 'Epilogue: Post-Modern Art in the Age of Obscenity' in *Blue Politics: Pornography and the Law in the Age of Feminism* (University of Toronto Press, 1994) 162.

[30] See further, the Preamble to the Obscene Publications Act 1959. It perhaps goes without saying that the Preamble's essential aim here is to distinguish between the protection of literature and the condemnation of pornography.

[31] Amy M Adler, 'Post-Modern Art and the Death of Obscenity Law' (1990) 99 *Yale Law Journal* 1359.

[32] See main text, Part III.

There is an implicit assumption within Article 10 of the European Convention on Human Rights that there may be a need for Contracting States to protect morality.[33] This assumption seems justified when relevant laws in the Contracting States oriented around such protection are identified. However, the degree to which it is appropriate for the law to impose criminal sanctions relating to obscenity, decency or blasphemy, for example, has always been, and continues to be, a matter of extreme contention. The liberal lobby maintains that limiting the availability of pornography unduly impinges on free expression and that there is no proven harm in its distribution and consumption. The antithesis of this is the moralists' position. They affirm that society must restrict access to pornography because it is immoral per se, independent of any considerations as to whether it causes harm or not. Feminists tend to posit their case against pornography in terms of harm to women rather than by reference to its intrinsic immorality, but in all stances there are, of course, shades of grey. Much depends on the notions we entertain about 'harm', and the intrinsically subjective colour of the idea of morality, together with the degree to which we believe sexual difference to be an important conceptual and practical form of distinction in this area.[34]

A central question in the current context is whether a distinction can be drawn between pornography and art in terms of potential harm caused. One argument is that because pornography, like art, has never been indisputably proven to cause harm to others, its consumption should be a matter of private rather than public moral judgment. If pornography were confined to the realm of the private, it would be arguable that there is no necessary nexus between it and the public-moral sphere, but, unfortunately, it does make its presence felt in public, through someone's deliberate or incidental action, to the annoyance and offence of certain other members of society. Despite the fact that one might consider sexual relations a 'citadel of privacy',[35] pornography tends to intrude beyond that dimension (but does not depend on the same degree of public accessibility as art in order to function efficiently). It is arguable, then, that it is only when pornography unusually encroaches on the public arena that the art-pornography distinction is crucial with respect to *public* morality since the consumption of

[33] This is usually a constitutional matter that is regulated by the criminal law.

[34] See, further, SH Bailey, DJ Harris and DC Ormerod, *Bailey, Harris and Jones: Civil Liberties Cases and Materials*, 5th edn (London, Butterworths, 2001) 682. When it comes to issues relating to the harm that pornography allegedly does, it can be argued that some gay men who feature in pornography are in a similar position to women in terms of allegedly harmful subordination, but one must be wary of over-generalisation in this sensitive area. There is a wealth of feminist literature available on the harm done to women by pornography and the author is far from indifferent to these claims. The author's general personal view is that pornography *can* in certain circumstances be extremely harmful. One point of his, though, is that such a view is not *conclusively* proven. Moreover, this essay's emphasis is on the relative harms of art and pornography rather than on pornography's harmfulness in general.

[35] There is, regrettably, insufficient space in this essay to comprehensively explore the conceptual issues connected with the public/private divide in the area of sexual morals.

pornography, from the point of view of John Stuart Mill[36], is not an other-regarding act, ie it does not impact on anyone else apart from the consumer.[37] The physical locus of the pornography thus becomes the determining factor in arguments in *public*-moral terms to repress it, rather than the alleged harm to any private individual, that may occur in any situation.

Whether pornography *should* be suppressed when it enters the public realm is still a matter of conjecture, but because there is evidence that it does no demonstrable harm to adults when in the public area, a distinction between art and pornography for legal purposes cannot convincingly rely on harm as the principal basis of any distinction between the two regarding the protection of *public* morality.[38] Nevertheless, the preservation of public morality may, of course, require the contribution of private approaches, and in this way, prima facie, pornography might be considered to have a more detrimental effect than art on the prevailing moral consciousness because of its content. However, a personal opinion is that, being conative rather than cognitive, pornography may actually have a less profound impact than art on an individual's ideas which are formed in private, and then transferred to the public sphere.

The more theoretical aspects of the regulation of art and pornography that should be addressed domestically under the European Convention on Human Rights must also be seen in terms of the era in which it is operating. This is postmodernism,[39] as mentioned earlier, which is notorious for lacking moral foundations of an immutable kind, and for being deprived of its own native culture. This furnishes a marvellous opportunity for artistic originality but that originality is not necessarily a matter of legal cognisance. One view is that the law can only appreciate new art after it has become a matter of convention, use and habit, ie when it has reached a condition familiar to a typically legal *modus operandi*.[40] This does not, of course, augur well for controversial art, at the cutting-edge of artistic discovery, that has innovative rather than immediately legally-recognisable qualities. However, in the context of freedom of artistic expression, one must be careful not to form a caricature of the role of law. Law under the Convention is not operating on art with condemnatory moral bluntness in the way that occurred in bygone eras of national moral hypocrisy. Now the law's role is still regulatory but 'in a broader machinery of dissemination in which erotica [are] differently treated according to an intra-legal specification of types of susceptible persons and dangerous places'.[41] The objective of the

[36] JS Mill, *On Liberty*, edited by G Himmelfarb (Harmondsworth, Penguin, 1974).

[37] See further, Noel B Reynolds, 'The Enforcement of Morals and the Rule of Law' (1977) 11 *Georgia Law Review* 1325.

[38] Firstly, it is widely contended that children should be protected from pornography, a position with which this author strongly concurs. Secondly, the author is evidently not concerned in his particular argument here with the practical issue of any public aspects of the *distribution* of pornography.

[39] See further, P Kearns, 'Postmodernism: A Critical Guide' in his book *The Legal Concept of Art* (Oxford, Hart Publishing, 1998) 185.

[40] Douzinas and Nead, *Law and the Image* (n 22) 1.

[41] I Hunt, D Saunders, and D Williamson, *On Pornography: Literature, Sexuality and Obscenity* (Macmillan, 1993) 53.

Convention is not ideological in the sense that it intends to reinforce an ancient dichotomy (Apollonian art versus Dionysiac pornography); instead, it seeks to create a delicate equilibrium between freedom of artistic expression and other genuine societal interests including those of the empirically-ascertained particularly vulnerable. Nevertheless, the Strasbourg Court's recalcitrant use of the margin of appreciation doctrine, which surrenders the regulatory initiative to the legal mechanisms of the Contracting States, means that art that is considered in some way morally delinquent will be at the mercy of the often arbitrary, and perhaps unduly oppressive, moral consensus of a particular state, or worse, one or more of that state's even more morally-restrictive provincial regions. This abuse of the Court's supervisory jurisdiction, that involves its refusal to establish supra-moral, principled guidelines for freedom of artistic expression, is more than lamentable, and will be illustrated in Part III of this essay.

The ambiguous nature of artistic expression conflicts with the definitive categorisations states habitually use in their legal regimes for admittedly necessary practical reasons.[42] In assuming that art is susceptible to definition, law is merely trying to impose parameters on it as it would on anything else. But art is a discrete, peculiar commodity that cannot be confined in this way; another legal route must then be found to permit its fair legal regulation. This is not an easy quest because, whereas criminal trials typically aim to ascertain the truth, when obscenity enters their arena there is only ever a clash of opposing opinions that distils no definitive answers.[43] Moreover, how is one clearly to distinguish between works of art of inherent value, and irredeemable others, based primarily on the artistically alien but legally relevant criterion of their perceived obscenity? This legally perennial problem is not resolved because the focus of the law is definitional, subjective and art-evaluative as far as art is concerned, and definitional, allegedly objective and potentially censorious as far as obscenity is concerned. To be more consonant with the right to freedom of artistic expression, the courts could profitably legally frame and project a new approach that arguably minimises uncertainties, inconsistencies and subjectivities. The essence of such reform would be the creation of a legal presumption of artistic character or relevance (not merit) in sexually explicit material that is alleged to contravene public-moral laws.[44] This would represent a legal acknowledgment of the value of art as well as affording some initial protection for the putatively offending material itself. It would prevent, for example, frequent accusations about the seemingly arbitrary, desultory and unprincipled condemnation of such material. With the existence of such a presumption, any suggested limita-

[42] The absence of a definition for art impedes legal efficiency particularly.

[43] Geoffrey Robertson, *Obscenity: An Account of Obscenity Laws and their Enforcement in England and Wales* (Weidenfeld and Nicolson, 1979) 6.

[44] It is relatively easy to establish artistic character or relevance at an objective level, whereas the ascertainment of artistic merit involves the exercise of essentially subjective judgement and a certain degree of expertise. A legal presumption of artistic character or relevance is not equatable with a legal presumption of free speech *simpliciter* since a legal presumption of artistic character or relevance is, inter alia, of a different cultural order.

tions on the right to freedom of artistic expression would then have to be justified on the basis of the actual resulting harm caused by individual artworks, in this way permitting courts to assess the validity of claims of real harm, rather than to assume the existence of a wholly hypothetical harm. This approach would affirm that the proper function of law courts is to eradicate the evil of actual (psychic) harm rather than hypothetical (moral) harm, rather than rely on the complex and highly subjective process of the evaluation of artistic merit, which is (frequently tacitly) commonly misleadingly projected as a viable, objective and fair juridical exercise. In fact, what this projection actually disguises is the palpable, though perhaps reluctant, and even ineluctable, judicial violation of the English common law principle that law-court judges should never be arbiters of taste. An unacknowledged resorting to the exercise of judicial taste undermines the need for legal certainty and consistency but, more crucially perhaps, legal transparency. It is respectfully submitted that my proposed reform, elaborated on above, removes such delicate and intractable problems.

III THE STRASBOURG COURT ON ART AND IMMORALITY: ARTICLE 10 ECHR

In this part of the essay, the author examines the seminal case law produced by the European Court of Human Rights on freedom of artistic expression and its ethical boundaries,[45] and analyses why the Court has been so reluctant to support artistic freedom; instead, it consistently reinforces local, national measures aimed at preserving the ambiguous concept of 'morality'. This substantive critique focuses on the cardinal constitutional laws of obscene and blasphemous libel,[46] laws which are designed to fulfil the paternalistic function of insulating the moral approaches of citizens from what is considered by legislators and judges to be undesirable corruption.[47]

Artistic freedom is only *implicitly* regulated under Article 10 of the European Convention on Human Rights, a provision which is phrased in comparatively general terms. That Article basically provides that everyone has the right to freedom of expression, and that this right shall include freedom to hold opinions and to receive and impart information and ideas without interference by public authorities, and regardless of frontiers. Under the Article 10 provision, the Convention therefore essentially protects freedom of speech in a very broad and undifferentiated way. Included in the idea of speech is 'symbolic' speech,

[45] There is only a small corpus of cases on artistic freedom per se.

[46] Although blasphemy law was abolished in England with effect from 8 July 2008 in accordance with s 79 of the Criminal Justice and Immigration Act 2008, the Convention case law based on blasphemy remains important for other Contracting States that still maintain a law of blasphemy or its equivalent, for example Austria.

[47] The Internet makes all manner of offensive publication available, which arguably negates the true efficacy of obscenity-related laws (based on the inordinately narrow selective scope of prosecutions for obscenity).

which is not specified in the Article, but which covers, inter alia, artistic works. Amongst the artistic works protected are visual art, creative writing, and film, which are the media featured here. Unsurprisingly, because the term 'speech' does not cover art, for example, it is freedom of expression rather than speech per se which is the Strasbourg system's preferred nomenclature for protection purposes in this area, and the term 'expression' obviously has a special resonance in the artistic context now considered.

What sort of dispute concerns us? The fundamental conflict between art and law under Article 10 occurs in the sphere of the proscription of immoral communications, an area that sometimes, lamentably, embraces morally controversial art. Art is not afforded a special place for public-moral purposes under the Convention; arguably, it should be.[48] Art has a distinct ontology, and is culturally recognised as a discrete body of value, being emergent from the creativity of individuals, which has a certain spiritual significance, that is reflected, for example, in the French intellectual property term 'oeuvres d'esprit' ('works of the mind/spirit').[49] From a purist, spiritual perspective, when art is pitched against public-moral considerations, the fruits of artistic expressivity should be accommodated and protected within the law's relevant tests and mechanisms. A personal opinion is that the culturally recognised autonomy of art should invite the special individual treatment of art by law-makers so that any perceived 'transgressions' of acceptable moral boundaries by it in a societal context are understood to be taking place within the artistic order, ie within art's normal internal canons of operation. This level of juridical selective treatment, as we will see, is yet to be achieved under the Convention, despite the alleged parity of each cultural sub-set of society, including art, within the central tenets of cultural recognition in the present era, which, as indicated in this essay's first section, is sometimes philosophically known as (egalitarian) postmodernism.

In *Handyside v United Kingdom*,[50] the applicant was the publisher of *The Little Red Schoolbook*, a book for children that included a chapter with subsections giving advice on sexual issues. He was prosecuted under the Obscene Publications Act 1959 and was convicted. By 13 votes to one, the European Court of Human Rights held that the conviction was not a breach of freedom of speech under Article 10. In reaching this result, the Court followed its own collective reasoning in terms which permitted a certain margin of appreciation or discretion to a defendant state in its assessment of what the public interest requires. In *Handyside*,[51] which was later to be treated as a seminal case, the

[48] By way of reform, artistic freedom could be explicitly included in the rubric of Art10 of the Convention. I support this idea, not least because it might increase judicial vigilance in protecting artistic freedom. I nevertheless acknowledge that that might militate against certain counter-suggestions of others mentioned in the introduction of this essay that a priori classifications of speech could be undesirable. Substantively, the important thing to achieve is a fair position for art whereby it is afforded legal treatment compatible with its essential characteristics.

[49] See further, I Cherpillod, *L'Objet Du Droit D'Auteur* (Lausanne, CEDIDAC, 1985).

[50] *Handyside v United Kingdom* E Ct HRR A 24 (1976) 1 EHRR 737.

[51] ibid.

Court pronounced that it was not possible to find a uniform European conception of morals in the domestic law of the various Contracting States. It opined that the view taken by their respective laws of the requirements of morals varies from time to time and from place to place, especially in our era, which is characterised by a rapid and far-reaching evolution of opinions on the subject. By reason of their direct and continuous contact with the vital forces of their countries, state authorities are, the Court said, in principle in a better position than the international judge to give an opinion on the exact content of these requirements. Unwittingly, the Court thereby opened the floodgates for narrow, and even antiquated, 'moral' standards in individual states to dictate the outcome of cases taken to it. This matters crucially because the Court represents the summit of an 'appellate' route the applicant expressly follows as the very consequence of his/her perception of the unfairness and narrowness of alleged domestic 'moral' conceptions, in the hope that the Strasbourg Court will take, as its remit suggests, a broader, supra-national approach to 'morality', appropriately unconnected with more restrictive scruples.

In the next relevant case, *X and Y v United Kingdom*,[52] the European Commission of Human Rights held that the applicant's conviction for the controversial crime of blasphemy was not a breach of Article 10. In that case, a poem and accompanying illustration depicting the sexual activity of a contemporary male soldier with the body of the dead Christ was the source of the complaint. It was not suggested in Strasbourg that because the material had featured in *Gay News*, which was designed for an audience of homosexual and bisexual people, the imagery may not have proved as potentially 'depraving' (a very old-fashioned concept that assumes a sort of innocent purity in an audience of adults). In fact, the allegedly offensive material may not have reached anyone at all for whom it may have been allegedly harmful, given the limited number, as well as the specialised sexual orientation, of the readership. Also, the Commission did not entertain the idea that it might be highly relevant that the condemned work was art, which is not meant to be taken literally, but, rather, as an invitation to a reaction not dissimilar to that habitually pertaining to humour (art, like humour, having an oblique rather than a literal intention of operating, which should be rightly and properly considered, with due respect to its distinctive ontology, by any given adult audience).

In a subsequent consistent case, *Muller v Switzerland*,[53] the first applicant was an established artist who was convicted under a Swiss obscenity law for publishing obscene articles in an exhibition of contemporary art. The three paintings involved were said by the Court of First Instance to give free vein to licentiousness and even perversion, a circumstance morally offensive to the vast majority of the population. At the European Court of Human Rights, by a majority of six votes to one, it was held that the artist's conviction was not in

[52] *X and Y v United Kingdom* (1982) 28 DR 77.
[53] *Muller v Switzerland* E Ct HRR A 113 (1991) 13 EHRR 212.

breach of Article 10, a result which was said to be consistent with the *Handyside*[54] ruling. In its judgment, the Court opined:

> [C]onceptions of sexual morality have changed in recent years. Nevertheless, having inspected the original paintings, the court does not find unreasonable the view taken by the Swiss courts that those paintings, with their emphasis on sexuality in some of its crudest forms, were [likely] . . . to offend the sense of sexual propriety of persons of ordinary sensitivity.[55]

The Court followed its own approach on the 'margin of appreciation' points formulated in *Handyside*,[56] so the result it achieved is unsurprising. However, the paintings concerned had not given rise to a public outcry, and the press was unqualifiedly on the artist's side. It was also true that the applicant, Muller, had been able to exhibit similar works in other parts of Switzerland without legal or other interference. What in effect transpired in *Muller*,[57] then, was that the Court used an even more provincial standard of art appreciation and moral over-sensitivity than it did in *Handyside*.[58] By neglecting to impose its own moral standards based on its members' arguably greater life experience and greater maturity of vision as well as superior status, the Court could be said to be in dereliction of its duty. It could have considered, and then asserted, a meta-standard of artistic and moral insight consonant with its supra-national foundational role.

In the next case chronologically, *Choudhury v United Kingdom*,[59] the Commission held that the fact that blasphemy protected the feelings of Christians only was not a breach of Article 9 on freedom of religion. Although this body had only to deal with the Article 9 issue, the case had important possible implications for art and Article 10, since the object of the proceedings was creative writing. Regarding the substance of the case, if a Christian, as opposed to a Muslim, had sought injunctions against Salman Rushdie and his publishers claiming that they had promulgated in Rushdie's novel, *The Satanic Verses*, a blasphemous libel pertaining to Christianity, then the Commission might have been obliged to adjudicate on whether it was conceptually feasible that a work of fiction, of an imaginative not factual dimension, could ever be capable of conveying literal blasphemous thoughts on the part of its art-intentioned and art-expressive author. As it was, the case result was determined solely on the fact that English blasphemy law did not protect Islam.

A similar line of enquiry on the limits of artistic capability could have been posed in relation to the important case of *Otto-Preminger Institute v Austria*.[60] Here, the applicant Institute, which operated an 'art cinema' in Innsbruck,

[54] *Handyside* (n 50).
[55] *Muller* (n 53) [35].
[56] *Handyside* (n 50).
[57] *Muller* (n 53).
[58] *Handyside* (n 50).
[59] *Choudhury v United Kingdom* (1991) 12 *Human Rights Law Journal* 172.
[60] *Otto-Preminger Institute v Austria* E Ct HRR A 295-A (1994) 19 EHRR 34, E Ct HR.

wished to show a controversial film called *Das Liebeskinzil*. Institute members received a bulletin that was also posted elsewhere in Innsbruck stating that in the film 'trivial imagery and absurdities of the Christian creed are targeted in a caricatural (sic) mode and the relationship between religious beliefs and worldly mechanisms of oppression is investigated'.[61] Despite the film possessing this serious artistic remit, in relevant Austrian courts, culminating in a decision by the Innsbruck Court of Appeal, the seizure and forfeiture of the film was permitted on the basis that Mr Zingl, the Institute manager, had committed the criminal offence of 'disparaging religious doctrines'. When the case went before the European Court of Human Rights, its judgment followed the Austrian courts' enmity towards the film, which it said portrayed '[t]he God of the Jewish religion, the Christian religion, and the Islamic religion as an apparently senile old man . . .'[62] It continued:

> Other scenes show the Virgin Mary permitting an obscene story to be read to her . . . The adult Jesus Christ is portrayed as a low grade mental defective and in one scene is shown lasciously (sic) attempting to fondle and kiss her breasts, which she is shown as permitting.[63]

The film's merit as a work of art was adjudged by the Strasbourg Court not to outweigh its essential offensiveness to the local general public. This judgment was reached even though Article 17a of the Austrian Basic Law specifically protects freedom of artistic expression, and Article 10 of the European Convention on Human Rights protects freedom of expression generally, including artistic expression. The result of the case was surprising because the film was explicitly characterised by its promoters as an 'art film' which was to be shown in an 'art cinema'. As in the case of art in an art gallery, no-one of a sensitive religious persuasion, who did not wish to see it, was in any way obliged to go and see it. Moreover, the 'art film' was located within an appropriate 'art' environment so the intended artistic impact of it was contextually clear. The film can therefore be easily legally defended and morally vindicated: the film was far from an imposition on local people, and it was designed to be viewed with the appropriate psychic and aesthetic attitude appropriate to art so that ordinary factual offence simply could not result. It was also situated in a place specifically designated for art appreciation, and art appreciation only. In view of this profile, the film could not fairly be judged to be a public hazard or to be literally blasphemous; its clear remit was artistic stimulus not factual irreverence.

In a following consistent case, *Wingrove v United Kingdom*,[64] the European Court of Human Rights had to adjudicate on whether a video film by the applicant was blasphemous, as had been decided by local censoring bodies in the

[61] See further, SH Bailey, DJ Harris and BL Jones, *Civil Liberties: Cases and Materials*, 4th edn (London, Butterworths, 1995) 839.
[62] ibid.
[63] ibid.
[64] *Wingrove v United Kingdom* [1997] 24 EHRR 1.

United Kingdom. The film, *Visions of Ecstasy*, controversially portrayed the erotic experiences of a putative St Teresa of Avila with a figure representing Christ. The Court upheld the validity of national blasphemy measures and emphasised yet again the doctrine of the 'margin of appreciation' to avoid replacing the judgment of the national authorities with its own, pursuing the conveniently dismissive and politically expedient logic that the national organs were in a better position to judge local sentiments regarding blasphemy and related matters. The Court thereby again declined to do its highly important duty to render considered justice as a human rights supervisory court, electing instead to defer to the legal wisdom of national authorities despite the fact that the whole point of applying to the European Court of Human Rights is to have an issue actively resolved by that superior court.

What has happened more recently to the art versus morality dynamic that the above cases exemplify? Article 10 on freedom of expression is quite a commonly used provision, but it may be the case, firstly, that, in view of the decisions adumbrated above, artists as a particular class are now relatively reluctant to turn to the European Court of Human Rights because its record for supporting them is so poor. Secondly, it might also be the case that national laws are now more attuned to artistic processes, including their occasional, revolutionary moral excesses, and consequently there is a failure to prosecute. Thirdly, it might be the case that art in general has become less opposed to conventional morality in its various depictions. It is submitted, however, that it is premature to think that art's cultural autonomy is now recognised by a European-wide legal exemption from criminal investigation since such an exceptional category of immunity to legal process in this realm has not been officially pronounced upon, or even more informally registered by arts critics and the general public.[65]

In some written national constitutions, such as the German and Austrian models, art is explicitly deemed to be free.[66] The above case law analysis shows that even that sort of ultimate assurance does not necessarily guarantee a presumption in favour of artistic freedom when art traverses accepted conventional moral boundaries, even when it reaches the utmost stage of European legal proceedings in an endeavour to protect itself. Indeed, as indicated in my introduction, under the European Convention on Human Rights, not all aspects of freedom of expression have been adjudged by legal commentators to be equally valued. It is now generally accepted, arguably erroneously, outside the Court itself, that a three-tiered scheme of priority of freedoms of expression has been established by the Court: the most prized is freedom of political expression; this is followed in terms of importance by freedom of artistic expression; and freedom of commercial speech is said to be the least protected, or to put it another way, the most vulnerable freedom in the Court's practice. It is the author's con-

[65] However, very shortly after the abolition of blasphemy law was enforced in the UK, the British Board of Film Classification invited Nigel Wingrove to reapply for a licence to show his film *Visions of Ecstasy*.

[66] See further, E Barendt, *Freedom of Speech* (Oxford, Clarendon Press, 1985) 244–79.

viction that the correct order of such a hierarchy may have to be reappraised in view of the facts revealed by the above critique of the Court's habitual practice. That analysis shows, quite conclusively, the severe degree to which artists have been disadvantaged when appearing before an important international body which has, in practice, left artistic freedom on the bottom rung of its free speech priorities, despite being explicitly, and precisely, foundationally designed to protect rights such as those connected with honourable artistic enterprise.[67]

IV THE STRASBOURG COURT ON POLITICAL ART AND SEDITION: ARTICLE 10 ECHR

Karata v Turkey[68] is an unreported case that progressed to be heard before the European Court of Human Rights in 1999. Its importance to artistic freedom will become obvious in the following analysis of the case. Although this is an Article 10 case, its focus differs from that of previous cases mentioned above since it is concerns, in broad terms, the issue of sedition as opposed to morality. Nevertheless, it has serious implications for artistic freedom that extends throughout the ambit of Article 10, including matters connected with public morals and the literary and visual arts. It is highly significant not least because it is the first case before the Court that has resulted in a victory for artistic liberty over other societal concerns. It is strange, therefore, that such a key case in Strasbourg jurisprudence should remain unreported and little commented upon by jurists, even by those writing specifically in the realm of freedom of expression. My aim here, accordingly, is to fill that important lacuna in legal awareness and knowledge by closely scrutinising the freedom of expression aspects of the case.

The applicant in the case, a Turk of Kurdish origin, published a volume of poems in Istanbul called *The Song of a Rebellion*.[69] The Turkish National Security Court, which comprised three judges, including a military judge, found the applicant guilty of disseminating separatist propaganda, in the form of this collection of poetry, which was detrimental to the unity of the Turkish nation,

[67] See further, Richard A Posner, *How Judges Think* (Harvard, Harvard University Press, 2008). In this work, the author argues that judges are really closet political actors even when they mouth the rhetoric of legalism. By way of illustration, on 15 February 2010, the Strasbourg Court issued its judgment in the case of *Akdas v Turkey*, as yet officially unreported. The applicant in the case was the publisher of the 1999 Turkish translation of *The Eleven Thousand Rods* by Guillaume Apollinaire, which was first published in 1907. The book is an erotic novel containing graphic descriptions of sadomasochism and vampirism, inter alia. Condemned in Turkey on the grounds of immorality, the European Court of Human Rights nevertheless found in favour of the book on the basis of freedom of expression. However, this is an exceptional case because the book was specifically saved on the grounds of its status as a venerable classic comprising a valued part of Europe's literary heritage. There is no assurance given by the Court that the decision has any more general implications for contemporary literary works.

[68] *Karata* (n 10). It is submitted that this case should be officially reported in view of its seminal importance in the area of artistic freedom.

[69] ibid [10].

and sentenced him to a term of imprisonment.[70] In addition, it ordered the confiscation of the publication concerned.[71] The applicant complained that, inter alia, his conviction for the publication of the poems constituted a violation of his right to freedom of expression under Article 10 of the Convention.

Before the European Court of Human Rights, it was not in dispute that the applicant's conviction amounted to an interference with the exercise of his right to freedom of expression under Article 10(1), but the interference was closely examined under Article 10(2) to determine whether there had been a legitimate restriction of the applicant's right or whether Article 10 had been breached. The case is crucial because of its serious implications for artistic freedom. In summary, it was held by the Strasbourg Court that the relevant national law formed a sufficient basis for the applicant's conviction and the resultant interference with his right to freedom of expression was therefore 'prescribed by law'.[72] The sensitivity of the security situation in south-east Turkey, and the need for the authorities to be alert to acts capable of fuelling additional violence, meant that the measures taken against the applicant could be said to have been in the furtherance of the protection of national security and territorial integrity, and the prevention of disorder and crime. However, the applicant was a private individual who (allegedly) 'expressed his views' through poetry, which 'by definition' was addressed to a very small audience rather than through the mass media.[73] That fact limited the potential impact on 'national security', 'territorial integrity' and 'public order' to a substantial degree. Furthermore, the severity of the penalty imposed, and the persistence of the prosecution's efforts to secure his conviction, were disproportionate to the aims pursued and, accordingly, not 'necessary in a democratic society'. It clearly followed, the Court concluded, that there had been a violation of Article 10 of the Convention.[74]Looking at the complete history of the case in appropriate detail, an important fact during its course was that the poet consistently maintained that his artistic work 'in no way reflected [his] own opinions'.[75] In stating this, he was asserting the philosophical and cultural phenomenon of the autonomy of art.[76] The poems may have emanated *from* him without being *of* him, in the sense that his art did not encapsulate any personal cherished (political) ideals. The Turkish National Security Court, oblivious to the distinct ontology of art, concentrated on the poems' content alone as if it represented the poet's inartistic political views. To that Court, the poems in issue referred to a particular region of Turkey as 'Kurdistan' and glorified the insurrectionary movements in that region by identifying them with

[70] Turkey is notorious for its high level of human rights violations, a fact which, inter alia, currently precludes its membership of the European Union.
[71] *Karata* (n 10) [12].
[72] ibid [40].
[73] ibid [49].
[74] ibid [54].
[75] ibid, for eg, at [11].
[76] Art, including literary art, possesses its own unique internal canons of operation that signify its cultural and sociological independence which frequently goes unrecognised by the law.

the Kurds' fight for national independence. Accordingly, the Court concluded that the expression of praise for those movements apparent throughout the work amounted to separatist propaganda that was detrimental to the unity of the Turkish nation, and the territorial integrity of the Turkish state, and thus justified Mr Karata's conviction. At no stage was a concession made that his work was art. In his arguments before the European Court of Human Rights, the applicant stated that the real reason for his conviction was that he had referred to the Kurds and 'Kurdistan' in his poems; thus, his only crime, in the eyes of the authorities, was that he had not followed the official line.[77] He stressed that it had to be borne in mind that the work in issue was a volume of *poems*, in which the author had expressed thoughts, anger, feelings and joy through colourful language that contained some hyperbole. He therefore quite logically concluded that his book was first and foremost a literary work and should be treated as such.[78]

Prior to the Strasbourg Court's deliberations, the Commission propounded its own views. Surprisingly, this body supported, in the main, the approach of the Turkish authorities, and dwelt on the 'duties and responsibilities' mentioned in the second paragraph of Article 10, which, it said, made it important for people 'expressing an opinion'[79] on sensitive political issues to ensure that they did not condone unlawful political violence.[80] It therefore ignored the fact that an artist's creations do not embody his own political beliefs; rather, they embody artistic artifices. Shakespeare wrote of murder but was not a murderer, even though some of the characters in his plays were murderers.[81] This simple awareness of art's *modus operandi* eludes the Commission. Accordingly, when conceding some ground to art, and compatibly with its art-ignorance, it stated that freedom of expression included the right to engage in open discussion of difficult problems such as those with which Turkey was confronted, with a view to analysing, for example, the underlying causes of the situation, or expressing opinions on possible solutions, it omitted to say that an artist is not in any way obliged to constrict his or her art for such discursive, pacific, or anodyne ends.[82]

The Commission went on to admit that a special feature in the instant case was the fact that the applicant had chosen to express himself through poetry. However, it affirmed, even taking into account the prerogatives of a poet, that part of the applicant's poetry glorified armed rebellion against the Turkish state and martyrdom in that struggle. Read in context, it continued, some of the expressions used were capable of creating among readers the impression that the applicant was encouraging, or even calling for, an armed struggle against

[77] *Karata* (n 10) [45].

[78] ibid.

[79] Art does not project the opinions of its creators but, rather, reveals messages peculiar to the artistic canon, often of an imaginative dimension.

[80] *Karata* (n 10) [46].

[81] Not to recognise that protagonists in art have characters unlike those of their makers undermines the entire integrated culture known as fiction.

[82] Karel Appel, of the Cobra art movement, always claimed that art must shock.

the Turkish state and was supporting violence for separatist purposes. Consequently, in the Commission's judgment, the Turkish authorities had been entitled to consider that the poems were harmful to national security and public safety, and, in those circumstances, the applicant's conviction and the penalty imposed on him could reasonably be regarded as answering a pressing social need, and therefore be necessary in a democratic society.[83]

Adopting a contrasting stance, the majority of the Strasbourg Court had other ideas.[84] It pointed out that freedom of expression is one of the basic conditions necessary for an individual's self-fulfilment, and that Article 10 protects even offending, shocking and disturbing ideas in accordance with the demands of the pluralism, tolerance and broadmindedness, without which there cannot be a truly democratic society. The Court went on to acknowledge that the work in issue, through the frequent use of metaphors and pathos, was in part aggressive; but that, it averred, was a legitimate aspect of poetic endeavour. With respect to the latter, the Court's view was that Article 10 protects not only the substance of ideas and information expressed, but also the form in which they are conveyed, including through the culturally recognised medium of poetry. In this regard, the Court observed that in the instant case the poems had an obvious political dimension. Using colourful imagery, they expressed deep-rooted discontent with 'the lot' of the population of Kurdish origin in Turkey. With respect to that, the Court recalled that there is little scope under Article 10(2) for restrictions on political speech or on debate on matters of public interest. Furthermore, it continued, the limits of permissible criticism are wider with regard to the Government than in relation to a private citizen, or even a politician. In a democratic society, the actions or omissions of a government must be subject to the close scrutiny not only of the legislative and judicial authorities but also of public opinion. Moreover, it opined, the dominant position which the Turkish Government occupies makes it necessary for it to display restraint in resorting to criminal proceedings against alleged adversaries, particularly where other means are available for replying to their allegedly unjustified attacks and criticisms.

In defence of the Government's actions, the Court confirmed that it certainly remains open to the competent state authorities to adopt, in their capacity as guarantors of public order, measures, even of a criminal-law nature, intended to react appropriately and without excess to the remarks of alleged adversaries. Where such remarks constitute an incitement to violence against an individual or a public official or a sector of the population, the state authorities enjoy a wider margin of appreciation when examining the need for an interference with freedom of expression. Furthermore, the Court took into account the background to the case submitted to it, particularly problems linked to the prevention of terrorism, and, on that point, noted the Turkish authorities' concern

[83] *Karata* (n 10) [47].
[84] ibid [48]–[54].

about the dissemination of views which they consider might exacerbate the serious disturbances that have been going on in Turkey for some 15 years. Nevertheless, the Court ultimately supported the poet, emphasising that poems make a limited impact on society in general and are of an artistic nature. In the instant case, it made the refreshing observation that the applicant's poems were less a call to an uprising than an expression of deep distress in the face of a difficult political situation. Even in art-related cases, it is unusual for the court to engage in literary interpretation of this kind, which in a small way augurs well for both the literary and the visual arts in the future, should an art-based case like this arise again. As already recorded, Mr Karata's conviction was held to be disproportionate to the aims pursued, and accordingly unnecessary in a democratic society, resulting in a finding that there had been a violation of Article 10.[85] Such a conclusion is worth emphasising because it is such a dramatic and unusual triumph for art in this particularly important court.

In accordance with the majority of the Court, Judges Palm, Tulkens, Fishbach, Casadevall and Greve proffered a joint concurring opinion.[86] They reached the same result as the majority but by a different route, which involved what they called 'the more contextual approach'. In their opinion, the majority assessment of the Article 10 issue attached too much weight to the form of the words used in the publication and focused insufficient attention on the general context in which the words were used and their likely impact. This group affirmed that, undoubtedly, the language in question could, legitimately, be intemperate or even violent, and that it could include 'fighting' words (a term imported from American constitutional law). Interestingly, given that the subject matter of the action was poetry, this group of judges maintained that an approach that is more in keeping with the wide protection afforded to political speech in the Court's case law is to focus less on the inflammatory nature of the words employed and more on the different elements of the contextual setting in which the speech was uttered. Was the language intended to inflame, or incite to violence? Was there a real and genuine risk that it might actually do so? Was the author influential in society? Was significant media coverage given to the work? Were the words employed far away from the centre of violence or on its doorstep? This group considered that it is only by a careful examination of the context in which the offending words appear that one can draw a meaningful distinction between language that is shocking and offensive[87] and that which forfeits its right to tolerance in a democratic society. This approach, though conscientious and relevant to freedom of expression cases in general, does not focus

[85] ibid.

[86] The numbering of the paragraphs in the transcript of the case stops at the beginning of this opinion. In the present essay, I deal with this and further opinions in the case in the order in which they occur in the transcript.

[87] The whole point of the law of freedom of expression is that it ensures that one can legitimately say many things that are shocking and offensive. The UK Obscene Publications Act 1959, for example, permits those governed by it to say shocking and disgusting things, but not things that deprave and corrupt.

on artistic expression as a judicially and juridically recognised sub-category within freedom of expression. This means that this judicial group's approach is not specialised enough in the instant case. More pertinent to that case is the separate concurring opinion of Judge Bonello. He emphasised that if any invitation to use force is intellectualised, abstract, and removed in time and space from the foci of actual or impending violence, then the fundamental right to freedom of expression should generally prevail. Nevertheless, in the instant case, it is clear to this author that the applicant would strongly deny that his poetry could be seen as such an 'invitation', a term which misrepresents a central goal of art which is to use its role primarily symbolically and obliquely, not directly, party politically or literally.

Another illuminating source of alternative judicial approaches to freedom of artistic expression under the Convention is the joint, partly dissenting opinion of Judges Wildhaber, Pastor Ridruejo, Costa and Baka. This cohort of judges did not share the majority view that there had been a breach of Article 10. They found that the applicant's poems exhort readers to armed violence through the use of expressions that are particularly insulting (such as references to 'the whelps of the Ottoman whore'), alarmist ('genocide is being prepared') or a call to insurrection ('I invite you to . . . death'; 'blood shall be washed in blood'; and, inter alia, 'we will sacrifice our heads drunk on the fire of rebellion'). This judicial group also disagreed with the majority about the likely impact of poetry as a form, and criticised the majority's 'ivory tower approach'.[88] In the opinion of this judicial sub-group, metaphors and other stylistic devices did not remove a clear revolutionary message contained in a publication that was not just intended for a cultural elite. The general public, it ventured, would take the document at face value, and not, impliedly, artistically. This judicial approach denudes art of its own cultural identity and is reprehensible for its indifference to the parity of cultures in the contemporary, prevailing, equalising spirit of postmodernism. This group can also be criticised for ignoring the very essence of artistic freedom and for ignoring its profile as an increasingly discrete category within Convention freedom of expression law.

In a solitary dissenting opinion, Judge Golcuklu was guided by the majority of the European Commission of Human Rights who, by 26 votes to six, had concluded that there had been no breach of Article 10 in this case. The Commission had highlighted as reasons for its decision the poetry's exhortations to Kurds to promote warfare against Turkish authority and the wide margin of appreciation afforded to 'embattled' state authorities in such circumstances. These considerations, in its view, and subsequently Judge Golcuklu's, overwhelmed all the possible prerogatives of a poet. The Court's contrasting majority of 12 to five on the freedom of expression issue, in favour of the poet, reaffirms the gap that grew

[88] It is not only those in ivory towers who understand the value of artistic freedom, hence why its specific protection is provided for in several national constitutions, as well as more generally under the European Convention on Human Rights.

between the Commission and the Court in terms of mutual co-operation in deciding freedom of expression cases in particular. Usually, though, it was the Commission that upheld the freedom, and the Court that subsequently expunged it.

The *Karata*[89] case raises three important points that are art-related. First, it is evident from the majority judgment in particular that it is an advantage for controversial art before the Court to have a political dimension. This is compatible with the Court's informal but definitive decision to prize political expression as the expression most in need of protecting, a commitment that has infiltrated its case law *ab initio*. However, to protect artistic expression primarily because of its political content creates conceptual difficulties because 'art' is then equated with 'opinion'. The applicant in *Karata*[90] did not see his art as expressing his opinions and made that fact plain to the Court. However, it is expedient for an artist to concede that point if his or her art can achieve legal protection principally on account of its perceived political import. Whether that is a good thing is debatable because it is artistic form rather than content that should primarily ensure art's freedom. This approach alone protects art as a genus from public-moral or anti-seditious accusation because form alone pertains to art as a complete category. Nevertheless, 'political art' as a genre does exist,[91] but in a more specialised sense than the Court's generalised conception of it in *Karata*.[92]

[89] *Karata* (n 10).

[90] ibid.

[91] 'Political artists' include Joseph Beuys, Wolf Vostell, Dieter Hacker, KP Brehmer and Gustav Metzger. See further, M Archer, *Art Since 1960* (Thomas and Hudson, 2002) 109–41. Political art has featured more prominently in Strasbourg jurisprudence in a private law context than in the context of sedition. In the European Convention human rights case of *Vereinigung Bildender Kunstler v Austria* [2007] ECHR 68354/01, a provocative painting called *Apocalypse*, by Austrian artist Otto Muhl, constituted a collage of various public figures depicted naked in various sexually explicit positions. Among those figures was a Mr Meischberger, who was a member of the Austrian National Assembly. He brought proceedings under the Austrian Copyright Act claiming injury had been caused to his legitimate interests. The Vienna Commercial Court, the Court of Appeal and the Supreme Court all supported the grant of an injunction to him to curb the alleged debasement of him and his political activities. However, the European Court of Human Rights held, under Article 10 of the Convention, that the public exhibition of the painting contributed to a debate between the artist, the exhibitor and the public. It reflected, the Court said, the painter's conception of the interrelation between power and sexuality, and the Court then confirmed that freedom of expression extended to offending, shocking or disturbing works of art. The Court accordingly rejected the argument that the injunction protected public morals and emphasised that the painting constituted a satirical counter-attack against the FBO, of which Mr Meischberger was a former general secretary until 1995, and which had always strongly criticised Mr Muhl's work. The Court added that the painting only affected Mr Meischberger's political standing, which was public, and not his private life. A politician, the Court opined, should display a wider tolerance in respect to criticism of his public role. It must be noted, however, that the Court was finely divided in this case, the decision resulting in favour of the applicant by the slimmest majority. Although this case appears prima facie to reveal the Strasbourg Court explicitly upholding freedom of artistic expression, the rationale for its decision was mainly based on the importance of free political comment rather than on free artistic expression. For the Court, the fact that political comment was made by way of art was of relatively little consequence, although highlighted by myself here. Significantly, since the case was conducted on a private law basis, it should be carefully distinguished from the art and public morality cases which are central to this essay.

[92] *Karata* (n 10).

Secondly, it is important to notice that in *Karata*[93] the Court, and here we mean the majority, adopts a pragmatic approach as opposed to a concept-based one. In accordance with this emphasis on practicality, it is the fact of art's limited audience that finds favour with the Court as the key factor in its legal exoneration. This is not developed by the Court into a more thorough contextual analysis, to the chagrin of the group of judges who presented a joint concurring opinion in favour of a more developed practical analysis by the Court. However, in the area of freedom of artistic expression specifically, it is vital to adopt a conceptual approach because a practical approach can easily be applied to any human product and does not distinguish art on its own cultural terms. The quantity of the art and its associated range of dissemination is an extra-artistic consideration. What the regulation of art requires is that art's unique cultural identity and ontology single it out for special legal treatment. This necessitates an art-educated approach in the Court. The Court must register and understand art's peculiar societal recognition and status, and concomitant singular methods of operation, in order to render it true justice when it enters the legal arena. The Court could profitably engage in a detailed appreciation of the art process and demonstrate an informed awareness of art. To facilitate this end, the Court evidently needs cognitive or educational enhancement in this specialist field. This step would better protect art but also be of juridical use to the Court to better ensure the certainty and consistency of the legal judgment of art, because it would necessitate a more principled and detailed line of reasoning when art is the object of legal regulation.

Thirdly, the case of *Karata*[94] reveals that the sub-category of freedom of artistic expression within the general Convention framework of freedom of expression is seldom judicially recognised and utilised as a thematic development in the case law even though such a theme exists. This neglect of the development of artistic freedom specifically is perhaps exaggerated by the fact that there is no rule of precedent in Convention law. Judges are not conspicuously encouraged to be consistent in their decision-making and this might explain why, in *Karata*,[95] there is no recognition of the established line of art-law cases that could lead to a consistent legal doctrine in Strasbourg relating to the protection of artistic freedom specifically. This oversight in judicial practice does not encourage art-related legal issues to be streamlined usefully and productively; and, as a result of this lacuna in judicial attention, the theme of artistic freedom in the relevant case law is only judicially developed in a relatively arbitrary way. In the *Karata*[96] case, there are only the slightest allusions to other art-related cases under Article 10, and these allusions never emphasise the art connection between such cases. This jeopardises the necessary continuation of the doctrinal development of the

[93] ibid.
[94] ibid.
[95] ibid.
[96] ibid.

law relating to freedom of artistic expression,[97] and does not promote a principled approach to the perennial problems relating to art-related questions that are periodically raised in this legal arena.

V AMERICAN PROTECTION OF ARTISTIC FREEDOM UNDER THE FIRST AMENDMENT: A COMPARISON WITH THE STRASBOURG APPROACH

It is instructive at this juncture to succinctly compare the Strasbourg approach to the protection of artistic freedom with that adopted by the United States of America under the First Amendment to the US Constitution, not least to better appraise the Convention system's efficacy in guaranteeing freedom of expression through the medium of art. One commentator has said that '[A]rt and aesthetics are the forbidden fruit of the First Amendment. They enjoy a tortured history in the annals of constitutional law.' [98] As this quotation indicates, from the very first years of First Amendment jurisprudence, artistic expression has been frequently excluded from US constitutional protection. It is arguable that the roles of art may have seemed trivial when compared to freedom from being in need, freedom from inequality, freedom of political participation, and freedom of religion, which were fundamental liberties in which free speech law was initially grounded in accordance with principles that were oriented around very basic and practical needs. The evocative, affective quality and associated transformative power of art were originally considered to be essentially private matters, with little public significance. They were also less important and formative than social and political collective goals, which were conspicuous features of the public realm, and necessary for the evolving construction of an incipient nation. These factors are reinforced by the fact that subjective aesthetic judgement tends to be in direct opposition conceptually to the more objective tools for political development of cognition and rationale. Any perceived importance in art is also hampered by the lack of a clear definition[99] of what it is, which tends to suggest that it is inherently vague, and of little tangible use. An additional reason for the US Supreme Court's tentative approach to artistic freedom emerges from the ontological consideration that art may overlap with obscenity in quite a core, rather than purely incidental, way. This is compounded by the truism that, unlike the Court, art is generally at least indifferent to the social requirements of public decency.[100]

[97] The case of *Karata* has been consistently followed by that of *Alinak vTurkey*, a judgment of 29 March 2005 (officially unreported). In that case, the applicant had written a novel, using fictional characters, which criticised the hostility by Turkish security forces against residents of an actual village. The Turkish security forces seized the book. The Strasbourg Court held that this action was unlawful because it was a disproportionate reaction to the book. The legal context was again sedition-related.

[98] Randall P Bezanson, *Art and Freedom of Speech* (University of Illinois Press, 2009) 1.

[99] See further, Amy M Adler, 'The Folly of Defining Art' in M Shapiro, *The New Gatekeepers: Emerging Challenges to Free Expression in the Arts* (Columbia University Arts Journalism Program, 2004).

[100] See further, Amy M Adler, 'What's Left?: Hate Speech, Pornography, and the Problem for Artistic Expression' (1996) *California Law Review* 1.

It is an orthodox observation that to qualify for full protection under the American free speech guarantee, even art should aim to do some or all of the following: contribute to the pursuit of truth, serve individual freedom, assist political realisation, and enhance the process of self-governance. These imperatives are in accordance with the traditional justifications for free speech policy in the USA. They rest on reason. This has led the Supreme Court to exclude obscenity from First Amendment protection because it is inimical to reasonable thinking, as embodied in the above-mentioned free speech goals, potentially generating harm and/or illegality through its apparently arbitrary effects that are independent of rationale. This is oblivious and antithetical to, inter alia, the poet Shelley's well-known expert judgment, repeated by many, that even a sensual, ethically controversial artistic imagination is in fact ultimately a great instrument of moral good.[101]

Broadly comparable to the method systematised by the European Court of Human Rights, the US Supreme Court's modern jurisprudence, particularly regarding freedom of expression, is founded upon a scheme of general categories. As in Strasbourg, the highest and most protected category is political speech. However, a second category in the American system, unlike under the Convention, is a less strenuously protected category of 'indecent' speech (as opposed to obscenity). Indecent speech is entitled to constitutional protection provided that it involves expressive and communicative content (as is likely to be the case with material that might be regarded as art). Such speech does not tend to overlap with political speech; instead, it involves issues such as sex and violence. But if indecent speech uncharacteristically does impinge upon politics, it is usually fully protected. On such rare occasions, it may be an aspect of hate speech that is politically related; and sometimes political speech can be inappropriate for the audience to which it is addressed, such as children, which again taints it with the stigma of indecency. Although other indecent speech is also habitually protected under the First Amendment, it is generally considered to be of comparatively low value, warranting only modest protection. Further down the scale, some types of expression simply do not qualify for First Amendment protection at all. A residual, additional general category of expression recognised in American free speech law is accordingly that which is deemed to fall outside the ambit of constitutional free speech protection. This form of expression includes words that produce an immediate violent response ('fighting words') and obscenity. Obscenity is excluded from the protection of the First Amendment because it comprises depictions of sexual conduct that offend community values, appeal to the prurient interest, and, where art is in issue, lack serious artistic value. This formula is the culmination of case law developments reviewed below. Government can prohibit or regulate such speech freely, as if it were equivalent to mere conduct.

[101] Bezanson (n 98) 258.

With respect to the art emphasis in this essay, it is interesting and important to note that, under US law, although art might be regarded as pornographic or obscene, this does not mean that the law will automatically categorise it as such. Sometimes, art is explicitly excluded from the scope of obscenity provisions. For example, a legal definition of what is obscene may be used to this end. In the leading and seminal case of *Roth v US*,[102] the Supreme Court employed the test that for something to be obscene, and thus excluded from free speech protection, it had to be 'utterly without redeeming social value'. This provided a much higher level of protection for art than is afforded under the European Convention on Human Rights. As we saw earlier in this essay, under the Convention artistic freedom is in practice seriously undermined in favour of the protection of morality when those two factors are in opposition. The American *Roth*[103] test, on the other hand, could be interpreted very broadly as protecting all art that had a claim to artistic merit, however tenuous. This test's practical effect was that art only lost its expressive freedom if it provided absolutely no social value, which was very difficult to prove. However, in the later, equally important case of *Miller v California*,[104] this standard was dramatically altered because the Supreme Court considered that it placed a burden on the prosecution that was virtually impossible to discharge. Instead, a new test was established by which a work could be held to be obscene if it lacked 'serious artistic value'. According to this new standard, which is still extant, even if a work has some artistic merit, and concomitantly, a degree of social value, it can nevertheless be deemed to be obscene if that merit is judged to be insufficiently serious.

The European Convention on Human Rights permits Contracting States, under the margin of appreciation doctrine, virtually unlimited discretion to censor artwork that they consider infringes the protection of morality in any given local area within the national jurisdiction. In US law, there is a comparable restrictive legal mechanism as a result of *Miller*,[105] where it was decided that state law does not permit the jury to assess any work by reference to national standards (as opposed to local ones) because such reference might involve imposing material on a conservative community that is only found tolerable in more permissive districts. Local standards therefore prevail and can involve the application of unduly narrow and conservative parochial morality to morally controversial art endeavours, which seems inappropriate given art's highly topical, avant-garde ontology and role. The *Miller*[106] approach is also potentially unfair to the artistically expressive in a more significant way, ie because of the ambiguity which is inherent in the relative criterion of 'seriousness' in the 'serious artistic value' test, which is highly susceptible to subjective interpretation, and which can lead to legal inconsistency. However, this difficulty for artists in

[102] *Roth v US* 354 US 476 (1957).
[103] ibid.
[104] *Miller v California* 413 US 15 (1973).
[105] ibid.
[106] ibid.

the USA is countered somewhat by the First Amendment's solemn commitment to forbidding laws that abridge freedom of speech, which does to some extent restrict any opportunity for unduly broad discretion here by loading the balance in favour of the artwork under examination by the strong presumption of liberty. The Strasbourg system, in contrast, provides no such dominant and emblematic constitutional safeguard.[107] In Article 10(2) of the Convention, explicit mention is made of a host of legitimate restrictions that Contracting States can put on free speech. Moreover, the US Supreme Court habitually only targets hard-core pictorial pornography as 'obscene' and therefore falling outside the First Amendment's strong protection of free speech. Pornography laws in the USA are also usually interpreted very restrictively so that works of art of even poor quality are in practice unsuppressed, which suggests that the liberalising effect of the *Roth*[108] test has endured at a grass-roots level despite the more censorious, later standard emergent from *Miller*.[109]

More generally, if the premises of the free speech doctrine are centred on the notion of a rational speaker with a cognitive message, then art may require a different set of constitutional rules to be applied to it than those of the First Amendment because art is an instrument through which new meanings and modes of perception can be communicated in at least a non-rational way, and sometimes in an unanticipated and uncontrolled way. An artist should not be blamed for executing the essential ingredients of artistic creativity since this would be inherently paradoxical, unless we are intent on condemning artistic creativity *in toto* as a standard juridical exercise. If art is a commodity that is ontologically separate from speech,[110] then it is clearly arguable that, as a different form of valued expressivity, the First Amendment (or an equivalent constitutional rule) should confer on art an absolute privilege to go uncensored because of its distinct qualities that emerge from its independent cultural order. This suggestion is predicated not on considerations of the intrinsic superiority of the artistic order but on the proposition that art is inherently a completely different genre of communication from literal speech. With respect to the idea of artistic obscenity (which itself may seem at least oxymoronic as a notion), what is legally ignored is that 'sexual' art is not literally obscene but simply a necessarily sensuous *de novo* representation of sexual images in accordance with the unique cultural canon of its implicit workings. The problems relating to obscenity and art, notably their inter-relation, are ones that have often challenged the US Supreme Court, and it may well be that the *Miller*[111] formula is a compromise that was a legal inevitability given the complexities involved, especially for

[107] See further, S Douglas-Scott, 'The Hatefulness of Protected Speech: A Comparison of the European and American Approaches' (1999) *William and Mary Bill of Rights Review*. See also, more generally, *Law after Modernity* (Oxford, Hart Publishing, 2013).

[108] *Roth* (n 102).

[109] *Miller* (n 104).

[110] See further, Edward J Eberle, 'Art as Speech' (2007–08) 11 *University of Pennsylvania Journal of Law and Social Change* 1.

[111] *Miller* (n 104).

a tribunal unspecialised in art matters. As suggested above, an answer for American law may be to redirect morally controversial art onto a new (presumably legal) route that protects it alone from legal condemnation in all instances of alleged obscenity. This may be preferable to trying to formulate a legal test involving criteria for artistic recognition and approbation (designating a work as 'non-obscene') which has been found in the USA to be conceptually (and regularly) unsuccessful. This approach does not solve the perennial problem of 'what is art?' but it respects the autonomy that postmodernism confers on art as a culturally recognised, unique sphere, within a social structure now containing a plurality of equal cultures. Moreover, in response to the *Miller*[112] test specifically, it is arguably the work of commercial pornographers, not sexually-related artistic imagery, that is gauged to appeal to the prurient interest, and to, perhaps inadvertently, offend community values with its superficial unseriousness.

The legal situation in the USA in regards to artistic freedom is far from as advantageous as that in Canada, where the scope of protection is much broader, and where, in one leading case,[113] even hard-core pornography without artistic merit, and without any other redeeming qualities, was held by the Supreme Court to be protectable as free speech (following the reasoning that even such pornography has expressive content and cannot be equated with mere conduct). It is therefore clearly arguable, by analogy with the Canadian Supreme Court's stated position,[114] which was not an aberration, that in any jurisdiction, a case involving legal consideration of the fact that the material is art should protect any work that can reasonably be considered to be art. It is also submitted that the question whether something is art should always be interpreted generously so as to be in accordance with the forward-thinking, and aptly postmodern, Canadian approach. In the light of this consideration, the contrasting absence of a legal mechanism to negate obscenity by a fresh consideration of artistic character or relevance at the supervisory level under the Convention is clearly an indictment of the Strasbourg system's illiberal approach to morally controversial art. The American approach, at least at a doctrinal level, is also vulnerable to criticism when compared to Canadian law's more truly contemporary and progressive stance because the Canadian approach avoids imposing an unpredictable qualitative standard on morally challenging art (such as America's 'serious artistic value' test). The Canadian Charter of Rights and Freedoms is an entrenched domestic mechanism for human rights protection and its workings are not inhibited by the international and political considerations that afflict the Strasbourg Convention (and which arguably necessitate attenuating, in practice, that Convention's ultimate authority in free speech and other rights areas by the use of the margin of the appreciation doctrine). In addition, the Canadian Charter is a more flexible instrument than the US Bill of Rights, not

[112] ibid.
[113] *R v Butler* [1992] 1 SCR 452.
[114] ibid.

least because it is less absolutist, achieving a more ameliorative justice by orchestrating a delicate balance between state and individual interests rather than focusing almost exclusively on the preservation of individuals' freedoms. Under the First Amendment, free speech is often protected to the point of sacrificing what can be seen as very legitimate countervailing interests, such as a right to freedom from intimidation in the context of hate speech. Having said this, whereas in the USA free speech per se is treated as a value whose protection is of paramount importance, the specific protection there of freedom of *artistic* expression is more limited, and less frequently emphasised. The Strasbourg Convention makes no reference to culture or to artistic freedom specifically in its treaty rubric, and that may indicate to some degree why the Strasbourg Court's jurisprudence is also not fundamentally geared to treating artistic freedom seriously. It is evident, by way of conclusion to this necessarily concise comparative analysis, that art's freedom appears to be guarded most vigilantly not in the USA or in Strasbourg but, rather, in Canada.

VI GENERAL CONCLUSIONS

The protection of artistic freedom is, sadly, not a major concern of the Strasbourg system, and the Convention in its practical working lacks a detailed concern for culture as a specific entity in comparison to other international human rights legal instruments.[115] The terms of Article 10 of the Convention are set out to protect freedom of expression in general without explicitly including a special place for the protection of the arts when they are faced with the charge of immorality. This means that the protection of artistic freedom is only implicitly protected under Article 10 and has become only a loose theme in the related case law rather than a persistently judicially recognised separate category of concern. This has led to the unfortunate situation where artistic freedom has been jeopardised by the Strasbourg Court's inappropriate over-protection of morals, when art and morality have conflicted in Strasbourg jurisprudence. The undesirable and shocking result is that the interests of contemporary artistic freedom have been defeated in every morality-oriented case under the Convention. The leading case of *Karata*[116] has introduced for the first time a victory for the arts, but this was in the context of a different, if related, subject area.[117] That case nevertheless shows that any demonstrably political aspect of an artwork will improve the likelihood of its success in Strasbourg in any future Article 10-based proceedings. This is because the Strasbourg Court chooses to safeguard political expression above other forms of expression. However, artistic freedom should be protected on its own terms rather

[115] The Universal Declaration of Human Rights, the International Covenant on Civil and Political Rights, the International Covenant on Economic, Social and Cultural Rights, the African Charter on Human and Peoples' Rights, and the American Convention on Human Rights, all include specific provisions on culture.

[116] *Karata* (n 10).

[117] The *Karata* case has been followed in the same subject area by that of *Alinak*. See n 97.

than having to appeal politically to the Court, as political content or connotation comprises only one incidental attribute of art as a cultural phenomenon. Artistic freedom is a well-recognised liberty, in society if not in law, that should be formally protected as a distinctive concern under Article 10 in accordance with its unique, usually esteemed, cultural significance. In any conflict with abstract conceptualisations about a hypothetical, rather than real, cohesive social morality, art should, as a palpable entity, prevail, hence this author's proposed reform of the legal approach to the 'art versus morality' problematic at the end of the first main part of this essay. In addition, as also elaborated on above, the author has severe doubts about the current fairness of the operation of the margin of appreciation doctrine in relation to artistic freedom. Finally at this juncture, but importantly, the indifference and even hostility displayed towards controversial artistic endeavour in Strasbourg jurisprudence undermines the image and reality of artistic life as a worthy cultural activity. The Strasbourg Court is quite unaware that art which seems to gratuitously contravene standards of accepted morality actually does so for a reason, which is to test the continuing validity of that morality. This critical-moral role is one that the Court tends to overlook, to the severe detriment of its own, as well as art's, perceived integrity.

Other controversial trends in the European Court of Human Rights are discernible in the context with which we are dealing. The Court displays a preference for protecting religion above the protection of art even though art is now participated in, actively and passively, by more individuals than organised religion. Moreover, the priorities of the Court have not altered over time which is incompatible with the Convention's living instrument doctrine that is meant to ensure that the Convention rights are protected according to the prevailing societal trends and consciousness in the states it governs; and art, in particular, is at the cutting-edge of societal development. In addition, since it is in urban areas that new moral approaches tend to find the most exposure, it is surprising that the living instrument doctrine permits the moral outlooks of rural areas to govern art-related moral matters, associated as such areas can be with narrow, parochial, frequently demoded mores. It is also an historical fact that the Commission and the Court often disagreed within this subject area, with the Commission being historically the better protector of artistic freedom, which is juridically and institutionally incongruous. Even though the Court's jurisdiction is supervisory, in the central era under examination it was its own job, not the Commission's, to be the final decision-maker and upholder of rights at this supra-national level, especially relating to important justiciable matters relating to artistic rights protection. One can more generally disapprove of the Court's anti-rights stance and wrong decision-making in the area of freedom of artistic expression by a close analysis of its reasoning (such as in the close critiques which this text has provided).

As a result of the *Karata*[118] judgment, we also become apprised of the fact that arguments based on sedition are less successful before the Court when

[118] *Karata* (n 10).

opposed to artistic interests than are those respecting morality, despite the fact that sedition is a more obviously real, objective threat to social welfare and cohesion than any more gradual, subjectively-determined infiltrations of 'immorality', that arguably present only an alleged danger to the notional moral fabric of society. It is also apparent that the judges who sit in the Strasbourg Court tend to lack appropriate expertise regarding the complexity and delicacy of the issues before them when art confronts its more pervasive conventional opponent in the form of establishment morality. There is little in any Strasbourg judgment on artistic freedom that even approximates to the level of detailed scrutiny that Part II of this essay reveals is required of judges in this area. Salient art issues are generally ignored by the Court, even though it purports to uphold the principle of effectiveness, a principle it cannot observe from the position of art-ignorance. A fortiori, there is no judicial recognition in the Court that art possesses its own cultural system that some even see as hermetically autonomous. Most people know the expression 'artistic licence', and it is also commonly acknowledged that art is not to be taken literally, but rather appreciated within the canons of its own workings including its symbolic, fictive dimension. The Court could easily be equipped with artistic knowledge but appears to prefer the imposition of regulation to the acquisition of information even when the latter is indispensable for the former. Moreover, the Court displays a strangely confused value system. As mentioned earlier, *Karata*[119] demonstrates that if art has a political content its right to exist is strengthened. This appears to legitimise 'political' art, and other art is disfavoured: in the Court's eyes, 'political' art has an extra, crucial dimension which saves it legally. However, art is firstly artistic, and only secondarily of any political import: the Court should protect art as a genre; just because one *oeuvre* is incidentally 'political' does not elevate it in artistic terms since it is arguable that all art is in principle worthy of protection irrespective of form or detail. By rescuing from censure only 'political' art, moreover, the Strasbourg Court is also diminishing the general category of protection to the disadvantage of 'non-political' art. The artistic nature of the expression should be enough in itself to guarantee its protection, despite whatever sub-categories the Strasbourg judges erroneously may favour.

Other problems with the Strasbourg Court's approach to allegedly immoral art include those connected with the Court's lack of differentiation between art and pornography. In Part II of this essay, it was demonstrated that a distinction between these two phenomena can be drawn, albeit with difficulty. The Court appears to be indifferent to the importance of such a division practically, as well as (merely) conceptually. This gives one no confidence in the seriousness of its intentions in this field. In addition, the Court pays little regard to the environmental or purely physical context of the art before it. One can normally assume that if a work is in an art gallery, its creator and the gallery curators obviously consider it to be of artistic significance. Similarly, if the art is shown in an 'art

[119] ibid.

cinema', it can be assumed to be art if no other considerations suggest otherwise. If the art is in the form of a video, it can be presumed that someone has to acquire the video first, so no-one could come across its controversial or other artistic content merely accidentally. The Court also usually fails to address the highly pertinent related fact that the art is not generally foisted on an unwelcome audience: the art-interested habitually have to make an effort to access art (in a gallery, for example); it is not crudely forced upon them. Moreover, the Court should take cognisance of the reality that any possible offence given by art these days is now negligible in comparison to the exotic range of contemporary abject, hard-core, meritless pornography freely available on the Internet.

The discerning intellectual appreciation of art is obviously pivotal to art mechanisms, and, perhaps less obviously, to the credibility of art law. The art experience is misplaced in the midst of relative art-ignorance. This is unfortunate because the Strasbourg Court could be a pioneer when it comes to art appreciation and could support art's defenders. The Court could also be usefully pedagogical, as a refreshing complement to, or replacement for, its sometimes outmoded, restrictive approach. If the Court thinks that certain sexually graphic artwork is unsuitable for children, it should recommend placing a warning to this effect in the gallery where the art is exhibited, and it should explain its decision to so recommend. If the Court feels that certain art aimed at adults is morally controversial, it should give adequate reasons why it feels that way (beyond its customary censorious reflex to condemn it outright in a misplaced deference to local moral standards). In a democracy, and particularly in an international judicial forum that prides itself on its democratic processes, art must be judicially considered with gravity as the important cultural phenomenon it is, not simply dismissed as an unwanted interference with untutored, raw, purely emotional reactions. An expensive and time-consuming application to the Strasbourg system is deserving of more judicial time than that taken by in effect just rubber-stamping a prior national authority decision. Justice in Strasbourg should be seen to be done at an appropriately higher level than that in the Contracting States. This change must be implemented quickly and effectively so that artistic expression can rise from its position of inferiority to even the least creditable commercial speech in the practice of the Strasbourg Court. To leave things as they are could be perceived to be a mistake of some magnitude, and highly detrimental to the legitimate interests of artists, who form an important and substantial cultural sector of European society.

11

Controversial Art and the Legal Enforcement of Morality in England

I INTRODUCTION

THE RADICALISATION OF art's typical content in the current era has threatened to jeopardise attempts within our public law to ensure that a certain, if qualitatively unspecified, standard of public morality is efficiently enforced for the moral protection of English contemporary society. This is not least because there has been a recurrent, recent trend in art in England towards extreme presentations, sometimes castigated as immodest, immoral or offensive, that have occasionally disturbed the general public. These have great relevance for constitutional law in particular. Exponents of such uncompromising art include Helen Chadwick, Tracey Emin, Tierney Gearon, Marcus Harvey, Damien Hirst, Chris Ofili, Marc Quinn, Andres Serrano, and Nigel Wingrove. Typically, such art involves the use of human and animal excrement, hard-core sexual imagery, ambiguous photographs of naked children, dissected animals, controversial depictions of disability, sensationalist portraits of heinous criminals, and irreverent portrayals of sacred figures. It is arguable that the public should be protected from exposure to such very challenging art, that appears to confront defiantly long-held, cherished, accepted moral standards; and, indeed, traditionally, the criminal law has sought to ensure such protection. However, artistic objectives are fresh and dynamic, assisting human pleasure and development, which is arguably a significant cultural role. The principal aim of this article, consequently, is to appraise the continuing validity of the morally paternalistic stance adopted by the law regarding artistic impact and concomitant social progress. To this end, it examines the relationship between, on the one hand, public-moral laws, notably innovative laws proscribing extreme and violent pornography, and, on the other, ethically contentious, avant-garde art, which, explicitly or implicitly, adopts a specialised, critical-moral[1] position

[1] In the context of the present analysis, art can be said to have a critical-moral function in the sense that it challenges society's accepted moral thinking so that established social morality develops rather than stagnates. Philosophers have frequently characterised artists as the 'antennae' of society, picking up and then developing ideas that are ahead of their time. Aspects of this, and other art law-related themes, are examined in a precursor of this essay, namely the author's article 'Very Challenging Art and the Contemporary Enforcement of Morality in England'. This appears in 2013

in relation to more conventional societal mores. It is, therefore, a study of an interface of pivotal importance for art, art-appreciative audiences, the public and the law.

Exposing art to criminal prosecution puts art in a legal context that is alien to it. It is often denuded here of its artistic status and prosecuted instead not as purely symbolic but as literal fact. It is this deaestheticisation that is key to condemning art as immoral because it is arguable that art cannot be harmful at any level if it is viewed, according to its own canons of operation, appropriately meditatively and aesthetically. Nevertheless, the practical reality is that the criminal law habitually tries to prevent the risk of harm, even of a purely psychic nature, by using obscenity and related laws. It does this in a general way that rarely respects art's autonomy[2] of cultural operation. But before fully analysing the resultant tension between artistic freedom and its censure by law in several instances, it is apt to briefly outline philosophical insights which illuminate the nature of the problematic.

In his *Essay on Liberty*, first published in 1859, John Stuart Mill wrote:

> The object of this Essay is to assert one very simple principle, as entitled to govern absolutely the dealings of society with the individual in the way of compulsion and control, whether the means used be physical force in the form of legal penalties, or the moral coercion of public opinion. That principle is, that the sole end for which mankind are warranted, individually or collectively, in interfering with the liberty of action of any of their number, is self-protection. That the only purpose for which power can be rightfully exercised over any member of a civilised community, against his will, is to prevent harm to others. His own good, either physical or moral is not a sufficient warrant.[3]

Thus, Mill argues that society has no 'right' to enforce its moral perceptions where their violation would not entail objectively perceptible 'harm' to others. In the absence of 'harm', it can be inferred that Mill is of the belief that diversity is a very positive factor in society and that it is dangerously threatened by moral repression. Mill advances his harm principle as an oriflamme of individual liberty, but it is clearly arguable that he leaves several questions unresolved, such as what exactly comprises harm and how such harm is to be proven.

According to Rolf Sartorious,[4] on the one hand, legal moralists, such as James Fitzjames Stephen, and, subsequently, Lord Patrick Devlin, and libertarians like John Stuart Mill, followed by HLA Hart, on the other, actually agree that

in the law journal *Art, Antiquity and Law* but, at the time of writing, the publishing editor has not yet decided in which precise issue it will be placed.

[2] Theodor Adorno contends that it is easy to imagine that art's autonomous realm has nothing in common with the external world other than borrowed elements that have entered into a fully changed context. See further, Theodor Adorno, *Aesthetic Theory* (London, The Athlone Press, 1999) 5.

[3] See further, JS Mill, *On Liberty*, edited by G Himmelfarb (Harmondsworth, Penguin, 1974).

[4] See further, Noel B Reynolds, 'The Enforcement of Morals and the Rule of Law' (1977) 11 *Georgia Law Review* 1325. The famous primary sources of Stephen, Devlin, Mill and Hart comprise, respectively, *Liberty, Equality and Fraternity* (New York, Holt and Williams, 1857); *The Enforcement of Morals* (Oxford, Oxford University Press, 1965); *On Liberty* (London, Longman, Roberts and Green, 1859); and *The Concept of Law* (1961).

individuals and communities are entitled to prevent what they believe to be potentially harmful.[5] The principal disagreement, he argues, arises when one asks what actually comprises 'harm',[6] which is a philosophically and practically unresolved question. The basic position of Mill is that when the state interferes with personal conduct it often interferes unjustifiably. According to Mill, only if such conduct risks harm to others can any such interference be legitimate. Devlin's legal moralism, on the other hand, justifies the enforcement of morality to preclude a different type of more abstracted and hypothetical harm based on protecting society from disintegration. His emphasis on society's desirable solidity of integration rather than, for example, individual liberty of expression, bodes ill for the artist, who is frequently characterised as a social non-conformist.[7] Mill's theory would entail the non-interference of society with a person's fulfilment in creating art, but a crucial issue would remain as to whether morally controversial art can actually 'harm' others when they are exposed to it, in which case Mill would have to accede to a non-absolute[8] artistic freedom. However, one might pose the question whether, if art is ideologically autonomous and teleologically neutral, it should ever be understood to strike the morals of individuals or society in a literally harmful way. The harm that Devlin might preclude in this context would be the insidious injury of moral corruption, even if this is an unproven effect of art, and, some argue, pornography. If Mill's position would permit societal interference to prevent psychological harm resultant from the art experience, this could be countered by the argument that art does not wield harm but is an invitation to soberly consider art's messages, a process to be met with a calm rather than emotive reaction, and subsequent intellectual digestion.[9] Unfortunately, such an analysis of art appreciation and its possible harmfulness

[5] There are different degrees of harm, and any alleged harm caused by art cannot be equated, in terms of severity, with, for example, physical injury.

[6] Joel Feinberg argues persuasively, for example, that the law should not treat offence as if it were as serious as harm. The principal objection to 'immoral' artistic expression is that it might damage others' moral probity. A secondary objection is that such expression might insult others or deride their religion. See further, J Feinberg, *The Moral Limits of the Criminal Law: Offense to Others* (New York, Oxford University Press, 1985).

[7] According to Jean Duvignaud, the artist is by nature a radically unconventional person, considered to live on an altogether higher plane of reality, alien to the everyday life of society, which attempts to justify his apparent peculiarities by attributing them to an 'essence'. See further, Jean Duvignaud, *The Sociology of Art* (London, Paladin, 1972) 24.

[8] It is too idealistic to envisage a society in which artists are completely free from legal or other societal constraint. Under Art 10 of the European Convention on Human Rights (ECHR), for example, where artistic expression is not differentiated from other modes of expression, the right to freedom of expression is qualified by the competing interests of others. Typically, free speech can be legitimately restricted when it defames others, disturbs public morals when obscene, or is unconscionably racist. However, when one examines the cases relating specifically to contemporary artistic freedom, the European Court of Human Rights can be rightly criticised for unduly favouring public-moral interests over artistic liberty to the extent that the latter is wholly defeated when a countervailing moral priority features in a given case. This is surprising and highly ironic when the key objective of the ECHR is precisely to support rights and freedoms. See further, Paul Kearns, 'Art's Demise in the European Court of Human Rights' (2007) XII *Art, Antiquity and Law* 2, 137–69.

[9] See further, Arthur R Howell, *The Meaning and Purpose of Art* (Sussex, England, The Ditchling Press Ltd, 1957) Ch 5.

is a conundrum rarely judicially considered philosophically in the context of the criminal law's enforcement of morality.[10]

II CONSTITUTIONAL CONSIDERATIONS AND THE NATURE OF ART AND LAW

Within the United Kingdom's unwritten constitution, there has always been provision for the enforcement of morals, largely as a result of the Christian foundations of our law, notably the criminal law. Historically, there was also the purported legal protection of civil liberties, including freedom of artistic expression, although such protection was precariously residual, and arguably quite ineffective, especially when freedoms conflicted with the law's firmly established moral positions. This weak position of liberties was because of the then negative form of rights protection: a liberty only amounted to the citizen being able to do all that the law did not forbid him or her to do. However, with the advent of the Human Rights Act 1998,[11] which came into force on 2 October 2000, positive rights became available, which can be activated by individuals to commence legal actions, and this development naturally strengthens traditional liberties, not least because they are now guaranteed by quasi-constitutional[12] legislation. The balancing of moral concerns with the right to freedom of expression has also become more juridically explicit, and it appears that the enforcement of a collective sense of morality is now legally more attenuated when pitched against free speech, for sociological as well as constitutional reasons. The choices available for the exercise of free speech, and its wider promulgation, have been increased by the Internet, for example; and the era we now inhabit, known culturally as postmodernism,[13] provides for the gradual lessening of sociologically-endemic native religious values in favour of relativism. This is enhanced by the increasing

[10] It is not asking much for the law to acknowledge how art simply cannot 'harm' morality (whatever 'morality' as a corporate notion precisely connotes) when art is received in an apposite way according to the rules of art. Artists should not be condemned when their art is misperceived since this misperception is due to the fault or ignorance of the perceiver. The canons of art appreciation on the correct perception of art are specified clearly in virtually every book on art theory.

[11] The Human Rights Act 1998 is usually said to 'incorporate' most of the provisions of the ECHR into UK domestic law, although legal commentators sometimes disagree as to the absolute precision of this formulation. The Act is said by some political analysts to be in jeopardy because the Prime Minister, David Cameron, seems keen to revoke it, and replace it with an exclusively national bill of rights. However, this would be extremely difficult to do in practice because, through judicial application and interpretation, the provisions of the Act have infused the whole common law, making it impossible to extricate its now fundamental presence and influence.

[12] The UK has an unwritten constitution, but the Human Rights Act 1998 could be a precursor of a written one. Because it deals with rights, which have a basic connection with constitutionality, the Act is considered by some to be a wholly constitutional document, but others contend that, because it is not entrenched in our legal system, it is only quasi-constitutional, which seems, to this author, to be the better view. This does not mean that, in the future, the Act might not be fully constitutional, if integrated as an element of a new written constitution.

[13] See further, D Harvey, *The Condition of Postmodernity: An Enquiry into the Origins of Cultural Change* (Oxford, Blackwell, 1990) and F Jameson, *Postmodernism, or, The Cultural Logic of Late Capitalism* (London, Verso, 1991).

religious pluralism of the United Kingdom, in which context Christian values now compete with other religious norms for moral validity. In addition, this is an époque of cultural self-legitimation, and different sub-sets of society have attained more autonomy in a broader spectrum of societal diversity. The subject of this essay, art, has particularly enjoyed such enhanced freedom, with legal-moral constraints on it decreasing incrementally.[14] However, there still remain criminal law constrictions on artistic enterprise so artistic freedom is qualified, not absolute.[15] Why this is so is partly explicable by an intrinsic tension between law and art, which exist in different spheres of the socio-cultural spectrum, and which have markedly different functions, some of which are almost irrevocably incompatible.[16]

Freedom of artistic expression can be justified in at least two ways. First, to express oneself artistically is part of an individual's right to personal fulfilment. Secondly, in the course of artistic expression it may be discerned that certain truths are made apparent, and these truths contribute to the noble search for truth as a general human endeavour. But art possesses other virtues more peculiar to it that militate in favour of promoting artistic efforts. On a spiritual or religious plane, it is arguable that being creative is a natural imitation of our Creator's creativity, whatever form one considers that principal creative entity to take. It is also possible to assert, as John Finnis does,[17] that aesthetic experience is an objective value, as important to human beings as play and knowledge, for example. To exercise or enjoy artistic creativity, accordingly, is to experience something intrinsically good. Art has its own distinctive ontology and, because of this, should be respected as an autonomous phenomenon,[18] as evidenced by its own rules, within its own canons, however much these might mutate over time. A difficulty faced by the art-law relation is that law tends, in its public-moral capacity, to censor putatively offensive objects in a contrary, undifferentiated way which sometimes results in art's cultural autonomy being ignored, even though its independence of characteristics and operations is socially and culturally acknowledged. The law, of course, is not assisted here by the lack of a watertight general definition of art to help achieve legal certainty of

[14] The relatively new 2008 laws regulating extreme and violent pornography, examined in the main text of this essay, below, may in time replace other provisions regulating the morality of art and pornography. At the moment, however, a variety of laws exist that morally censor both commodities. See further, P Kearns, *The Legal Concept of Art* (Oxford, Hart Publishing, 1998) Ch 1.

[15] See n 8.

[16] There is frequently a misunderstanding of art by law which exacerbates such incompatibility. Part of the problem lies in the fact that art is drawn into law's arena where it is devalued by being subjugated to legal controls heteronomously, whereas art, in contrast, imposes no constraints on law, making their relationship unequal and, consequently, problematic. Art's functions become almost irrelevant when art is treated by law like any other fact when in law's domain. This qualifies art's legitimate integrity as well as its cultural autonomy.

[17] See further, J Finnis, *Natural Law and Natural Rights* (Oxford, Clarendon Press, 1980). Finnis's theory is quite controversial. He claims that there are self-evident basic values that are objectively good. The problem is that there is no evidence for self-evidence, so believing Finnis, like believing other branches of natural law, becomes a matter of faith alone.

[18] See Adorno (n 2).

operation.[19] It is also arguable that the law has more important priorities than distinguishing art from other facts when law is conceived and constructed for operating on all facts. One problem here is that art is not an ordinary fact since it does not comprise literal fact; and art is obliquely symbolic rather than being a literal 'opinion'.[20]

The art-law problematic is further complicated by the indisputable fact that art and law are very different entities. The criminal law tends to be made for relatively wide application, whereas artworks are peculiarly individual in conception and result, and it could be argued that the criminal law may *have* to be applied heteronomously when art is in issue, since special treatment for art, for example, may not be consonant with the just, objective and consistent application of public-moral laws to everything potentially caught within their ambit. Conversely, from an art perspective, it may be considered that law should be tailored to accommodate art according to the latter's specialised character; otherwise the law is unjust to it. In certain circumstances, the *modus operandi* of art may simply be *unable* to conform with law's public-moral norms.[21] This may be especially the case if art is conceived to be shocking or disturbing to shake society out of complacent moral stagnation, and to challenge the legal approbation, and protection, of such a morally static stance. Art is geared to being new, original, and of dynamic impact, whereas law's role is inevitably shaped by more general, conservative, inherited processes. The application of law, moreover, results after a lengthy process of law's creation by painstaking and cautious traditional techniques. Law's role, especially in contrast to art's,

[19] Some things defy definition and can only be described. For the purposes of legal consistency, it is convenient to work with definitions which can be applied time and time again to render the law internally coherent. The enduringly protean nature of art as a concept threatens to destabilise legal categorisation when art is in issue, and exposes the law to charges of subjective and inconsistent, rather than objective and consistent, operation. It also leads to questions about the real character of legal certainty.

[20] In the law of defamation, a difficulty arises because, rather than being fact or opinion, a distinction on which defamation law depends, art is a different type of entity that could be called a 'value'. Art is more than an ordinary 'fact' because, for example, it is culturally esteemed, and possesses a distinct essential code of being; and it is not an 'opinion' because, inter alia, it lacks the political and rhetorical slant of that term. In the USA, the picture is further confused because of the existence of the 'defamation by fiction' doctrine, according to which defamation within a novel, for example, is legally considered to be a litigious possibility.

[21] To provoke moral change, art sometimes has to be sensationalist. The most original art tends to break existing rules of art, and this type of art is often the most valued. Impressionism and Cubism, for example, revolutionised artistic style, and were not accepted as 'good' art by the art establishment until after a substantial passage of time. The development of art movements is an aspect of the way art culturally evolves, and art's habit of continual internal metamorphosis inevitably brings about changes in art history. This is similar to law's growth case-by-case, but legal developments are rarely as iconoclastic as art's revolutionary effects, because law tends to comprise a conservative system of accruing precedents within one constant model. Art has the capacity to bring changes to things that surround it, and that includes its legal regulation. This is particularly the case when that regulation is based on moral premises that new art rejects. If part of art's role is moral amelioration, however heterodox and unwelcome that might initially appear, then it is almost inevitable that art cannot always conform to morally-founded legal norms, when they attempt, in any way, to morally restrict it. The battle is then set up between accepted and critical morality. See n 1.

can be broadly characterised as often regulatory and pragmatic rather than revelatory and edifying; and because art is inherently subjective, and law aims for objectivity, a clash of cultural mechanisms is almost inevitable when law attempts to assimilate art within its own framework of consistent decision-making. Consequently, criminal cases involving art tend to fascinate the legal philosopher and frustrate the purist practitioner.[22] This is because art-related cases have a habit of confuting the straightforward and uniform development of legal doctrines since their art elements sometimes defy clarity of treatment, notably in definitional terms. Often, art will not allow the smooth application of general legal tests on it because the latter have usually simply not been adequately designed to accommodate the regulation of something as conceptually specialised and volatile as art (usually because the lawmakers, whether legislative or judicial, have, quite understandably, not predicted any conceptual or ontological difficulty that art may cause).

III RELATIONSHIP BETWEEN OBSCENITY AND RELATED LAWS AND ART

Traditionally, the criminal law has used a range of atomistic laws to regulate public morality. These include obscenity law; the common laws, formulated sometimes as conspiracies, of outraging public decency and corrupting public morals; certain more specialised legislation including the Indecent Displays (Control) Act 1981(hereinafter sometimes referred to as the 1981 Act); other miscellaneous offences; and the common law offence of blasphemy, which has only very recently been repealed. Significantly, the extant measures specified have been supplemented recently by laws regulating 'extreme' pornography. Despite this array of provisions, only under section 4[23] of the Obscene Publications Act 1959 (hereinafter sometimes referred to as the 1959 Act) has there been a specific provision to try to insulate art against legal-moral condemnation, and this, a defence, relates only to meritorious[24] art for the public good.

[22] It is a truism that difficult cases make bad law but good jurisprudence.

[23] The relevant provision provides: '(1) Subject to subsection 1 (A) of this section a person shall not be convicted of an offence against s 2 of this Act . . . if it is proved that publication of the article in question is justified as being for the public good on the ground that it is in the interests of science, literature, art and learning, or of other objects of general concern.' In this essay, the author includes creative writing under the terms 'art' and 'artistic' for facility of exposition.

[24] It is arguable that the creation of art is always for the public good, but if one concedes that some art is of greater merit than other art then the question arises as to how such merit is calculated. It is forbidden in English law for a judge to judge matters of taste, but it appears ineluctable that in evaluating artistic merit the exercise of taste is unavoidable. Under s 4, it is for the jury to determine artistic merit but the judge may influence its opinion during the course of proceedings. As well as the likelihood of the jury being very subjective in its deliberations on merit, once the level of merit is determined, that has to be balanced against the jury's preliminary finding of obscenity so as to negate it and exonerate the art. It is submitted that this is too tortuous a process for the jury to undertake convincingly. Similarly, in the USA, to protect an artwork from being condemned as obscene, the jury has to consider if it has 'serious artistic value', a process as problematic as that conducted by an English jury.

Even this relatively minor legal contribution towards a more paternalistic approach to art has been undermined by the unconscionable prosecution of art by what have become 'alternative' common law offences[25] (that in fact illicitly[26] circumvent the Act's section 4 defence and contain no defence for art themselves). Nevertheless, the 1959 Act was innovative in providing a defence for art, and other publications for the public good, when such publications otherwise faced indictment. This is because it was introduced with the partial remit of protecting literature and, logically, the defence of the useful arts[27] from unfair prosecution.

The obscenity crime under the 1959 Act is a strict liability offence and targets all publications that have 'a tendency to deprave and corrupt', a phrase interpreted conjunctively. If a work has sufficient artistic merit to counter such a tendency, as decided by the jury, it will be exonerated. However, it is difficult to categorise 'art' for such exculpation, and, in particular, to balance its merit, for the public good, against its obscene tendency. The jury must calculate whether the merit cancels out the obscenity in the given object and this is a subtle, necessarily intellectual, exercise.[28] The jury can be assisted, however, by expert witnesses[29] on art, to make its decision. This might be constructive for the cause of the art but is not always welcomed by the judge in the individual case. This was the situation in the first case brought under the 1959 obscenity legislation involving the emphatically art-hostile Justice Byrne. Nevertheless, in that case,[30] DH Lawrence's novel *Lady Chatterley's Lover*[31] was saved from the draconian fate of destruction by an art-attentive[32] jury. However, it is lamentable that, for

[25] These offences are the common law crimes of outraging public decency and corrupting public morals. The Police have used these offences so that the s 4 defence in the 1959 Act can be circumvented. This means that defendant artists cannot raise art as a relevant issue in their defence. The aforementioned common law crimes are strict liability offences so the absence of an opportunity to claim artistic intent results in particular unfairness.

[26] In 1964, the Solicitor-General gave a firm assurance that no 'alternative' common law crimes could be charged to avoid the s 4 defence's availability to defendants under the 1959 Act. See further, *Hansard*, HC Deb 1964, vol 695, col 1212. It appears that the Solicitor-General had in mind the crime of corrupting public morals, in particular, since that offence shares the component of corruption with legislative obscenity, but in practice the statement applies more to outraging public decency, which he could not have predicted would become such a menace in eliminating the possibility of pleading the public good defence under s 4.

[27] For art to be defensible in the obscenity context, it must be for the public good. To be charitable, an art trust has to be for the benefit of the public. To be copyrightable, a work must have, in the art context, artistic character. These requirements differ according to the prevailing policies in each respective legal category. However, in all of them, there is some sort of minimal quality criterion the art must satisfy.

[28] See n 23.

[29] Section 4(2) provides: 'It is hereby declared that the opinion of experts as to the literary, artistic, scientific or other merits of an article may be admitted in any proceeding under this Act either to establish or negative the said ground.'

[30] See further, P Kearns, 'Obscenity Law and the Creative Writer: The Case of D. H. Lawrence' 22 *Columbia-VLA Journal of Law and the Arts* 4, 525–31.

[31] DH Lawrence *Lady Chatterley's Lover* (London, Penguin Group, 2011)

[32] The testimony of EM Forster and Dame Rebecca West was particularly influential. The case was instrumental in making the sales of *Lady Chatterley's Lover* soar in number.

our purposes, it was not recorded whether the jury simply found that the novel was not obscene or whether it did find the novel obscene, but was justified as having sufficient literary merit to counter the obscene content so as to warrant exoneration. Subsequent cases have proceeded relatively smoothly in the application of the obscenity test and public good defence but in no trial has it been advocated by defence counsel that, ontologically, it is impossible for art ever to be obscene since the aesthetic contemplation it requires involves an artistic distance from the work that negates the possibility of the reader becoming 'depraved and corrupted'. Moreover, these are archaic and severe terms that demand more than shock or disgust[33] on the reader's part, amounting to a gravity of psychological state that an appropriate meditative attitude to art clearly precludes. Another line of argument sadly ignored by defence counsel in obscenity cases involving art is that if the supposedly offensive article is situated in an art gallery, a presumption might exist that it is not just art but art of sufficient artistic quality to be placed on public display. Art's physical public context can therefore not only affirm it is art but confer its merit for the purposes of the 1959 Act. In comparable French law, art has not been prosecuted for outraging public decency (*outrage aux bonnes moeurs*) since the mid-nineteenth century,[34] and what such French law[35] targets is now, exclusively, unduly violent, inartistic films, and non-art objects that might damage children. However, Anglo-American[36] law persists in prosecuting, inter alia, sexually explicit[37] art.

In England, there has been a surprising development in the obscenity law field. In the joined cases, *R v Gibson, R v Sylveire*,[38] the prosecution resurrected an, until then, redundant, ancient common law offence to prosecute the accused, an artist and a gallery curator respectively, for 'outraging public decency'. Gibson had made an art exhibit called 'Human Earrings' which comprised a model's head bearing earrings made of real foetuses, of three to four months' gestation. Sylveire agreed to display it in his art gallery. Before the exhibition

[33] However, most modern authorities reveal that for the commission of the common law crimes of outraging public decency and corrupting public morals, to shock or disgust, rather than to deprave and corrupt, is an adequate formula. Evidently, this is a less demanding test than that for legislative obscenity. An exceptional case is that of *Knuller (Publishing, Printing and Promotions) Ltd v Director of Public Prosecutions* [1972] 2 All ER 898, in which Lord Simon of Glaisdale made it clear that outraging public decency went 'considerably beyond' offending the sensibilities of, or even shocking, reasonable people.

[34] These cases involved Flaubert's *Madame Bovary* and Baudelaire's *Les Fleurs du Mal*. Both these works are now greatly esteemed as very fine literature.

[35] See further, the penal code that entered into force on 1 March 1994. The old code's Article 283 (ff) became Article 227-24 of the new code. It was under the old code that the seminal law of *outrage aux bonnes moeurs* developed.

[36] American obscenity law only proscribes the offensively sexually explicit that appeals to the prurient interest, whereas the law of England also prohibits depictions of drug-taking and excessive violence.

[37] Censoring unduly graphic sexual material is an Anglo-American facet of obscenity law that arguably reveals an immature preoccupation with sexual mores. Whereas, for example, a hard-core pornography star (Ilona Staller) can become a politician without controversy in Italy, such an association with the sex industry would be likely to abort political careers in England and the USA.

[38] *R v Gibson, R v Sylveire* [1990] 2 QB 619, [1990] 3 WLR 595.

began, the police arrived and charged both men with outraging public decency. They were not charged with contravening the Obscene Publications Act 1959. In this way, the section 4 defence in that legislation was circumvented, despite the fact that such circumvention is formally discouraged.[39] The duo were duly convicted of outraging public decency, an offence of strict liability that permits no consideration of art matters by the jury. A sister antique offence, called corrupting public morals,[40] was presumably not used by the prosecution because of the obvious overlap with the corruption element of the legislative offence of obscenity. It has, though, been employed in other, non-art cases.[41] However, both offences, one already in practice, and one in theory, clearly threaten artistic liberty. This is unacceptable when, in the 1959 obscenity legislation, a defence of artistic merit for the public good was added to the law specifically to protect worthy art from conviction for obscenity *and* crimes that conceptually or practically overlap with it.[42]

The Indecent Displays (Control) Act 1981 is an Act of Parliament applicable in England, Scotland and Wales but not Northern Ireland. Since it is concerned with preventing the display of 'indecent' material to an unsuspecting public, it is slightly surprising but welcome that museums and art galleries are excluded from its field of application.[43] Prosecutions under this Act are very rare. There have been only three guilty verdicts under it, all in 2004. Unhelpfully, 'indecency' is not defined in the rubric of the offence. What is clear, however, is that the legal standard for proving indecency is less demanding than that for obscenity so it would be easier to convict someone of displaying the indecent. If the Act were to apply to art exhibitions, it could therefore potentially catch more art than the 1959 legislation. Displays are not caught by the 1981 Act if they appear behind a warning notice *in a shop*, so it is evident that one aim of this legislation is to protect sex shops for adults who wish to use them. It is also evident that the Act is somewhat residual as it does not cover several things that are subject to other controls. However, the Act could be relevant for art because, for example, in 2004 a provocative nude sculpture had to be concealed from outside view after a warning about the Act. This means that artists, particularly sculptors, who are especially inclined to display work outdoors, could be caught by the Act if any of their nudes, for example, were sufficiently 'indecent'. The more abstracted the piece, the more unlikely it is that it would be prosecuted under the Act, so the Act would not affect the works of Henry Moore,[44] for example;

[39] See n 26.

[40] The crime of corrupting public morals is very rarely utilised in the modern era.

[41] For example, in *Shaw v DPP* [1962] AC 220.

[42] It could be argued that, terminologically, outraging public decency does not essentially possess the same *actus reus* as legislative obscenity. However, in practice, outraging public decency is used to target virtually the same alleged evil as the 1959 Act. Section 73 of the Coroners and Justice Act 2009 has now abolished related archaic crimes.

[43] The Act targets sex shops that might display items in their windows that could offend certain adults and adversely affect the psychologies of children.

[44] Tate Britain hosted an important exhibition of Henry Moore's work in the summer of 2010.

and nudity per se is not in issue, as opposed to nudity that is in some way 'aggravated',[45] as evidenced by the proliferation of naked stone cherubs and gods habitually openly displayed in British gardens (that are never subject to prosecution under the Act). Visual artworks may be affected by other areas of the law that in some way relate to immorality. Section 42 of the Customs Consolidation Act 1876, as amended, makes it a crime to import into the United Kingdom indecent or obscene prints, paintings, photographs, books, cards, lithographs or other engravings, or any other indecent or obscene articles. Very similar restrictions apply to the export of obscene and related material. It is noteworthy, first of all, that customs officers[46] determine what is of relevance here. A jury decides at a later stage. Obscenity here is not synonymous with obscenity as defined under the 1959 Obscene Publications Act, and such inconsistency is antinomic and potentially confusing. Under section 54 (10) of the Metropolitan Police Act 1839, every person who sells or distributes or offers for sale or distribution, or exhibits to public view, any profane book, paper, print, drawing, painting or representation, in any London thoroughfare or public place, shall be guilty of an offence. There is no case law defining what 'profane' means in this particular context. It may be a combination of obscene and blasphemous since one antonym of profane is 'sacred'. What appears certain is that under the 1959 Obscene Publications Act, 'profane' and 'obscene' are not identical in meaning. This definitional doubt again renders the law frustratingly uncertain. Exactly the same problem occurs under a comparable ancient provision, which is section 28 of the Town Police Clauses Act 1847, which is also still extant. In addition, artwork in a public place could be caught by section 5 of the Public Order Act 1936 (now 1986, as amended). The germane issues here are somewhat different as the terms of the offence indicate. These terms are as follows: any person who in any public place or at any public meeting or museum to which the public have access distributes or displays any writing, sign or visible representation which is threatening, abusive or insulting, with intent to provoke a breach of the peace or whereby a breach of the peace is likely to occur, shall be guilty of an offence. This crime was created to proscribe Nazi Party propaganda but may be of concern to artists, not least because of the specific mention of 'museum' in the offence's rubric. There is some overlap and inconsistency here with the Indecent Displays (Control) Act 1981 which renders the law inconsistent, and impossible for artists to construe coherently so as to be certain of avoiding prosecution.[47] Provocative art,[48] in particular, could be jeopardised by the relevant provisions of the Public Order Act, as referred to above, the terms

[45] It is difficult to pinpoint exactly what would constitute a sufficiently indecent object to be caught by this Act.

[46] It is surprising that customs officers have adequate expertise for this role.

[47] It is important that the criminal law is clear enough to inform artists about what they can and cannot display in public. Some official guidelines would be welcome in this area.

[48] Presumably, the Public Order Act 1986 would also seek to regulate intemperate *reactions* to fairly extreme political art or related representations.

of which also inevitably overlap with those of the common law offence of outraging public decency. Moreover, Karel Appel of the Cobra art movement[49] said that art *must* shock. However, it cannot comfortably do so in public situations in the United Kingdom without fear of criminal prosecution for a variety of offences that are not always adequately differentiated from one another.

Section 11 of the Post Office Act 1953, as amended, provides that it is an offence for a postal packet to be sent through the mail which contains any indecent or obscene print, painting, photograph, lithograph, engraving, cinematograph film, book, card or written communication, or any indecent or obscene article; or for a postal packet to have grossly offensive, indecent, or obscene matter on it. What is meant by 'indecent' is undefined and, idiosyncratically, the relevant obscenity test requires the application of a single objective standard but not the one prescribed by the Obscene Publications Act 1959. This unspecified objective standard is higher and more rigorous than that for indecency but, since 'indecency' is undefined in this provision, it is impossible to hypothesise about the precise elements of the prescribed obscenity standard. What is clear, however, is that the obscenity involved is not ascertained in relation to the item's impact on the addressee, or anyone else who happens to open the mail in his or her stead. This post office regulation to deter the communication of offensive matter by mail is characterised by a lack of attention to ease of legal interpretation. It should be centred on one unambiguous offensiveness[50] standard, and should not imply a host of implicitly different standards (indicated by different emotive adjectives, such as 'grossly offensive', 'obscene' and 'indecent', in the same definitional region).

The Coroners and Justice Act 2009, as well as abolishing the anachronistic common-law offences of sedition and seditious, defamatory and obscene libel, makes it illegal to own any pornographic picture depicting under-18s participating in sexual activity in the presence of someone under 18. This consolidates another reform measure in the Act which criminalises the possession of pornographic non-photographic images depicting under-18s, and of adults where the 'predominant impression conveyed' is of a person under the age of 18. The Act has been condemned by a coalition of graphic artists, publishers and MPs, who fear it will criminalise graphic novels such as *Lost Girls* and *Watchmen.* [51] However, the Act does provide an exemption for classified films. The relevant sections came into force on 6 April 2010.

[49] Not every art movement concurs with Appel's imperative, but new art tends to surprise or cause consternation even if its content appears to be innocuous. This was the case with Impressionism and Fauvism, for example.

[50] It is arguable that offensiveness is what public-moral laws really aim to proscribe in the current era. However, offended responses are surely too subjective to regulate per se.

[51] A Moore, *Lost Girls* (London, Knockabout Comics, 2012) and A Moore, *Watchmen* (London, DC Comics, 1987)

IV BLASPHEMY AND ART

A public morality offence that should not be forgotten in an art context is that of blasphemy,[52] which has recently been abrogated, but which still has repercussions in public-moral law, not least because of its case law's associations with the general theme of offensiveness,[53] which renders it still relevant in the deciding of cases involving all cognate crimes. Historically, there has also always been a close connection between obscenity and blasphemy, since both reflect the preoccupation of early lawmakers with Christian values, especially regarding the reputation of God and its abuse, particularly by the exercise of profane or obscene language. Until its repeal, blasphemy law specifically protected the traditional image of the Anglican God, and religious personae associated with Him, from vilification.[54] A blasphemy prosecution succeeded in *R v Lemon, R v Gay News Ltd*[55] in 1979, which was surprising because most legal commentators had assumed that the offence had fallen into desuetude.[56] In *Lemon*,[57] the editor of *Gay News* was prosecuted for publishing in that magazine a poem by James Kirkup, and an accompanying illustration, which artistically portrayed homosexual love for Christ. He was found guilty of blasphemy irrespective of the fact that the production was specifically designed for a gay or bisexual readership rather than the general public. The art was considered scurrilous, but it was not judicially considered whether literal, intemperate blasphemy could ever be illegally achieved through artistic media that were calmly permanent and had only an oblique, symbolic relationship with real life. Moreover, would Shakespeare, for example, be guilty of blasphemy in the real world through the mouths of one of his invented, fictive protagonists? If so, a lack of a basic artistic insight by the law here would undermine the wholly different, non-factual dimension of the well-recognised culture of fiction. In *Lemon*,[58] it is likely that the judge and jury were inappropriately inartistic given their lack of attention to the obviously intellectual medium and serious literary focus of this case. A lamentable, similar ignorance could pertain when the cognate offence of obscenity is applied to art.

In another blasphemy-related case, *R v Chief Metropolitan Stipendiary Magistrate, ex p Choudhury*,[59] a very controversial set of facts was set out for

[52] Historically, blasphemy was a very grave matter, especially given the very close relationship between Church and State in earlier times.

[53] See n 50.

[54] The law of blasphemy did not condemn sober arguments about the deity; it comprised, rather, a prohibition on scandalous styles of blaspheming.

[55] *R v Lemon, R v Gay News Ltd* [1979] 2 WLR 281.

[56] Few reports to the police relating to blasphemy occurred, probably arising from public indifference to the subject, in an increasingly religiously plural and agnostic society. Very few people were as vigilant about blasphemy as Mary Whitehouse, the self-styled guardian of family values, who instigated the *Lemon* proceedings.

[57] *Lemon* (n 55).

[58] ibid.

[59] *R v Chief Metropolitan Stipendiary Magistrate, ex p Choudhury* [1990] 3 WLR 986.

legal scrutiny. The creative writer Salman Rushdie had produced a novel called *The Satanic Verses*[60] and this work allegedly contained blasphemous elements. Mr Choudhury sought a summons to prosecute the novelist and his publishers for blasphemy, inter alia.[61] The relevant magistrate refused to issue such a summons because he considered the law of blasphemy in England to pertain only to the Christian religion, while Mr Choudhury had alleged blasphemy against Islam. The appeal court agreed with the magistrate and his reasons for refusing the summons. What went unconsidered was whether the novel could have infringed English blasphemy law via its alleged vilification of Islam since Christ is a prophet within Islam. Another aptly intellectual question, raised above relating to Shakespeare, that could have been profitably engaged by the courts, might have been whether the defamation of Mohammed in *The Satanic Verses*, which occurred during dream sequences of one of the characters in the novel, could be *literally* attributed to Rushdie when only expressed by one of his fictional protagonists in a state of sleep. That matter is crucial because the unwritten constitution of the United Kingdom is said to uphold free speech, including freedom of artistic expression, as an intrinsic democratic right (a right more explicitly and positively secured now under the Human Rights Act 1998). Perhaps the courts in *ex p Choudhury*[62] avoided these issues as a way of defusing further religious tensions, as a matter of pragmatic, inter-faith, reconciliatory realpolitik.[63]

Blasphemy's repeal came into force on 8 July 2008 after much campaigning against it by free speech activists, so there is no longer a law which operates prejudicially in favour of one religion in the United Kingdom, which was an indefensible situation in a religiously plural state. Primarily to include Muslims within the ambit of legal protection, the Racial and Religious Hatred Act 2006 criminalises incitement to religious hatred to supplement the equivalent provision applicable to race derived from the Public Order Act 1986. This demonstrates a move away from the exclusive upholding of Christian morality in favour of a more pragmatic approach to try to ensure social harmony in a religiously mixed community. The growing religious plurality of the English public over a number of years has been appropriately accommodated by the legislature which, instead of protecting all religions under blasphemy law, which could feasibly have led to inter-faith criminal proceedings, has reacted sensitively by providing for the insulation of all established religious groups from insult, and associated psychological harm, which could lead to breaches of the peace. These 2006 measures, however, do not specify that such harm cannot be communicated by art.[64] They therefore share this omission with the former

[60] S Rushdie, *The Satanic Verses* (London, Viking Press, 1988).

[61] Mr Choudhury also sought a summons regarding seditious libel, a request that was also refused.

[62] *ex p Choudhury* (n 59).

[63] The courts chose to restrict discussion within the case to its simplest *ratio*.

[64] The 2006 legislation also threatens to restrict religiously focused humour, as frequently emphasised by the comedian Rowan Atkinson.

blasphemy law, and the related and still extant common law offences of outraging public decency and corrupting public morals. It is to be hoped that the law in this sphere develops in a reasonable, rather than unduly defensive, way, in light of possible inappropriate extremist reactions[65] to the purely artistic. As alluded to earlier, not to protect art in this way would be contrary to freedom of artistic expression, that is firmly guaranteed under the Human Rights Act 1998. There is no countervailing right in that document that promises equivalent freedom from being offended by art.[66] This is quite proper in a society that upholds cardinal rights like freedom of expression as part of its wholly democratic character.[67]

V FREEDOM OF ARTISTIC EXPRESSION UNDER THE HUMAN RIGHTS ACT 1998

The Human Rights Act 1998 (referred to hereinafter as the Act) enhances the protection of artistic expression in the United Kingdom in a number of respects, even though artistic expression is not yet specifically distinguished from free speech in general under this relatively new legislation, which only came into force on 2 October 2000. There have been very few domestic cases that have had art at their core, but art's protection under this national legislation can be inferred from its protection under the European Convention on Human Rights (hereinafter referred to as the Convention), which the Act incorporates, and to which it gives effect. The protection of free speech in general under the Act is therefore embracing of art's specific domestic protection in human rights terms in the United Kingdom.

Under the 1998 Act, artists are able to rely directly on Article 10[68] of the Convention on freedom of expression when bringing a claim under the Act alleging that a public authority has violated that right. In this context, the courts in the United Kingdom are allowed to refer to Strasbourg jurisprudence to decide whether any interference with the right is prescribed by law, has a legitimate aim, is really necessary in a democratic society, and is non-discriminatory. Of particular significance is section 12(4) of the Act whereby a domestic court, in considering the granting of any relief which could affect freedom of expression specifically, must have 'particular regard' to the importance of this Convention right under Article 10. Prima facie, this appears to require the court to give freedom of expression an enhanced status in proceedings that involve a conflict between that right and other countervailing rights or interests. Moreover, where the proceedings relate to material which is artistic, literary or journalistic, the court must, firstly,

[65] It is important for the law not to pander to undemocratic arguments to censor free speech, which is the pre-eminent human right in civil and political terms, and an intrinsic element of traditional culture in England.

[66] ibid.

[67] ibid.

[68] For the full rubric of Art 10, see above, main text, under the next section.

have particular regard to the extent to which that material has, or is about to, become available to the public. Secondly, it must also have particular regard in these circumstances to the extent to which it is, or would be, in the public interest for the material to be published; and, thirdly, in relation to such material, it must have particular regard to any relevant privacy code. In certain cases involving freedom of expression, the relevant information might have already reached the public arena, and the court may therefore decide to discontinue any existing injunctions because they are then relatively useless. This course of action is presumably reinforced under section 12(4) when the material in question is of an artistic, literary or journalistic character. However, this is far from an unqualified rule, since a court may still grant such an order if it believes that further publication would cause even greater harm to the claimant's interests. This was done in *Barclays Bank Plc v Guardian News and Media Ltd.*[69] In this case, the High Court emphasised that section 12(4), and the fact that material had already become accessible in the public domain, did not give carte blanche to the press to further disseminate such information. With respect to the determination of whether the publication of certain material is or would be in the public interest, a court must have particular regard to the advantages of supporting press freedom and the public's right to freedom of information. Strasbourg jurisprudence would normally be drawn upon to assist a domestic court in assessing the necessary weight to be given to such rights.

The central and tangled area relating to section 12(4) of the Act relates to whether the courts have a duty to give enhanced status to freedom of expression when it conflicts with other rights or interests. Initially, courts in the United Kingdom displayed caution regarding this, but more robust attitudes stressing the importance of free speech gradually emerged. Instead of the establishment of a certain rule here, flexibility of approach is evident in court practice. In *Cream Holdings v Banjaree*,[70] the House of Lords affirmed that section 12 did not require the courts to afford freedom of expression a higher value than other Convention rights, and in *Douglas v Hello! Magazine*,[71] the Court of Appeal agreed with the House of Lords in principle, emphasising that the explicit acknowledgment of restrictions on free speech under Article 10(2) of the Convention clearly implied that no necessary additional weight should be given to free speech over other countervailing rights such as privacy. However, in *Venables and Thompson v MGN*,[72] the Court said that section 12 did give freedom of expression an enhanced status, above that of other rights, and in *A v B Plc*,[73] freedom of expression was strongly supported by Lord Woolf CJ, and the rest of the Court of Appeal. There, Lord Woolf CJ opined that the effect of section 12 was that there was no justification for courts to interfere with freedom

[69] *Barclays Bank Plc v Guardian News and Media Ltd* [2009] EWHC 591 (QB).
[70] *Cream Holdings v Banjaree* [2005] 1 AC 253.
[71] *Douglas v Hello! Magazine* [2001] 2 WLR 992.
[72] *Venables and Thompson v MGN* [2001] 2 WLR 1038.
[73] *A v B Plc* [2002] 3 WLR 542.

of expression simply because there was no identifiable public interest in particular material being published. Nevertheless, in *Re S (Publicity)*,[74] the House of Lords reaffirmed its position, stating that freedom of expression under Article 10 did not have an automatic trump card status under the Act, but in *A Local Authority v A Health Authority*,[75] Dame Butler-Sloss P stressed that, by virtue of section 12(4), freedom of expression had an elevated status. On the facts of that case, she asserted that the correct approach was to publish freely unless such publication would be so disadvantageous to others that the court was *driven* to restrain publication in whole or in part.

By way of conclusion, it is evident that freedom of expression under the Act has an ambiguous status, ironically, courtesy of section 12(4)'s precise phrasing. It is sometimes said to be the cardinal right in a democracy but in the domestic law of the United Kingdom its status, relative to other rights, is unclear. It requires clarification otherwise it will lead to confusion within the law, where there is already inconsistency. As far as artistic freedom is specifically concerned, it remains to be seen, in an appropriate case, whether our domestic courts have a comparably fluctuating idea about its particular importance.

VI FREEDOM OF ARTISTIC EXPRESSION UNDER THE EUROPEAN CONVENTION ON HUMAN RIGHTS

Freedom of artistic expression is implicitly protected by Article 10 of the European Convention on Human Rights, the specific rubric of which provides for the more general protection of freedom of expression *simpliciter*. The law under Article 10 is developed in Strasbourg jurisprudence, ie the case law of the European Court of Human Rights. Such case law, inter alia, must be taken into account by courts in the United Kingdom, in relevant cases, in accordance with section 2 of the Human Rights Act 1998, which incorporates most of the Convention articles into United Kingdom domestic law. Article 10 of the Convention reads as follows:

1. Everyone has the right to freedom of expression. This right shall include freedom to hold opinions and to receive and impart information and ideas without interference by public authority and regardless of frontiers. This Article shall not prevent states from requiring the licensing of broadcasting, television or cinema enterprises. 2. The exercise of these freedoms, since it carries with it duties and responsibilities, may be subject to such formalities, conditions, restrictions or penalties as are prescribed by law and necessary in a democratic society, in the interests of national security, territorial integrity or public safety, for the prevention of disorder or crime, for the protection of health or morals, for the protection of the reputation or rights of others, for the disclosure of

[74] *Re S (Publicity)* [2005] 1 AC 593.

[75] *A Local Authority v A Health Authority* [2004] 2 WLR 926.

information received in confidence, or for maintaining the authority and impartiality of the judiciary.

The case law on Article 10 regarding artistic freedom specifically has developed incrementally, commencing doctrinally with the case of *Handyside v United Kingdom*.[76] This case concerned a publication called *The Little Red Schoolbook*[77]. This text was the subject of a prosecution under the English Obscene Publications Act 1959 on the ground that it allegedly encouraged early sexual intercourse. Following an application to the European Court of Human Rights, the Strasbourg Court found interference with freedom of expression justified under Article 10(2) for the 'protection of morals'. The domestic authorities were permitted a wide 'margin of appreciation' here, which did not imply a totally unlimited discretion, but which nevertheless enabled the local authorities to judge whether censorship was required on the particular facts of this case, in accordance with local moral needs, as a matter of their own discretion. This notion of a 'margin of appreciation' was adopted in subsequent artistic freedom cases, inter alia, to permit Contracting States to the Convention to regulate that freedom to the point of its virtually complete negation by countervailing moral factors, which is shocking given the specific remit of the Strasbourg organs to uphold rights and freedoms. Such negation of artistic freedom happened in the leading art-related cases of *Muller v Switzerland*,[78] *Otto-Preminger Institute v Austria*[79] and *Wingrove v United Kingdom*[80], which are examined in chronological order below. It is arguable that, in supporting conservative morality based on ancient tenets of institutional Christianity over contemporary artistic freedom, the Strasbourg Court is not paying adequate attention to the demands of pluralism, tolerance and broadmindedness in a democratic society, virtues which it confusingly extols in some of its fundamental governing principles but which are in fact in stark contrast to its clearly contradictory, very restrictive approach in this particular free speech context. In *Muller*,[81] one of the first Convention cases on artistic 'speech', the facts of the case were straightforward. Muller, a distinguished artist, produced and exhibited three large paintings that depicted a variety of sexual acts including some between men, women and animals. He was consequently prosecuted for obscenity under Swiss law. He was duly convicted under the Swiss Criminal Code and had his paintings seized by the relevant authorities. The relevant Swiss Court opined: 'Comment on the confiscated work is superfluous; their vulgarity is plain to see and needs no elaborating upon.'[82] Muller and his supporters favoured a more detailed, contextual approach to the issue of obscenity in an artistic context and

[76] *Handyside v UK* E Ct HRR A 24 [1976] 1 EHRR 737.
[77] J Jensen and S Jensen, *The Little Red Schoolbook* (New York, Pocket Books, 1973).
[78] *Muller v Switzerland* E Ct HRR A 113 [1991] 13 EHRR 212.
[79] *Otto-Preminger Institute v Austria* E Ct HRR A 295-A [1994] 19 EHRR 34, E Ct HR.
[80] *Wingrove v United Kingdom* [1997] 24 EHRR 1.
[81] *Muller* (n 78).
[82] ibid.

wished for greater emphasis to be placed on the need for artistic freedom, saying that it was not for the Swiss Court to undertake direct censorship of the arts. The European Court of Human Rights did not subsequently ask itself whether the censure of Muller's work was necessary; instead, it considered whether the Swiss Court was entitled to think it necessary. However, it offered no substantive reasoning to support its conclusion that they were so entitled. In addition, it did not consider the Swiss Court's action disproportionate in effectively banning the paintings from being shown anywhere at all, even though only three people in a small canton had claimed to have been seriously offended by them. The Swiss approach here was one that the Strasbourg Court should have condemned in accordance with its pivotal role as a guardian of the freedoms for which it had been founded to protect.

Very worryingly, the stance that the Strasbourg Court took in *Muller*[83] was repeated in the later case of *Otto-Preminger*.[84] In brief, the case concerned a film, *Das Lieberkinzil* (*Council in Heaven*), which caricatured aspects of Christian doctrine, and which was based on a nineteenth-century satirical play. It was deemed offensive on religious grounds in the Innsbruck district of Austria, and was consequently seized and forfeited. Subsequently, the Strasbourg Court affirmed the Austrian province's action of censorship by stressing the very high number of Catholics who lived in the area where the offence was allegedly given. It is clearly illogical to allow such reasoning to justify measures that made it impossible to show the film anywhere in the world. The two cases, *Muller*[85] and *Otto-Preminger*,[86] demonstrate that local interference with artistic freedom is easily justified by the European Court of Human Rights on the basis of very little evidence and almost entirely without regard for the Court's own operative principle of proportionality. The Court's stance here is in marked contrast to its vigilant protection of *political* expression, interference with which is subjected to the very closest scrutiny.

In the 1997 case of *Wingrove*,[87] the facts were as follows. Nigel Wingrove produced a video-film entitled *Visions of Ecstasy*, which depicted the tale of Saint Teresa of Avila, who had ecstatic visions of Christ. Wingrove chose to add an erotic element to the traditional story, which led to the entitlement to distribute the film being denied by the British Board of Film Classification (BBFC), and, subsequently, the Video Appeals Panel, on the ground that it could be found to be blasphemous. The European Court of Human Rights affirmed the ability of the national authorities to censor the film based on this rationale. Its judgment here clearly resembles that in *Otto-Preminger*[88] since it reveals an inexplicable failure on the part of the Strasbourg Court to give appropriate weight to what in

[83] ibid.
[84] *Otto-Preminger* (n 79).
[85] *Muller* (n 78).
[86] *Otto-Preminger* (n 79).
[87] *Wingrove* (n 78).
[88] *Otto-Preminger* (n 79).

other free speech contexts would be very familiar free speech justifications. In addition, the fact that a law proscribing blasphemy may give rise to a prosecution does not in itself require the condoning of such a prosecution at supranational level, let alone necessitate affirming a total ban on the distribution of the allegedly offensive subject matter.

Although there have been a few more recent decisions of the Strasbourg Court on the general theme of artistic freedom, none of them are direct authorities on the issue of the protection of morals under Article 10 of the Convention in relation to cutting-edge art. They include cases that link art and sedition, art and private law, and the law relating to the translation of classic works that may engage public morality concerns. The Court's position on current artistic production and the offensiveness of such art on moral grounds per se, continues to be completely negative regarding artistic freedom. This is a surprising and lamentable situation, especially since in many national jurisdictions there are presumptions that art is free and/or can be legally tolerated even when shocking or disgusting. The whole point of having a free speech principle is that it does not just protect the morally anodyne or pure alone. Moreover, the Strasbourg Court does not pay enough attention to the positive attributes of art in relation to contemporary European society. It ignores the formal aspects of art that indicate its unique ontology; it is unaware of art's role as a crucial litmus test for the moral development of society; and it fails to praise art's widely recognised function as a medically-proven therapeutic agent for members of society, including the mentally ill, who sometimes produce morally controversial art known as 'outsider art' or *art brut*. A fortiori, the Court's parameters of reference when morally-challenging works of art are in issue are too narrow for it to render a necessarily specialist type of justice.

VII A CONCISE COMPARISON BETWEEN THE STRASBOURG APPROACH AND OTHER SYSTEMS OF ARTISTIC FREEDOM PROTECTION

One similarity between the American approach, under the First Amendment to the US Constitution, for example, and that of the Strasbourg Convention system, is that freedom of expression is protected in both instances according to schemes of general categories. In both systems, the most protected type of speech is political speech. A second category under the American system is indecent speech (unlike under the Convention). If this type of speech also happens to be a form of political speech, it is habitually fully protected. However, other types of indecent speech, usually involving sex and/or violence, tend to attract only relatively modest protection. Constitutional protection is still in principle, and in practice with regularity, afforded to indecent speech if it has expressive and communicative content, as is likely to be the case with indecent artistic expression. However, if the level of indecency is characterised as obscenity, that obscenity is excluded from constitutional protection under the First Amendment, as are violent responses which are customarily called 'fighting words'. Obscenity is excluded from such protection if it comprises depictions of sexual behaviour that offend community values, appeal to the prurient interest, and, where art is concerned, lack serious artistic value. A finding of obscenity has the legal consequence of such material being prohibited or regulated by government freely, as if it were 'mere' conduct.

Art can be redeemed in American law even if prima facie obscene. Under the seminal case of *Roth v US*,[89] for something to be obscene, it had to be 'utterly without redeeming social value'. This was for some time the constitutional standard against which to test material for obscenity. It was a conspicuously liberal standard because it was virtually impossible to prove that something was, factually, 'utterly without redeeming social value'. Under the *Roth*[90] formula, all bona fide art could qualify for First Amendment protection. However, because the attainment of the *Roth*[91] standard for obscenity was so difficult to prove, a new case brought a dramatic change of approach to assist prosecutors. Under *Miller v California*,[92] to avoid attracting the label of obscene, art had to possess 'serious artistic value'. This requirement is still extant. It creates much difficulty for morally controversial art. It is difficult to determine what art can satisfy this relative, subjective and demanding test. It invites individual courts, in individual cases, to entertain essentially subjective judgments on the matter of artistic merit. It contradicts the legal norm that law court judges should not be in the business of expressing their personal tastes in any way. In addition, *Miller*[93] parallels the Strasbourg system in inviting contemporary morals at a local, not even national, level to dictate the legitimate circumference of artistic morality (the Strasbourg system via its previously discussed margin of appreciation doctrine). This potentially puts artistic liberty at the mercy of inappropriately parochial and conservative moral attitudes that tend to be more censorious in the provinces than in metropolitan environments, whose publics are usually more appreciative of morally challenging, avant-garde art. These urban centres, in housing a moral plurality in their citizens, can better evaluate art in accordance with enlightened, international attitudes that are not preoccupied with non-postmodernist, traditional moral scruples.

The commitment to freedom of expression is voiced more strongly in America than in Strasbourg since the American position under the First Amendment rubric is more absolutist than the freedom of expression advocated in Strasbourg, which is prey to so many legitimate restrictions on that freedom imposed by Contracting States. In addition, the US Supreme Court limits the freedom of artistic expression only slightly, by in practice targeting only hardcore pictorial pornography in its jurisprudence. In Strasbourg, the censoring of

[89] *Roth v US* 354 US 476 (1957).
[90] ibid.
[91] ibid.
[92] *Miller v California* 413 US 15 (1973).
[93] ibid.

artistic freedom is delegated to local authorities to authorise virtually at will, and such censorship is consequently much broader in scope than in the USA. Both the American and the Strasbourg systems of regulating artistic freedom could learn something about moral progress in this field from Canada. In the case of *R v Butler*,[94] the Canadian Supreme Court decided that even hard-core pornography without any redeeming features was protectable as free speech since its expressive content could not be equated with mere conduct. This judgment, which is not out of keeping with the general trend of Canadian human rights law, implicitly protects all morally provocative art from legal censure, and actively promotes its freedom in a mature and sophisticated way, in tune with the prevailing moral liberalisation and egalitarianism developed in the up-to-date and adventurous era of postmodernism. In particular, the Canadian approach avoids imposing unpredictable qualitative standards on morally challenging art, in contrast to the demoded systems of Strasbourg and the USA that are still tied to old distinctions between art and pornography, including archaic concepts of depraving and corrupting obscenity, and 'dangerous' appeals to the prurient interest. Having said this, we move now to an analysis of more obviously and seriously degrading types of pornography, the prohibition of which in the United Kingdom is arguably as imperative as the absolute proscription of child pornography, which is correctly considered morally intolerable.

VIII EXTREME PORNOGRAPHY AND ART

Section 63 of the Criminal Justice and Immigration Act 2008 is part of relatively new legislation in the United Kingdom that criminalises possession of what it refers to as 'extreme pornographic images'. The law came into force on 26 January 2009, and is not retrospective. It applies to pornographic images of such a nature that they must reasonably be assumed to have been produced solely or principally for the purpose of sexual arousal, which are grossly offensive, disgusting or otherwise of an obscene character, and which portray any of the following in such a way that a reasonable person looking at the image would think that any such person or animal was real:

(a) An act which threatens a person's life.
(b) An act which results, or is likely to result, in serious injury to a person's anus, breasts or genitals.
(c) An act which involves or appears to involve sexual interference with a human corpse.
(d) A person performing or appearing to perform an act of intercourse or oral sex with an animal (whether dead or alive).

[94] *R v Butler* [1992] 1 SCR 452.

An extreme pornographic image covers staged acts, whether or not the participants involved consent to be in them. Classified works are exempted. Section 64 of the Act excludes from the ambit of the new 2008 offence persons who possess a video recording of a film which has been classified by the BBFC, even if the film contains an image or images which nevertheless fall foul of the section 63 offence in the 2008 Act. The fact that the images are held as part of a BBFC classified film takes them outside the scope of the offence. Significantly, the definition of 'obscene' in the 2008 Act is not the same as that used in the Obscene Publication Acts; instead, the ordinary dictionary definition of 'obscene' is used, which includes such terms as 'grossly offensive' and 'disgusting'. Section 68 and schedule 14 of the 2008 Act are to ensure that the operation of the extreme pornography offence is consistent with the United Kingdom's commitments under the E-Commerce Directive (Directive 2000/31/EC) with regard to services provided by the Internet industry. Section 71 of that Act increases the maximum penalty for publication of obscene material, and the possession of such material for gain, under the Obscene Publications Act 1959. The 2008 new offence only relates to material which, by virtue of the Obscene Publications Act 1959, is illegal to publish or distribute in the United Kingdom. The Criminal Justice and Immigration Act 2008 thus contains provisions on extreme and violent pornography that could impact negatively on art, in particular films that are not officially classified. The Government justified the measures on the basis that extreme pornography may encourage or reinforce interest in violent and aberrant sexual activity to the detriment of society as a whole.[95] Such extreme material was already illegal to publish and distribute in the United Kingdom under the Obscene Publications Act 1959. The 2008 Act now criminalises possession of it. Relevant material has become increasingly accessible from abroad via the Internet, so these 'new' laws on violent and extreme pornography make it illegal to possess it both on and offline.[96] These 2008 laws are stated to build on the fundamentals of the 1959 Act, suggesting a moral justification for them.[97] Banning the possession of extreme pornographic material mirrors the existing offence of possession of child pornography under section 160 of the Criminal Justice Act 1988. The necessity for legal provision for the protection of children from seeing violent and extreme pornography is, of course, little disputed.

[95] See further, Home Office, *Consultation: On the Possession of Extreme Pornographic Material* (London, Home Office, 2005). Section 63 of the Criminal Justice and Immigration Act 2008 criminalises possession of 'extreme pornographic images' and the law came into force on 26 January 2009. The central legal test prescribed, and which is most pertinent for the theme of this essay, is whether a reasonable person looking at any such image would think that any person or animal featured was real.

[96] See further, J Rowbottom, 'Obscenity and the Internet: Targeting the Supply and Demand' (2006) *Criminal Law Review* 97.

[97] For an informative analysis of the extreme pornography laws and an argument that harm to women should be the object of such legislation as opposed to morality-based factors, see C McGlynn and E Rackley, 'Striking a Balance: Arguments for the Criminal Regulation of Extreme Pornography' (2007) *Criminal Law Review* 677.

Framers of the original consultation document preceding the enactment of the new 2008 offences maintained that there would be no restriction on political expression or public interest matters, or on artistic expression.[98] Section 63 (3) of the 2008 Act clearly states that an image is 'pornographic' if it is of such a nature that it must reasonably be assumed to have been produced *solely or principally for the purpose of sexual arousal*. Theoretically, at least, this excludes artistic images because art is non-conative, ie it does not embody any will on the part of its creator that viewing it results in action. This is what, at least partly, distinguishes art from pornography.[99] Only if an artwork is viewed unmeditatively can its impact be effective literally and negatively, as opposed to appropriately positively and aesthetically. Moreover, the physical context of an artwork implicitly informs the viewer to appreciate it as art not pornography; for example, an object in an art gallery must, of course, be viewed aptly as art, ie in accordance with the traditional art environment provided. There should be, for example, no paternalistic necessity for warnings if the art appears to be sexually controversial, since the fact that the venue is designated as for the exhibition of art should be enough to indicate that what is featured may be in some way artistically stimulating. Any incidental alleged 'arousing'[100] should, of course, be put within an artistic context, which should transform any inappropriate physical effect into a psychic art-specialised one that results in reflection only. Crucially, in addition, the actual impulse to create artistically is rarely vitiated by any venal or ulterior pornographic intent.

Section 63(7) of the 2008 Act states that an image is only caught under the provisions of the Act if it portrays certain unpleasant events, such as an act which threatens a person's life, *in an explicit and realistic way*. This could be ominous for art that so portrays such an event, since art frequently imitates life, and is often praised for its 'verisimilitude'; and, since art is always 'pushing boundaries', it is not inconceivable that art forms, especially films, might have something quite extreme as their theme, which might be presented in an explicit and realistic way. Such imitation of aspects of real life, known in the arts as 'mimesis', is commended in the artistic sphere but would be condemned, for the same representational power, under the 2008 Act. It is arguable too, from an artistic perspective, that the *best* art is that which appears lifelike, and thereby contributes real life insights from its realistic portrayals. Some protection for such art arises from the explanatory notes to the Act which, in its paragraph 456, assure us that where an image is integral to a narrative, which, taken as a whole, could not reasonably be assumed to be pornographic, the image itself

[98] ibid.

[99] The distinction between bona fide art and unacceptable pornography is a complex matter. A primary consideration is the objective of the respective materials, but there can also be content-based differences that are apparent from the degree of the explicitness of sexual and violent depictions. The context of the materials is also sometimes highly relevant.

[100] Sexual arousal is the principal effect of pornography but the creation of art is only prompted by a desire to appeal to the prurient interest when a cynical motive is present which is extrinsic to artistic method.

may be taken not to be pornographic, even though, considered in isolation, the contrary conclusion would have been reached. This could help protect avant-garde horror films from the bite of the legislation, for example, which have the occasional extreme moment. Moreover, paragraph 459 of these aforementioned explanatory notes, states that persons portrayed in a legally unacceptable image must appear to be real, the effect of which requirement is to exclude animated characters, sketches, painting and the like. This should reassure the Campaign against Censorship and the Bar Council which, respectively, worried about the possible proscription of classical art such as *Leda and the Swan*, and a video of the play *Romans in Britain*.[101] Nevertheless, the explanatory paragraph in question protects principally classical artforms, and does not accommodate art-films, for example, in which the moving imagery is almost inevitably more explicitly imitative of reality. What does not fall foul of the law, though, as adverted to above, is the content of DVDs which have received a certificate, notably R18, from the BBFC. This follows on logically from the lack of criminal prosecutions of films under the Obscene Publications Act 1959 that have received such a certificate. It is a personal contention, however, that such certificates have regularly been given to films that, at least prima facie, appear to transgress the traditional 'deprave and corrupt' standard under the Act (and similar ones at common law), as illustrated by the relatively innocuous type of obscene matter seen to be condemned in the existing case law under the Act (and analogous common law offences).[102] In April 2009, the BBFC issued a rare rejection notice for a 'disturbing and realistic' DVD called *NF713*. A spokeswoman for that body denied that the decision was influenced by the 2008 Act. Vigilant opponents of the Act, relying on the veracity of that statement, maintain that that BBFC scenario proves that in practice certain material that it is not illegal to possess is nonetheless illegal to 'publish'. On the evidence, *ex quocunque capite*, this appears a likelihood, and, in the absence of considerable legal vigilance, unavoidable.

What is surprising about the extreme pornography laws is that they do not outlaw all excessively violent mainstream films, which is now habitually done in France. Also, they strangely fail to make the crucial moral distinctions between, firstly, real and fictional activity and, secondly, non-consensual and consensual activity. This is anomalous when the 2008 Act is so closely connected with the morally-based 1959 Act. According to the pro-pornography contingent, this may mean that pornography as well as art should be conspicuously defended against moralistic complaint[103] because the evidence that pornography is harmful is not, they say, indisputable.[104] Such commentators also argue that law that

[101] See further, McGlynn and Rackley (n 97) 684–85.

[102] See further, C Munro, 'Sex, Law and Videotape: The R18 Category' (2006) *Criminal Law Review* 957.

[103] The principal argument in favour of pornography is that it is arguably a safety-valve to prevent potential sex offenders from committing illegal sexual acts.

[104] ibid.

regulates pornography seems geared to conservatism and demoded approaches. They submit, for example, that a defence based on the therapeutic effects of pornography still appears in practice legally untenable following the outdated case of *DPP v Jordan*.[105] In addition, they identify a conceptual problem connected with the 2008 Act, which is that it will be difficult to juridically ascertain exactly what constitutes a 'realistic' portrayal of the proscribed undesirable activities. They ask how such a subjective criterion can be consistently applied. Moreover, they suggest that what they consider to be wasted time relating to hypothetical harms and ambiguous terminology could be better spent on eradicating evils that are known and agreed to be harmful, such as *real* acts of *non-consensual* violence.[106] In the context of extreme pornography, they contend that it might be preferable to formulate a single distinct offence of knowingly acquiring any material featuring such acts. However, despite pro-pornography arguments, behind the extreme pornography laws is the laudable desire to prevent sexual violence against women, and there is some evidence that such pornography, at least, could be linked to violent or aberrant sexual activity. Moreover, it is difficult to see anything meritorious in the workings of the pornography industry, and it is clear that extreme pornography does appear to legitimate certain despicable activities, including rape. This can lead to the argument that the pornography problematic should not even be considered to be a free speech issue, despite the argument of some liberals that every curtailment of pornography carries the risk that individual self-expression is jeopardised, and that that endangers, in turn, the equality afforded to phenomena through which the moral environment evolves. Nevertheless, a personal submission is that restrictions on violence, in particular, in extreme pornography, are very prudent and necessary. The objective of this essay is not to try to condone such pornography but to ensure that artistic expression is differentiated from more heinous activities that, it appears to this author, are more clearly deserving of moral and legal condemnation.

IX CONCLUDING REFORM PROPOSALS AND REMARKS

It remains to be constructive about legal reform in relation to the principal argument presented here. As well as the reforms implicit or suggested in the text, the following are further recommendations. One constructive approach would be to make the section 4 defence in the Obscene Publications Act 1959 applicable in all obscenity-related offences.[107] Another would be to repeal the 1959 Act[108] and

105 *DPP v Jordan* [1976] 3 All ER 775.

106 This point was made in a variety of responses to the Government's consultation document. See further, McGlynn and Rackley (n 97).

107 See further, P Kearns, 'Obscene and Blasphemous Libel: Misunderstanding Art' (2000) *Criminal Law Review* 660.

108 See further, P Kearns, 'The Ineluctable Decline of Obscene Libel: Exculpation and Abolition' (2007) *Criminal Law Review* 676.

the Indecent Displays (Control) Act 1981 entirely, especially since the latter, in particular, is so seldom used, and allow the 2008 extreme pornography laws, in an amended form to protect bona fide artistic endeavour, to stand alone as moral monitors of offensive creations. If these include a defence for art along the lines of that currently available under the 1959 Act, the possession of only the vilest pornography would be proscribed; and, if considered desirable, the introduction of an accompanying publishing offence derived in principle from the 1959 Act, but applicable only to extreme and violent pornography, could be considered by legislators. The inclusion of a defence for art in the 2008 Act would protect, inter alia, art that imitates pornography or art that includes very challenging imagery of a type that could be confused with pornography. In addition, with regard to the crimes designated in this text as miscellaneous,[109] the law should be clarified and modified to make them mutually consistent and streamlined, especially in terms of the *actus reus* details of what they purport to prohibit. These offences occur randomly in the English criminal law and could usefully be brought together in a single piece of appropriate legislation. Another more general suggestion is that the criminal law provisions upholding Christian morality, for historical reasons, should now target real harm done, not hypothetical moral debilitation. In this respect, it is scientifically proven that violent representations are more directly harmful to adults and children than sexual ones, as acknowledged in contemporary French obscenity law; and the constant protection of children from exposure to violent images is also commendably provided for in England and the United States of America as well as in France. Finally, it is arguable, as mentioned earlier, that the criminal law should aim, as a first priority, to tackle the true evil of recording real acts of non-consensual violence, before then concentrating on unacceptable artificial representations of them. The former are sometimes illicitly included in the most repugnant pornography, and constitute a proven menace to society.

In a philosophical context, contemporary English criminal law could, arguably, focus less on the equation of a crime with a sin and more on the scrupulous proving of actual harm to others, from a John Stuart Mill argument, whereby an individual is free from legal restraint apart from where he or she abuses his or her liberty by harming others. This libertarian approach is now reflected in the relatively high standard of adverse influence required to make the worst pornography criminally indictable under the 2008 Act. Whether this is a desirable state of affairs is clearly disputable. What appears to this author to be relatively certain is that, especially with the gradual radicalisation of art in the postmodern era, art should be legally acknowledged to be of a different character from pornography, even if its extreme examples seem prima facie to replicate pornography. Mel Gibson's disturbingly graphic film *The Passion of the Christ*, featuring much blood and gore during Christ's dismal progress to the cross, and Gunther von Hagens's *Bodyworks*, which displays constructs of dead human beings

[109] See main text.

using his novel plastination techniques, which combine art with education, are examples of very challenging artistic representations that should be afforded legal protection from censorship because their artistic ontology is of a different cultural order from that of pornography (even though drawing a line between such extreme art and abject pornography sometimes becomes objectively exacting for those unacquainted with aesthetics). Distinguishing art from pornography is nevertheless essential if the terms of the 2008 Act on extreme and violent pornography are not to jeopardise art's unique contribution to society by confusing it with hard-core pornography's arguably illicit representations of potentially offensive defilement.The criminal law's moral regulation of art is ramified in terms of relevant offences, and complex regarding conceptual matters. Struggling to find, usually implicitly, a workable definition of art itself, the law finds no comfort in the fact that there is not even a conclusive philosophical definition of it.[110] Neither are morality and obscenity concepts that are susceptible to exhaustive definition. The appearance within the law of such a subjective maze creates significant debate but yields few answers. Judges have to wrestle here with both natural law and positivist issues, in the sense, for example, that they tend to accept 'morality' as being naturally immanent or self-evident in human life but some might find it fit for legal critique only if divorced from unempirical faith in such a notion and treated more scientifically. In addition, the cultural autonomy of, and a certain general reverence for, art suggest a corresponding judicial recognition of its status and worth within law, even though the extremism of some contemporary art threatens the veracity of ethical and legal distinctions between it and pornography. These and related, complex and sometimes seemingly intractable art-law matters, require a great sophistication of analysis. Consequently, justice can only be done, and be seen to be done, in this tangled field of what could be perceived to be subjective preferences, if courts become more receptive to intellectual discourses on the value of art, and integrate them more subtly into adjudications that tend to be habitually morality-biased and unduly conservative. In addition, art's socially-recognised worth and independent ontology, should not be inequitably neglected in favour of uninformed prejudices against artistic portrayals that are sometimes misrepresented as literally immoral rather than merely symbolic. A fortiori, there must always be concrete proof in resolving legal issues, and, in the context with which we are dealing, sufficient proof of actual harm by art, in specific instances. Such harm must be clearly identified in each legal case: if not, inappropriate and random convictions could unjustifiably result.[111]

[110] Theodor Adorno maintains that '[t]he concept of art is located in a historically changing constellation of elements; it refuses definition'. See Adorno (n 2).

[111] In 2009, the Comic Shop Voice, for example, said that the law as it stands might result in the banning of certain collections of comic books that could be considered contemporary artworks. See further, *The Daily Telegraph* (29 January 2009) 3. In *The Guardian* (3 August 2011) 15, it was reported that Lars von Trier's art-film, *Nymphomaniac*, could fall foul of the 2008 Act. The film examines the taboo subject of child sexuality.

Part V

European Union Law and Culture

12

The Culture Problematic in European Union Law: A 2002 Perspective

IT IS UNSURPRISING that culture did not arise as a primary concern when EU law was in its infancy since the European Economic Community's (EEC) eponymous concerns were purely economic. However, with the development of the EC then EU, incorporating not just economic objectives as the remit, culture emerged as a growing new area of European interest, notably post-Maastricht. Allied more substantive initiatives were the foundation of EU citizenship and the increased EU development of human rights, both of which had legal precedents for the EU to follow within or outside the EU. Cultural protection did not fit easily within the ambit of either of these related concerns and there was a conceptual difficulty as to in what established legal zone culture could be regulated. This need to fit culture under another umbrella was because there was originally no legal autonomy granted to cultural provisions in EU law. As a result, cultural aid, for example, thrived as a matter of state aid, whereas cultural rights were very slow in developing in the EU context because there was no comparable established route for their regulation even though certain human rights were protected as a matter of EU law. This fracturing of the cultural area was intended to be remedied at Maastricht, and the current Cultural Title XII, originally conceived at Maastricht, promised a more pronounced independent role for culture within EU competence. The principal dramatic development was the coming into force of what is now Article 151. Article 151 is set out as follows:

> Article 151 (1) EC. The Community shall contribute to the flowering of the cultures of the Member States, while respecting their national and regional diversity and at the same time bringing the common cultural heritage to the fore.
>
> 2. Action by the Community shall be aimed at encouraging co-operation between Member States and, if necessary, supporting and supplementing their action in the following areas:
>
> improvement of the knowledge and dissemination of the culture and history of the European peoples;
> conservation and safeguarding of cultural heritage of European significance;

non-commercial cultural exchanges;
artistic and literary creation, including the audiovisual sector.

3. The Community and the Member States shall foster co-operation with third countries and the competent international organisations in the sphere of culture, in particular the Council of Europe.
4. The Community shall take cultural aspects into account in its action under other provisions of this Treaty. [In particular in order to respect and to promote the diversities of its cultures.]
5. In order to contribute to the achievement of the objectives referred to in this Article, the Council:

acting in accordance with the procedure referred to in Article 189b and after consulting the Committee of the Regions, shall adopt incentive measures, excluding any harmonisation of the laws and regulations of the Member States. The Council shall act unanimously throughout the procedure referred to in Article 189b;
acting unanimously on a proposal from the Commission, shall adopt recommendations.

There is a lot to observe about these provisions. In Article 151(1) there is the practical appeal to note that within the EU there are both common and individual cultural phenomena in the Member States. The homogeneity proposed is not a bland EU conformism but, rather, a complex holistic picture that has EU membership as a parameter. Article 151(2) indicates Community action in respect of the nature of cultural activities that are to be developed between Member States when they interact; the Article also anticipates Community action beyond these objectives but the specific character of such extra action seems to be restricted to the activities already given in the Article paragraph. Article 151(3) is an outward-looking provision that urges co-operation between the Community and Member States, presumably disjunctively and conjunctively, and third countries and apposite international entities. The Council of Europe is given special mention as one such body. This is not surprising because the Council of Europe is immersed in cultural concerns and is informally a sister supra-national European organisation. Article 151(4) is difficult to interpret. It foresees the Community taking cultural issues into account when acting under other provisions of its treaty law, with the additional stress that such measures must respect and promote the whole range of its cultures. The subsidiarity principle, by which decisions are permitted to be taken at a national local level, will be highly significant in this context. Article 151(5) is a principally procedural provision that involves in part consultation with the Committee of the Regions to achieve the substantive aim of incentive measures. Taken together, Articles 151(4) and 151(5) promote much cultural action at a domestic level in keeping with the subsidiarity principle and the nature of the work of the Committee of the Regions, which too has local issues as its primary concern. This dissolves irrational fears that the EU's programme of cultural law has EU undifferentiated cultural homogeneity as its objective.

Whether Article 151 embodies an EU policy is a highly controversial subject as some maintain that a policy must be explicit, not inferred. What is more, from case law, it is national policy that is more prominent in relation to culture, as a permitted vehicle for derogation from the EU principle of free movement. In *Cinetheque v Federation National Des Cinemas Francais*,[1] it was said that cultural aims may justify certain restrictions on the free movement of goods provided that those restrictions apply to national and imported products without distinction, that they are appropriate to the cultural aim which is being pursued and that they constitute the means of achieving them which affects intra-Community trade the least. From this case, it is evident that the protection of at least motion visual art can be added to the *Cassis De Dijon*[2] list of mandatory requirements which facilitate legitimate derogations from the free movement of goods principle. Similarly, in *Groener v Minister for Education*,[3] this time in the context of the free movement of persons, it was adjudged that the EEC Treaty does not prohibit the adoption of a policy for the protection and promotion of a language of a Member State that is both the national language and the first official language. The Court said, however, that discrimination against nationals of other Member States in the course of the free movement of workers was prohibited, and that any disproportionate measure to the object pursued was unacceptable. In the context of the related area of free movement of services, it was pronounced that a national cultural policy may constitute an overriding requirement relating to the general interest which justifies a restriction on the freedom to provide services. It was also held in this case that restrictions may be imposed in order to protect consumers against excessive advertising or, as an objective of cultural policy, in order to maintain a level of programme quality. Again, in the context of the provision of services, the European Court has held, in *Commission v Italy*,[4] that the general interest in consumer protection and in the conservation of the national historic and artistic heritage can constitute an overriding reason justifying a restriction on the freedom to provide services. Variations on this approach emerged in two subsequent cases: first, in *Commission v France*,[5] where it was said, somewhat differently, that the general interest in the proper appreciation of places and things of 'historical interest' *and* the widest possible dissemination of knowledge of the artistic cultural heritage can also underpin an overriding reason justifying a restriction on the freedom to provide services; and, secondly, in *Commission v Greece*,[6] where it was considered in broadly similar terms to those adopted in *Commission v Italy* and *Commission v France*, and perhaps conflating the two, that the general interest in the proper appreciation of the artistic and archaeological cultural heritage of

[1] *Cinetheque v Federation National Des Cinemas Francais* [1985] ECR 2605.
[2] *Cassis De Dijon* [1979] ECR 649.
[3] *Groener v Minister For Education* [1989] ECR 3967.
[4] *Commission v Italy* [1991] ECR I-709.
[5] *Commission v France* [1991] ECR I-659.
[6] *Commission v Greece* [1991] ECR I-727.

a country and in consumer protection can comprise an overriding reason justifying a restriction on the freedom to provide services. From this stream of related case law, we discern a narrow focus on national cultural policy without an accompanying explicit reference to EU cultural policy, if one indeed exists. There is no obvious relation between Article 151 and any such policy. We are left, therefore, with a somewhat disjointed picture of EU cultural regulation. Only the EU Commission has addressed cultural policy directly, and that body treats it as a mediator for integration rather than on its own terms. This is perhaps explained by the proposition that the inclusion of culture in the Treaty on European Union was at the relevant time generally agreed to have been an implicit part of a more general strategy to more closely involve the citizens of Europe in the process of European integration.

The scope of a specific cultural initiative in EU law can therefore be seen as very narrow. The text of Article 151, set out above, confines the competence in the audio-visual realm to artistic and literary creations, *including* in the audio-visual sector, rather than opening the whole of the audio-visual sector to Community intervention. Additionally, the Article's provision that the Council shall adopt incentive measures, excluding any harmonisation of the laws and regulations of the Member States, indicates the lack of availability of what can be termed hard law. This arguably results in the European Union being essentially confined to the establishment of financial incentives in the area of culture. A further potentially limiting factor is that Council decisions in the cultural area are to be taken unanimously as opposed to by qualified majority voting. Another inhibiting factor is that although cultural rights have gained importance within public international law in particular, they have not acquired the same status in European Union legal vocabulary and instruments, perhaps because they are normally viewed as group rights rather than individual rights; this is the case despite being cultural issues which fall within Community competence. Such difficulties for cultural development in the European Union are clearly problematic but they can, nevertheless, be cast in relief by the following observations. Until Maastricht, there was clearly no policy for culture but, even within the strictly economic competences of the Community, matters of cultural concern periodically surfaced. This was most apparent when the derogation to the free movement of goods for the protection of national treasures possessing artistic, historic or archaeological value was spasmodically invoked. Regulation 3911/92 on the export of cultural goods[7] and Directive 93/7 on the return of cultural goods and objects exported illegally,[8] although running in the opposite direction to the treasures derogation, also highlighted culture as a Community concern. In addition, it was introduced into the EC Treaty by the Treaty of European Union that state aid to promote culture and heritage conservation may be compatible with the common market as long as the aid does

[7] Council Regulation (EEC) No. 3911/92 of 09.12.92 = Official Journal L 395, 31.12.1992.
[8] Council Directive 93/7/EEC of 15.03.93 = Official Journal L 074, 27.03.1993.

not affect trading conditions and competition in the Union to an extent that is contrary to the common interest. Such irregular positive cultural developments in EU law form a placebo for the more general tortuous culture problematic that has accrued within it. European Union organs must combine to tackle culture in a less incidental way and address its growing importance as an autonomous concern within EU competence in accordance with the independent, if rather incomplete, profile of Article 151.

13

EU Law and Culture: An Holistic Overview (2004)[*]

THE OBJECT OF this essay is to offer, after a brief introduction, observations on the contemporary nature of culture, especially in the light of EU legal and political objectives; a short overview of the relationship between EU law and culture using the theory of autopoiesis, which is particularly suited to interfacial issues of the type with which we are dealing; a necessarily succinct commentary on Article 151[1] and selected associated case law; a reflection on EU legal subjects deemed relevant to culture; and finally, conclusions forming an assessment of the relationship between EU law and culture, having regard both to the law's apparent aims and the synthesis of law and culture in practice. The fact that this is a somewhat mixed bag serves to underline the difficulties and complexities which arise when two not obviously compatible entities are fused in a juridical structure lacking not only a clear focus but also any specific design for their particular inter-relation.

[*] A precursor of this essay (by this author) was 'Culture and EU Law: The Exploration of an Interface' in Rachael Craufurd Smith (ed), *Culture and European Union Law* (Oxford, Oxford University Press, 2004) Ch 13, 385–405. Regarding the principal provision of EU law analysed here, it is useful to know that original and seminal Article 151, becomes Article 167 under the most recent numbering system of the Treaty on the Functioning of the European Union, but, conveniently, that Article is still habitually referred to as Article 151. It is beyond the ambit of this essay to examine rights in the European Union Charter of Fundamental Rights that may have cultural relevance. For a detailed analysis of European Charter rights in general, see De Vries, Bernitz and Weatherill (eds), *The Protection of Fundamental Rights in the European Union after Lisbon* (Oxford, Hart Publishing, 2013).

[1] Article 151 reads: '1. The Community shall contribute to the flowering of the cultures of the Member States, while respecting their national and regional diversity and at the same time bringing the common cultural heritage to the fore. 2. Action by the Community shall be aimed at encouraging cooperation between Member States and, if necessary, supporting and supplementing their action in the following areas: –improvement of the knowledge and dissemination of the culture and history of the European peoples, –conservation and safeguarding of cultural heritage of European significance, –non-commercial cultural exchanges, –artistic and literary creation, including in the audio-visual sector. 3. The Community and the Member States shall foster cooperation with third counties and the competent international organisations in the sphere of culture, in particular the Council of Europe. 4. The Community shall take cultural aspects into account in its action under other provisions of this Treaty, in particular in order to respect and to promote the diversity of its cultures. 5. In order to contribute to the achievement of the objectives referred to in this Article, the Council: –acting in accordance with the procedure referred to in Article 251 and after consulting the Committee of the Regions, shall adopt incentive measures, excluding any harmonisation of the laws and regulations of the Member States. The Council shall act unanimously throughout the procedure referred to in Article 251; –acting unanimously on a proposal from the Commission, shall adopt recommendations.'

I INTRODUCTION

Given the economic priorities of the incipient EC, it is unsurprising that culture did not feature as an EC concern from the outset.[2] As the European Community developed, however, culture began to gain in prominence, emerging as a new EU concern at Maastricht. It is also possible to identify other arguably related initiatives: the notion of citizenship found a place in the treaty law, also at Maastricht, and human rights, inter alia, gradually infiltrated the *acquis communautaire*. Cultural protection was originally allied to both these evolving fields in an attempt to fit it under an appropriate existing umbrella for practical purposes, if not conceptually ideal ones.[3]

The notion of cultural rights, however, slowly evolved in the EC framework in contrast to other culture-related measures such as the provision of cultural aid, for example, for regional festivals and their ilk, which fell within the scope of the structural funds and well-established legal categories, and was therefore more easily assimilated into an existing pattern. Arguably, however, some of this funding did not actually have a legal base but was pushed through by the Parliament using its budgetary powers in a way which would now be considered unconstitutional. The current Cultural Title XII, initially established at Maastricht, nevertheless promised a more sound and pronounced role for culture as a distinct and legitimate EU concern, not least because founding such additional policy initiatives in existing EU law by the treaty route is historically something of a successful mechanism for the object concerned.[4] However, in the case of citizenship there was a Community precedent in the form of the free movement of persons which paved the way for the more all-embracing idea to become a legal reality. No comparable avenue pre-existed for culture and, in this way, it can be better compared to human rights in EU law, which were a somewhat residual EU concern, only gradually assimilated into EU law[5] as it broadened its socio-political as well as economic horizons. It is indisputable, though, that EU measures in the realm of culture have been seen as a less necessary and less pressing concern than adequate provision for basic freedoms and concomitant obligations.[6]

[2] The area is still little-covered, even in standard textbooks such as that of P Craig and G De Burca, *EU Law: Text and Materials*, 2nd edn (Oxford, Oxford University Press, 1998), and does not feature in G Glockler, L Junius, G Scappucci, S Usherwood and J Vassallo, *Guide to EU Policies* (London, Blackstone Press Ltd, 1998).

[3] See further, M Ross, 'Cultural Protection: A Matter of Union Citizenship or Human Rights?' in N Neuwahl and A Rosas (eds), *The European Union and Human Rights* (The Hague, Kluwer, 1995).

[4] From the time of its inclusion in an EU treaty, a given EU purpose is built upon and expanded with little fear for its future contraction, given the current constraints of unanimity.

[5] Through the mechanism of unwritten general principles of EU law established in Case 29/69 *Stauder* [1969] ECR 419.

[6] This is also a political reality in individual Member States.

II GENERAL PERSPECTIVES ON CULTURE AND EU LAW

The autonomy of culture as a concern within the EU reflects sociological conditions. As Clement Greenberg said,

> In societies below a certain level of economic development everybody works; and where this is so, work and culture tend to be fused in a single functional complex. Art, lore and religion then become barely distinguishable, in either intention or practice, from the techniques of production, healing and even war. Rite, magic, myth, decoration, image, music, dance and oral literature are at one and the same time religion, art, lore, defence, work and 'science'. Five thousand years of civilisation have separated these areas of activity from one another and specialised them in terms of their verifiable results, so that we now have culture and art for their own sake, religion for the sake of things unknowable (or, like art, for the sake of states of mind) and work for the sake of practical ends. It would seem that these things have now become separated from one another forever.[7]

This sense of fragmentation of different spheres is a typically postmodern phenomenon.[8]

Postmodernism has many distinct features but it follows a scheme of fragmentation, compartmentalisation, assimilation then integration. These traits are discerned in the various celebrated works of F Jameson, including his 1991 monograph, *Postmodernism*. The term 'integration' appears for the first time in the EU's formal development in the debates prior to the Treaty of Nice, so politico-legal practice here is shadowing theory and implicitly calling for reconciliation of theory and practice. The specific recognition of cultural trends in the EU regime suggests an appeal for closer associations[9] between Member States at a grass-roots inter-human level, an area for expansion under the Committee of the Regions. However, the specialised juridification of culture is not assisted by the lack of a suitable precedent to show the ways in which culture could be judiciable; the issue of human rights, by way of contrast, was clearly a justiciable field prior to the EU's *sui generis* regulation of it. Moreover, the controversial legal, notably judicial, application of the principle of subsidiarity could prove problematic for juridical applications of EU law's central institutional cultural conceptualisations at the local level.

It was always unlikely that EU law's regulation of culture would be holistic. When the wheel of EU law turns, it takes with it, in each of its relevant separate segments, a particular dimension of culture; the type of cultural concern regu-

[7] C Greenburg, *Art and Culture: Critical Essays* (Boston, Beacon Press, 1989) 32–33.

[8] Postmodernism occurs after modernism, as its name suggests, and embraces at least the last 50 years; its more precise timing is a matter of controversy. See further, P Kearns, *The Legal Concept of Art* (Oxford, Hart Publishing, 1998) 185–92 and F Jameson, *Postmodernism* (London, Verso, 1991).

[9] For a critique of the difficulties of closer cultural co-operation in the cultural sphere, see further, S Weatherill, 'Finding Space for Closer Co-operation in the Field of Culture' in G De Burca and J Scott (eds), *Constitutional Change in the EU: From Uniformity to Flexibility* (Oxford, Hart Publishing, 2000) 237–57.

lated will depend on which branch of EU law is at play. Despite the rubric of the cardinal EU culture provision, Article 151,[10] discussed later, this leaves a picture resembling crazy paving, with the random regulation of unspecified but allegedly culturally related factors which fail to unite under the one titular head of culture in a conceptually convincing way. Because there is no precise conceptual parameter to, or apparent constraint upon, the definition of culture, it would be naïve to assume that forthcoming cultural regulation will be strictly confined to the loosely expressed areas and processes specified in Article 151. European cultural integration is ready to be manipulated as a disguised political phenomenon as much as an explicitly legal one.

'Culture' means cultivation or the result of cultivation; the state of being cultivated; refinement in manners, thought, taste, etc; loosely, the arts; a type of civilisation; the attitudes and values which inform a society.[11] A definition of 'civilisation' is the state of being civilised, but civilisation can be defined as exactly synonymous with culture.[12] In his *Notes Towards the Definition of Culture*,[13] TS Eliot also tends to make the two concepts of culture and civilisation interchangeable throughout his analysis.[14] In addition, he tells us that culture is 'what is worthwhile' in a society.[15] If this is an acceptable conception of culture, as I would venture, then its implications are very interesting. To consider something 'worthwhile' cannot be construed as being other than a judgement of positive value; culture, accordingly, cannot embody anything other than commendable quality. Is this the meaning of culture we will find developed in EU law? That remains to be seen. Sometimes mere customary practice as a way of life does not invite evaluation as positive or negative but can nevertheless be described as 'cultural'. Let us then first explore further what culture denotes in cultural theory.

B Robbins recently observed that

> Never have the moral consequences of laying claim to membership in a culture, or accepting someone else's claim to such membership, seemed so far from self-evident. As a result, many are now wondering in some bewilderment how culture could ever have been allowed to expand until there was no one it didn't appear to include, nothing it didn't appear to explain – until it had become . . . 'everything'.[16]

F Mulhern and A Kuper, in different studies, one in the area of literary studies,[17] the other in the area of anthropology,[18] offer evidence that the concept of culture is itself experiencing cultural fatigue. This is a far cry from Raymond Williams's

[10] See n 1.
[11] *The Chambers Dictionary* (Edinburgh, W & R Chambers Ltd, 1995).
[12] ibid.
[13] TS Eliot, *Notes Towards the Definition of Culture* (London, Faber & Faber Ltd, 1983).
[14] ibid.
[15] ibid 27.
[16] B Robbins, 'No Escape' (London Review of Books, 1 November 2001) 34.
[17] F Mulhern, *Culture/Metaculture* (London, Routledge, 2000).
[18] A Kuper, *Culture: The Anthropologist's Account* (New York, New York University Press, 2000).

classic account of the idea of culture, which was a concept invented only at the end of the eighteenth century, and which was essentially a standard against which industrial modernity could be judged. In the last half-century, there has been a dramatic growth in metaculture, which is discourse about what culture is or does, which concludes counter-intuitively that culture is indeed everything. Gone are the antiquated but refined notions of C Geertz that culture is the epitome of values that rule in a society, embodied most immaculately in the revered religious rites and high art of an elite.[19] Postmodernists are much more concerned with the forging of extreme relativism and acute popularism in cultural analysis, which is undoubtedly the tenor and reflection of the age.

Kuper's scholarship does not indicate great hope for European Union political integrationists committed to common cultural identification. He distinguishes the German, French and English approaches to cultural thinking. According to him, the German is romantic and ethnic, the French is civilised, and the English is a synthesis of the other two. More worryingly for Europhiles, Mulhern insists that the concept of culture is, always was, and always will be, generative of a narrow nationalism. J Tusa is more optimistic. He says that

> [d]efining European cultural identity is a challenge of its own. Even without too specific a definition, thinking about the contribution that existing cultural experience makes to the political task of forging a new Europe is worthwhile, if only because it forces us to raise our horizons beyond our own seemingly ever-present [national] miseries.[20]

In addition, Tusa has a more negative opinion on the limited use of the power of culture as a unifying force:

> From Lithuania in the Baltic to Slovenia in the Adriatic, the new democracies of the former socialist bloc are desperate to become members of the European Union . . . As Eurocrats wrestle with the task of creating true adherence to the European Union in the countries of Central and Eastern Europe, the notion that a millennium or so of European cultural activity might be a good way of reinforcing and popularising the widening and deepening Europe has not featured strongly in what has been an overwhelmingly politicised process.[21]

Further, he believes that 'Europe's sheer cultural homogeneity might be used to build European identity.'[22] J Pietrse provides a definition of Europe's homogenous cultural backcloth:

> Europe is formed by the . . . community of nations which are largely characterised by the inherited civilisation whose most important sources are: the Judaeo-Christian religion, the Greek-Hellenistic ideas in the fields of government, philosophy, arts and science, and, finally, the Roman views concerning law.[23]

[19] Robbins (n 16) 35.
[20] J Tusa (ed), *Art Matters: Reflecting on Culture* (London, Methuen, 2000) 36.
[21] ibid 37.
[22] ibid.
[23] J Pietrse, 'Fictions of Europe' (1991) 32 *Race and Class* 3.

Drawing on this extensive corpus of basic cultural unity could prompt in EU citizens a more profound feeling of European, as opposed to mere national, cultural identification.

If culture were used more habitually in the politico-legal arena, it is arguable that it would also bring with it a livelier and more dynamic sense of European status. A feeling for European culture specifically could stop local cultures being introspective by placing them on a broader European footing while ensuring that they did not become submerged in a global quagmire and lose their identity. Time could be spent isolating truly European traits in the arts – European classical composers have always written to common rules of structure and harmony; European playwrights have regularly drawn on Greek drama; there have always been distinctively European visual-artistic canons.[24] There is now a wariness of fake internationalism[25] and the associated uniformity resonant in commercial brands utilising globalisation, but it is indubitable that occidentally-inspired international consumerism has reinforced a specifically European allegiance more effectively than dry political allegiances and purely legal ambitions. The seeming paradox of cultural diversity in a legal homogeneity designed to foster cultural identity is, in reality, practicable. This is the case despite the fact that the horizons of culture are far wider than the horizons of law. Culture clearly transcends the legal notion of jurisdiction, EU or otherwise, and is inherent in all societies, though it is not confined to merely societal culture. The 'worthwhile' permeates nature as well as civilisation, and though culture and civilisation can be synonyms, culture is not restricted to human enterprise. Culture also exists, for example, in the animal kingdom.[26] One school of thought[27] might consider that it would be undesirable for EU law to discriminate between cultural forms as a matter of EU priority because it cannot grasp the diverse nature of local or national culture by institutionally centralised, remote and unwanted selectivity; if EU law were to attempt to establish discriminatory prescriptive requirements for culture, the Europe that would evolve would be in that very discriminatory action already more penurious in cultural terms.

III AUTOPOIESIS, CULTURE AND EU LAW

It is instructive to attend to the more theoretical ramifications of the relationship between culture and EU law using the concept of autopoiesis[28] to enlighten

[24] See further, Tusa (n 20) 42.

[25] ibid 36 et seq.

[26] The underestimation or dismissal of animals' complex cultural systems is beginning to be reassessed, albeit somewhat belatedly.

[27] The author's opinion is that this school of thought is too exaggeratedly locally defensive.

[28] See further, N Luhmann, 'Autopoiesis, handlung, and kommunikative Verstandigung' (1982) *Zeitschrift fur Soziologie* 11, 366; H Rottleuthner, 'A Purified Sociology of Law: Niklas Luhmann on the Autonomy of the Legal System' (1989) *Law and Society Review* 23, 779.

us. Autopoiesis is useful to us because it is concerned with both the idea of the autonomy of systems and their interface. This can very pertinently illuminate the EU law/culture relation when EU law attempts to juridify the system or notion of culture in any way. It also provides an intellectual overview.

Autopoiesis comes in several forms but all of them have the same fundamental features. The legal theory of autopoiesis derives essentially from the work of the late German theorist, Niklas Luhmann, who utilised the work of the South American biologists, Maturana and Varela, who saw biological systems as entities which regularly reproduced their elements from their own elements in a self-generating way, becoming autonomous in so doing, and intrinsically insularised from their environment. Luhmann was responsible for divorcing autopoiesis from these biological origins and applying it to social systems. He defined social systems as systems of meaning, with communication at their heart. For cells and organisms, Luhmann substituted communications; and an autopoietic system for Luhmann constituted a representation of society within society. Each social system became a system of meaning-production.

Some see autopoiesis as an attempt by lawyers to impose their closed systems approach on the open systems view favoured by social science, but law is, of course, a more nuanced entity than the caricature this misconception engenders. According to autopoietic theory, law's components are self-constituted in self-referential cycles, and together become a hypercycle of self-reference; self-sufficiency and self-governing operations are therefore intrinsic to an autopoietic system. If external elements enter the realm of legal communication, they are transformed by law in a manner which permits their transmutation into identities that are recognisable as legal communications. Our specific theoretical enquiry is how EC law appears to, or attempts to, perform this operation on culture.

Essentially, autopoiesis as a legal theory offers valuable insights into the operation of the legal system and its relationships with other social systems including the cultural. Applied to our study it raises important questions, namely, whether the EU legal system is firmly closed to all external influences to defend and perpetuate a traditional hegemony (and to assert a potent form of legal positivism) and the way in which culture 'threatens' such a regime. Culture may do so by being all-embracing: it surrounds the traditional legal hegemonic area, influencing law from inside and without, saturating law with its ubiquity. We will test the accuracy of this suggestion in autopoiesis's specialised terms.

The conclusion of most recent systems theory is that the openness of legal and cultural systems is an essential prerequisite for equilibrium in the context of wider society. Autopoiesis, rather than using an input-output model, emphasises the internal operations in a given system of self-production, seeing that system as a system of meaning rather than as a group of people. The basic autopoietic premise is that culture will exist within the system of EU law only according to the meaning that the EU system assigns to it. But is culture too broad and unmanageable for that, too all-infusing? Will culture in EU law be simply, in Teubnerian[29] terms, a 'semantic artefact'? No; because it will interconnect with the remainder of its conceptualisation outside the EU system uninterruptedly, a process which is part of its own pervasive autopoietic system. EU law will reproduce within itself its version of the external social environment which culture permeates, amplifying the environmental complexity it has to master.

The test of EU law's degree of autopoietic self-sufficiency depends on how that system manages to constitute its own components and identity in a self-referential cycle. Culture threatens this cycle because EU law is just one part of culture's own hypercycle, a cog in culture's larger wheel. Another difficulty for EU law is that, in its interaction with culture, it may be forced to receive and produce non-legal communications which it may be ill-equipped to do, and a consequence of which may be the thwarting of its regulatory function and its legal autopoietic independence. However, once culture is in the EU legal domain, it is arguable that culture is likely to be transformed or reconstructed by EU law in ways which allow for its conversion into data recognisable as EU legal communications. But this is not inevitable, not least because EU law's role regarding culture is primarily facilitative rather than unduly prescriptive or punitive and very largely unconcerned with the dichotomy of legal and illegal. Culture is, however, 'shadowed' in the EU legal system when any of its facets are integrated into rules, as in EU customs law, under which art is non-dutiable. A counter consideration is that EU law can never have autonomous operation but is moulded by culture in its social environment. Culture will no doubt influence the content of legal communications but the question becomes can it determine legal communications in any direct way or in a way that is possible to predict? If the answer to this is yes, EU law ceases to be an autopoietic system because it is not then *normatively* closed. It is no threat to its autopoietic character, though, if it is simply *cognitively* open, which, in its relationship with culture, inter alia, it clearly has to be, for effective decisions to be made in relation to it. EU law then reconstructs cultural objectives as EU law in keeping with its autopoietic remit. There is no problem with the EU law being motivated by 'external' initiatives since that does not compromise its cycle of self-reference in EU legal terms.

If cultural issues *are* reformulated by EU law, they are reconstructed within EU law's system of meaning. This can seem dehumanising when culture involves as epistemic units personal dimensions, and neutralising when EU law processes creative and vital cultural versions of reality. Any parallel conclusive definition of culture by law suggests comparable power in the conceptual realm. The application of such power is perhaps inevitable in a formalist regime but, as we have seen above, it cannot be assumed that culture will be easily reduced to one of EU law's reality constructs, not least because its sheer multi-dimensionality and ubiquity may resist such formal reductivism. There also remains the hierarchical issue that

[29] G Teubner is a leading authority on autopoiesis. See further, M King, 'The Truth about Autopoiesis' (1993) *Journal of Law and Society* 20, 218.

EU law may be simply one element in culture's autopoietic hypercycle: depending on how broadly we configure culture, it may be that EU law's autopoietic character is of relatively minor stature in systemic terms. After all, is culture capable of being autopoietically confined by a legal regime when (a) culture's definitional parameters are so elastic and potentially all-inclusive and (b) its alleged central fabric is so endlessly contentious as a consequence?

IV CULTURE AND EU CASE LAW

Prior to the development of a treaty provision for cultural purposes in the form of Article 151,[30] it was easy to be negative about the EU law approach to culture. Critics have claimed that until that development European cultural identity was an essentially residual idea based on a precept of what Europe was not.[31] In particular, the original Treaty of Rome can be blamed for cultural stagnation given the paucity of references to culture within it.[32] Even the national treasures derogation from the free movement of goods in Article 30[33] can be interpreted as a way of achieving the economic goal of the internal market at the expense of leaving national culture static, underdeveloped, or repressed. The more conventional interpretation of the effect of the current Article 30 is that it actually performs the positive function of protecting 'national treasures possessing artistic, historic or archaeological value'.

The rather incidental inclusion of cultural matters in the original treaty law of the EC, such as that pertaining to the restriction of the movement of national treasures, implicitly indicates a lack of interest in cultural matters as a complete genus in EU law's early history. The first signal of a real concern for cultural issues per se came in 1969 when the Heads of Government of the Member States recognised the need to preserve Europe as an exceptional seat of development, culture and progress. The institutions of the EU nevertheless remained apathetic until, in 1977, the EU Commission issued a document called *Community Action in the Cultural Sector* which it followed up, lamentably slowly, with another in 1987 ironically and self-consciously entitled *A Fresh Boost for Culture in the European Community*. In the early 1990s one regulation and one directive involved cultural subject matter.

[30] See n 1.

[31] This original exclusive approach is partly explained by the then lack of sufficient development of supra-national institutions in Europe.

[32] The marriage of culture and EU law was obviously but lamentably not a perceived priority at this incipient stage of predominantly economic EC development.

[33] Article 30 provides that: 'The provisions of Articles 28 and 29 shall not preclude prohibitions or restrictions on imports, exports or goods in transit justified on grounds of public morality, public policy or public security; the protection of health and life of humans, animals or plants; the protection of national treasures possessing artistic, historic or archaeological value; or the protection of industrial and commercial property. Such prohibitions or restrictions shall not, however, constitute a means of arbitrary discrimination or a disguised restriction on trade between Member States.'

The position of the rather arbitrary treatment of cultural issues by the EU persisted until the scope for EC action in the area of culture was augmented at Maastricht. Article 3(q)[34] indicates that the activities of the Community will now include a contribution to education, training of quality and the flourishing of Members States' cultures. The rubric of Article 3(q) actually uses the term 'flowering' instead of flourishing, the poeticity of which has been subsequently criticised for its vagueness. 'Flowering' does, though, have an appropriately artistic appeal and captures the flavour of creative activity. The Article's linking of education, training and culture suggests that the former two terms are not self-evidently included in the latter, a situation which prefaces the definitional problems EU law ineluctably confronts in its attempted juridification of the term 'culture(s)'. It also anticipates the practical drafting technique that spells out different manifestations of culture whenever a given EU provision aims to assist or regulate one specific form or forms of culture in particular. Another treaty reference to culture appears in an amendment to former Article 87 which permits the granting of state aid to promote culture and heritage conservation. Again, we notice that heritage conservation is specified independently of culture, which could definitionally include it, because, somewhat obviously, the law's main objectives in the amendment have to be concretised rather than left at the mercy of imprecise inference. Nevertheless, an unwanted tautology occurs when the word 'culture' itself is juxtaposed with terms for one aspect of culture as if they were separate things. Such an approach also begs the question what is included within, and what is excluded from, the often residual generic term 'culture' in these contexts.

As mentioned previously, the principal dramatic development in EU law's treatment of culture occurred with the coming into force of what is now Article 151, set out in full at the beginning of this essay. A number of things are immediately noteworthy about this provision. In Article 151(1) there is a sensible appeal to appreciate that within the EU there are both common and individual cultural phenomena in the Member States. The homogeneity sought is not a uniform bland EU conformism, it is a richness of detail in a complex holistic picture that is European in its parameters. Article 151(2) spells out Community action regarding the type of cultural activities that are designed to be encouraged between Member States in their interaction; the Article also envisages Community action beyond those aims, though the specific nature of such additional action appears to be confined to the activities already enumerated in the Article's second paragraph despite the broad enterprise conceived of in the first. Article 151(3) is an outward-looking provision that urges co-operation between the Community and Member States, presumably disjunctively and conjunctively, and third countries and apt international bodies. The Council of Europe

[34] Article 3(q) provides that: '[For the purposes set out in Article 2], the activities of the Community shall include, as provided by this Treaty and in accordance with the timetable set out therein] . . . a contribution to education and training of quality and the flowering of the cultures of the Member States.'

is specifically mentioned as such a competent organisation. This is unsurprising since the Council of Europe is centrally involved in both cultural and rights issues and is a fellow European organisation with similar distinctive European cultural goals explicit and implicit in its activities. Article 151(4) is a provision which is important but not easy to interpret. It envisages the Community taking cultural matters into account when acting under other provisions of its treaty law, with the added emphasis that such measures should respect and promote the diversity of its cultures. There is an invitation here for the principle of subsidiarity to be utilised to its fullest extent. Article 151(5) is a mainly procedural measure that involves in part consultation with the Committee of the Regions to achieve the substantive objective of incentive measures. A reasonable assumption, taking Article 151(4) and Article 151(5) together, is that there will be the promotion of much cultural activity at a local level in accordance with the subsidiarity principle, and, optimally, the work of the Committee of the Regions, which has local concerns central to its remit. This militates somewhat against the fear that cultural uniformity is behind the EU's programme of cultural law.

In *Cinéthèque v Fédération Nationale des Cinémas Français*,[35] it was said that cultural aims may justify certain restrictions on the free movement of goods, provided that those restrictions apply to national and imported products without distinction, that they are appropriate to the cultural aim which is being pursued, and that they constitute the means of achieving them which affects intra-Community trade the least. From this case, it is evident that the protection of at least motion visual art can be added to the *Cassis De Dijon*[36] list of mandatory requirements. In *Groener v Minister for Education*,[37] in the context of the free movement of persons, it was pronounced that the EEC Treaty does not prohibit the adoption of a policy for the protection and promotion of a language of a Member State which is both the national language and the first official language. However, it was said that the implementation of such a policy must not encroach upon a fundamental freedom such as that of the free movement of workers. Consequently, the requirements deriving from measures intended to implement such a policy must not under any circumstances be disproportionate in relation to the aim pursued and the manner in which they are applied must not bring about discrimination against nationals of other Member States.

In *Stichting Collective Antennevoorziening Gouda v Commissariaat Voor De Media*, it was stated, with a rare explicit reference to policy, that a cultural policy may indeed constitute an overriding requirement relating to the general interest which justifies a restriction on the freedom to provide services.[38] Additionally, it was held in this case that restrictions may be imposed in order to

[35] Cases 60 & 61/84 *Cinéthèque v Fédération Nationale des Cinémas Français* [1985] ECR 2605.

[36] Case 120/78 *Cassis De Dijon* [1979] ECR 649.

[37] Case 379/87 *Groener v Minister for Education* [1989] ECR 3967.

[38] Case C-288/89 *Stichting Collective Antennevoorziening Gouda v Commissariaat Voor De Media* [1991] ECR I-4007.

protect consumers against excessive advertising or, as an objective of cultural policy, in order to maintain a level of programme quality. Also in the context of the provision of services, the Court held in *Commission v Italy* that the general interest in consumer protection and in the conservation of the national historic and artistic heritage can constitute an overriding reason justifying a restriction on the freedom to provide services.[39] In *Commission v France*, it was said somewhat differently that the general interest in the proper appreciation of places and things of 'historical interest' *and* the widest possible dissemination of knowledge of the artistic cultural heritage can also constitute an overriding reason justifying a restriction on the freedom to provide services.[40] Another variation on this theme arose in *Commission v Greece*,[41] where it was considered, along *Commission v Italy*[42] lines, above, that the general interest in the proper appreciation of the artistic and archaeological cultural heritage of a country and in consumer protection can constitute an overriding reason justifying a restriction on the freedom to provide services. However, despite the above rulings relating to three EU traditional freedoms, namely goods, persons, and services, the Court of Justice has not yet thoroughly examined the impact of cultural policy on competition law or other such prominent areas of EU law. It is incontrovertible, however, that cultural concerns will infiltrate most dimensions of EU activity in due course and prompt further related litigation and judgments.

The Court of Justice has thus acknowledged, albeit scantly, the notion of cultural policy in its nomenclature, and culture per se as an important concern of Member States. It is such judicial activism in this area that will ultimately determine the precise rules that will apply where any 'cultural policy' is a central issue. The comparative paucity of relevant EU legislation on the subject, and the fact that there is not really a discernible EU cultural policy to serve as a guide or blueprint, despite exiguous references to one in the Court's case law, will not assist the Court in its deliberations. This lacuna does not help culture and law prepare to marry in the EU law context, and Article 151[43] is not a firm enough foundation or even signpost for this exercise, despite being *lex lata* with a prospective vision. R Lane said of Article 151 that '[it] cannot be said to be an example of the draughtsman's finer arts'[44] on the grounds that it is not obviously justiciable and the Member States' common cultural heritage is relatively amorphous. My personal animus is that what has happened since Lane's prophetic insight is that, rather than having a doctrinal development of the EU law-culture inter-relation, precluded perhaps by culture's non-justiciability,

[39] Case C-180/89 *Commission v. Italy* [1991] ECR I-709.

[40] Case C-154/89 *Commission v. France* [1991] ECR I-659.

[41] Case C-198/89 *Commission v. Greece* [1991] ECR I-727.

[42] *Commission v Italy* (n 39).

[43] See n 1 above.

[44] R Lane, 'New Community Competences under the Maastricht Treaty' (1993) *Common Market Law Review* 30, 939.

there is currently only a judicial *theme* of cultural awareness dealt with on an ad hoc basis. This is not a satisfactory footing for an area lacking related precursors in EU substantive law to suggest the road ahead.

Neither is human rights law or citizenship an apt matrix from which to try to elevate the autonomous concerns of culture as a single monolith. Only the Commission has addressed cultural policy directly and it treats it as a mediator for integration rather than on its own terms. What emerges from this approach is what Kymlicka famously coined 'societal culture',[45] and yet, ironically, there is little overlap between culture and EU social policy. Additionally, art and literature, for example, embody cultural value in a way which does not immediately suggest a *societal* dimension except in the sense that they anticipate an audience. Those two entities could be said, rather, to comprise *immanent* or *inherent* culture, of a self-standing variety.

From EU case law on culture we have a very fuzzy impression of what culture actually is. The Court of Justice is prone to simply citing cultural forms, somewhat arbitrarily, as being linked to the type of culture it has in mind on a particular occasion. R Lane, considering education and culture, warned that

> the Court . . . will have to be on its mettle, both in defining the meaning and breadth of Community education and cultural competence and the subsidiarity and integration provisions, but also for another reason: much of its intrusion hitherto into sensitive national domains has been, and has been accepted as being, justified by the economic interests of the common/internal markets. Education and culture, however, are sensitive non-economic spheres, of which the Court has had little experience. Its reasoning may therefore be coloured by, and subject to attack on grounds of, not economic analysis but ideology.[46]

Since Lane's observations, we have had neither significant judicial insights into culture's definition or nature even for purely EU purposes, nor prominent dicta on culture's capacity or incapacity for being justiciable or even being simply *judicialised*, ie operated on by judges in the way that other relevant factors are habitually treated by judicial process. This is perhaps explained by the particular difficulty of the definitional task and the comparatively recent judicial acquaintance with the issue of cultural appraisal.

The inclusion of culture in the Treaty on European Union was part of a strategy to more closely involve the people of Europe in the process of European integration. Nevertheless, its scope can be perceived as very narrow. The text of Article 151[47] confines the competence in the audio-visual realm to artistic and literary creations, *including* in the audio-visual sector, rather than opening the whole of the audio-visual sector to Community intervention. In addition, the Article's provision that the Council shall adopt incentive measures, excluding

[45] See further, D Chalmers and E Szyszczak, *EU Law Vol. 2, Towards a European Polity* (Dartmouth, Aldershot, 1998). Will Kymlicka is a famous Canadian political philosopher best known for his work on multiculturalism.

[46] ibid 956.

[47] See n 1.

any harmonisation of the laws and regulations of the Member States, indicates the lack of availability of what can be termed 'hard law'. This arguably results in the European Union being essentially confined to the establishment of financial incentives in the area of culture. A further constraint is that Council decisions in the cultural area are to be taken unanimously as opposed to by qualified majority voting. Another inhibiting factor is that although cultural rights have gained importance, particularly within public international law, they have not acquired the same status in European Union legal vocabulary and instruments, perhaps because they are normally viewed as group rights rather than individual rights; this is the case despite there being cultural issues which fall within Community competence.

Such difficulties for cultural development in the European Union can nevertheless be put in perspective. Until Maastricht, there was no policy for culture but, even within the strictly economic competences of the Community, matters of cultural concern occasionally surfaced. This was most conspicuous when the derogation to the free movement of goods for the protection of national treasures possessing artistic, historic or archaeological value[48] was periodically invoked. Regulation 3911/92 on the export of cultural goods and Directive 93/7 on the return of cultural goods and objects exported illegally, though different in objective from the treasures derogation, also highlighted culture as a Community concern. In addition, the Treaty on European Union introduced into the EC Treaty a derogation from the state aid prohibition for aid which promotes culture and heritage conservation, provided the aid does not affect trading conditions and competition in the Community to an extent that is contrary to the common interest.

Traditionalist commentators, such as the late Mary Whitehouse, have expressed concern that cultural values have been degraded by the promotion of free speech to include all manner of violent and pornographic vulgarity. Many commercial products possess the label of culture without being 'objectively' cultural is the tenor of their argument. To them, the Television without Frontiers Directive 89/552, for example, is very disappointing because the European Union promotes the transmission of 'European works' rather than 'European cultural works', the latter term not necessarily equating with the former. The lack of a strong case for 'real' culture is also arguably reflected in the operation of the Treaty competition rules, which, absent the possibly disabling distractions of a cultural law dimension, may lead to the cultural interest being set aside in favour of maintaining competition in the internal market. However, this dynamic is not yet sufficiently developed in practice to make firm generalisations. The conservative reservations, and the whole question about the quality of culture promoted by the European Union, are crucial in the areas mentioned and raise evaluative difficulties that are seldom easy to resolve, and that are explored later in this essay. Is there a justifiable preference for 'high art' standards immanent in EU

[48] See text accompanying n 33.

policy or do more populist conceptions of cultural worth now dominate? It may be that, in the contemporary Union, decisions on cultural worth are still largely market-driven in accordance with the economic emphasis of the traditional Community; or it may be that such decisions are coloured entirely by the priorities of the specific EU legal area in the course of which they are now made, and are thus simply context-dependent and context-determined. The lack of a sharp, explicit cultural policy in the European Union arguably leaves the matter as one for mere educated inference.

V CULTURE-RELATED PARADIGMS IN EU LAW

One of the primary difficulties when addressing the problematic of culture's assimilation by EU law is the fact that there are many arguably culture-related subjects that are branches of EU law but which are not necessarily dealt with under Article 151[49] and which are not embraced by a putative EU cultural policy, explicitly, implicitly, or otherwise. The lack of a policy under which these subjects are, or can be, unified is potentially confusing as well as unhelpful for the development of a cultural head in EU law. The subjects are either directly or indirectly, firmly or loosely, connected to cultural matters, and the lack of a suitable EU legal definition of culture means that they all have possible relevance to cultural concerns as legally-conceived. There is no EU legal prescription of what is culture and what is not that can help form a unitary cultural identity for otherwise miscellaneous, independent legal categories.

What are these culture-related subjects? They are a wide-ranging group, and include: education, equality and gender, sport, consumer protection, language policy, copyright, the movement of national treasures, external policy, citizenship, human rights, visa and asylum policy, audiovisual policy, customs law as it pertains to art and artists' resale rights. No doubt this list is not exhaustive.

The perceived links between these areas and culture will be more or less close depending on the definition of culture taken as one's starting point. There was no provision for, or allusion to, education in the EEC Treaty, only 'vocational training' under former Article 128. Following amendments to the Treaty on European Union, the development of education falls expressly, albeit with significant constraints, within the Community's competence. There is little doubt that education has cultural dimensions. Matters of equality and gender have become central parts of Union activity, the law having moved on a great deal since the days of simply equal pay for equal work. In this respect, identity of a personal nature impacts on culture. A more doubtful cultural entity is sport. Kicking a football between players in a game does not seem intrinsically cultural but is, rather, more of a leisure time pursuit, which could also be said of all other forms of mere entertainment and participation in it. What we retain of

[49] See n 1.

primary value from Ancient Rome includes literature and philosophy but only peripherally details of antics in the amphitheatre. There is arguably a durable aspect to 'real' culture and something beyond the merely interactive and prosaic. In contrast, the movement of national treasures is of essential cultural importance because art is indubitably a cultural concern. External policy, citizenship, human rights, and visa and asylum policy all have human issues involved that are linked, rather like gender and equality, to cultural concerns, albeit relatively loosely. They are clearly not as self-evidently cultural as, for example, high art. Similarly, it can be argued that audio-visual policy impacts on popular culture, in particular, but is really only contingently cultural, as a vehicle only, and only incidentally a vehicle for culture. Customs law deals in cultural distinctions because art passes through customs controls duty-free, and a question often arises as to what is art for these purposes, which is a cultural enquiry. The legal area of the resale rights of artists is probably a legal category even more central to truly cultural issues. So, one can make such distinctions as to the degree of cultural import in a particular EU legal field but only on the firm understanding that the criteria employed are inevitably somewhat contestable, and thus need to be clearly articulated, even though they may be difficult to justify objectively. Nevertheless, despite the lack of such objective justification, they might strike a chord of integrity in many, and might be relevant when considering how to shape an EU *cultural* policy that merits that title.

Let us briefly profile EU customs law pertaining to art, and the EU law on artists' resale rights, to see to what degree they have cultural relevance. This exercise can be seen as an assessment of these legal sectors that prefigures the consideration of whether they, for example, should in principle be included within an EU cultural policy that deserves the dignity of that name.

First, let us consider EU customs law pertaining to art.[50] EU customs law has evolved within the Customs Union and the Common Customs Tariff. The Customs Union has regulated the common customs area's internal market and the Common Customs Tariff has regulated the external trade of the EU, with the Common Commercial Policy as a partner in this role. Customs duties within EU territory are eliminated as is desired by any customs union between Member States. The basic rule is that all art passes through customs control duty-free. Since art has been more privileged duty-wise than other items, there has been substantial litigation over its definition when used in this particular context, and it is evident that EU customs law often penalises innovative forms. By 'works of art', the customs tariff sense refers only to the fine arts and not to the useful, mechanical, industrial or commercial arts. In ascertaining whether an object can be considered a work of art, the Court has not only had recourse to whether its appearance meets some definition of one of the fine arts but has also examined the occupation of the person creating it and/or the purpose for which it was made. The EU customs approach can favour a commercial characterisation of an object

[50] See further, Kearns (n 8) 159–70.

over its habitual artistic designation too much. Whereas pop art has transcended the commercial character barrier and escaped customs duties, paperweights, irrespective of their having appeared in art exhibitions, have not, due to their functionality. All artworks have an incidental commercial potential because their artistic work gives them the possibility of commercial significance. If an object can be regarded as a work of art, it is arguable that any concomitant commercial potential it might have should not decree that it is placed outside the 'works of art' category for customs classification purposes. A contrary view renders the purpose of customs duty exemptions applicable to art unjustly jeopardised by giving inappropriate weight to factors inimical to the fiscal privilege, specifically conferred on art for reasons which go beyond the usual commercial rationale for customs duties. The centrality here of cultural concerns militates clearly in favour of bringing EU customs law under the aegis of a cultural policy, which could resolve some of the inherent problems of art identification in this area by directions on artistic character and quality.

Now, concisely, we move on to artists' resale rights in EU law.[51] In April 1996, the European Commission presented the European Council with a proposal for a European Parliament and Council Directive to harmonise national laws relating to artists' resale rights. The subsequent legislative progress was complex and slow, and remains problematic following the lack of conciliation between the Parliament and the Council. However, the so-called 'Common Position' was adopted by the Council in June 2000 providing, inter alia, that the resale right is inalienable and incapable of waiver. It applies only to a resale of an 'original work of art' that is subsequent to the first transfer of the work by the artist. The term 'original works of art' is defined and the phrase is said to embrace even numbered, signed or otherwise duly authorised copies. A royalty is payable to the 'author', or, after his death, those entitled under him. The term of the right is the same as the copyright term, which is the case for moral rights in certain Member States including the United Kingdom.

It is clear that, with the concern for artists at its heart, the EU position on the artist's resale right is of fundamental cultural concern. It joins the EU provisions on the national treasures derogation from the free movement of goods as an area of law intrinsically connected with art, which is indubitably a matter of cultural relevance. Like the EU customs law pertaining to art, the artist's resale right has fundamental and direct financial significance for artists, and it indirectly promotes, on a practical level, artistic productivity.

VI CONCLUSIONS

There are a number of observations that one can make in general terms about the EU and cultural policy. The first is that a distinct, explicit policy is not

[51] See further, S Stokes, *Art and Copyright* (Oxford, Hart Publishing, 2001) 65–86.

apparent from the current state of EU law. This causes obvious difficulties for the legal management of the area. There are too many diffused strands of law relating to culture that are in no way anchored together, and this is attributable to straightforward EU disorganisation. Secondly, it is difficult to evaluate the efficacy of EU legal measures on culture when there are such vague and generalised cultural objectives set, when set at all. Thirdly, it is evident that the EU's general vision of culture is not an elitist one containing solely high art or fine art matters; EU cultural interest appears to accommodate sport and television as readily as national treasures and artists' moral rights. The overall cultural perspective of EU law is not classical but, rather, incorporates popular culture, which is to be expected given the removal of hierarchies in, and the eclectic nature of, the postmodern era[52] in which the law is operating. This approach requires overt pronouncement in terms of policy objectives.

What are currently perceptible in EU law are different concepts of culture co-existing not necessarily inconsistently, just diversely. What is problematic is the lack of a collation of these concepts in a mainstream policy, which would be a very broad-ranging one if we simply inferred the policy from the facts of current cultural regulation in EU law. But, one could urge, a policy should be a dynamic forerunner of events, explicit not inferred, actively not passively constructed. At the moment, the theme of cultural regulation in EU law is infused somewhat haphazardly throughout the law. Something needs to be done to congregate disparate elements pertinent to culture into a reservoir where they can be collectively analysed and from which a policy can deliberately emerge.[53]

EU cultural policy is not definite, let alone coherent, and is open-ended. The autopoietic model elaborated on earlier in this essay shows that culture's relative immunity to justiciability means that it cannot be operated on as tightly as human rights or citizenship, which were both legal phenomena that benefited from clear internal or external legal precedents for EU law to follow. Culture has an elasticity in EU law that has the subtle advantage of seeming unpolitically-determined, except, perhaps, when the law is obliged to regulate a matter that is not self-evidently cultural, but which someone has to decide is cultural for one legal reason or another, which could have the colour of a subjective political decision. This is also likely to be the case when authority has to be expressed on cultural quality matters, including appropriate value judgments, which may be deliberations for which EU legal personnel are not particularly apt, and concerning which they are undoubtedly insufficiently expert.

Contemporary EU cultural policy should provide direction, and a nexus for culture-related law. Currently, any such policy is at best inchoate, has no apparent stamp of allegiance, no tendency to constructive selectivity, and no conceptual parameters with which to close its field of application. In its vagueness

[52] For a critical guide to postmodernism, see further, Kearns (n 8) 185–92.

[53] There is ample room for additional scholarship on the EU's approach to the regulation of culture that could potentially assist the more coherent development of the law in this area.

and variable incidence, it is close to being regarded as an uncoordinated non-event. That situation must be remedied by proactive EU institutional synergy of a concerted and effective nature in order to clarify EU cultural goals in the legal arena.

Envoi

WE ARE ALLEGEDLY at a turning-point in our common culture: postmodernism is ending, and, apparently, according to commentators more percipient than myself, post-secularism is beginning. With this in mind, especially regarding the artistic and literary content of this book, this poem by the author, which is not, of course, entirely, or even marginally, autobiographical, may be of at least fleeting interest at this ideological and sociological crossroads.

RENAISSANCE

An old spirit
in his last lifetime
observes

younger lives draining
material pleasure
without limit.

Imagination-free victims,
technocrachy's product:
no postmodern impulse to pray.

One day,
when the world is less mad,
people will start growing –

inside themselves,
cultivate gardens:
beauty for others, and God.

Index

www.ingramcontent.com/pod-product-compliance
Ingram Content Group UK Ltd.
Pitfield, Milton Keynes, MK11 3LW, UK
UKHW020802290926
15470UKWH00003B/910

9 781841 130804